UNDEREDUCATION IN AMERICA

UNDEREDUCATION IN
——————AMERICA——————
The Demography of High School Dropouts

Dorothy Waggoner

FOREWORD BY
José A. Cárdenas

AUBURN HOUSE
New York • Westport, Connecticut • London

Library of Congress Cataloging-in-Publication Data

Waggoner, Dorothy.
    Undereducation in America : the demography of high school dropouts
    / Dorothy Waggoner ; foreword by José A. Cárdenas.
      p. cm.
    Includes bibliographical references (p.) and index.
    ISBN 0-86569-043-X (alk. paper)
    1. High school dropouts—United States—Statistics. 2. Minorities
    —Education—United States—Statistics.
    3. Educational surveys—United States. I. Title.
    LC146.5.W34 1991
    373.12′913′0973—dc20   91-3980

British Library Cataloguing in Publication Data is available.

Library of Congress Catalog Card Number: 91-3980
ISBN: 0-86569-043-X

First published in 1991

Auburn House, 88 Post Road West, Westport, CT 06881
An imprint of Greenwood Publishing Group, Inc.

Printed in the United States of America

The paper used in this book complies with the
Permanent Paper Standard issued by the National
Information Standards Organization (Z39.48-1984).

10 9 8 7 6 5 4 3 2 1

Contents

CONTENTS

Figures and Tables

FIGURES

TABLES

Foreword

The next decade may well be the most challenging in the history of American education. Economic and technological changes in our society are demanding a highly skilled work force that will have to come predominantly from the type of students with whom the schools have had the least success.

For this reason we can expect that the most intensive focus in the schools will be on the education of that segment of the school population that traditionally has been undereducated: minorities, disadvantaged, immigrant, and children from non-English language backgrounds. The cumulative impact of these characteristics is such that a student in American schools today who is an immigrant Hispanic living in a poverty home using a language other than English has virtually no chance of surviving 12 years of schooling regardless of his or her inherent ability, motivation, and the family valuing of a high school education.

The education of mainstream children similarly will have to be addressed because, at least numerically, they form such a large segment of undereducated youth, although dropout rates are much smaller than rates for non-mainstream youth.

Dorothy Waggoner's pioneering research appears to be a logical starting point for the upcoming analysis of educational opportunity and the drastic reform efforts that are sure to follow. Any functional response to inadequacies in the existing systems must begin with a context evaluation, addressing the question "What is the nature of the problem?"

The data presented here give insights on the most dramatic failures of the American systems of education and prepare us for the formidable task ahead. The organization and subsequent analysis of information used in this publication will allow for the necessary flexibility in addressing educational problems of varying segments of the undereducated population.

One can only hope that the ultimate product of this study will be a drastically different educational system that enhances opportunity and the realization of the American dream for each individual and that capitalizes on the potential of all subelements of a culturally pluralistic society to meet the labor needs at the local, state, and national levels.

José A. Cárdenas
Intercultural Development Research Association

Acknowledgments

Many friends and colleagues made this study possible and encouraged and supported me along the way. I would like to thank José A. Cárdenas, executive director of the Intercultural Development Research Association (IDRA) in San Antonio, Texas, who hired me to analyze the 1980 census information on Texas dropouts in connection with IDRA's Texas School Dropout Survey Project and who enabled me to study similar data for the nation, all 50 states, and the District of Columbia. Without his help and encouragement and that of his staff, especially María del Refugio Robledo, director of IDRA's Center for the Prevention and Recovery of Dropouts, this book would never have been written. Through Cárdenas' intercession, funding for the special analysis was provided by the Ford Foundation, for which I would also like to thank Edward J. Meade, Jr., formerly chief program officer of the foundation's Education and Culture Program. The presentation and interpretation of the findings are entirely my own and are not intended to reflect the views either of IDRA or the foundation.

I owe special thanks to Gina Cantoni, Northern Arizona University; John Leach, University of Connecticut; Antonio Simões, New York University; Anita Tegu, Montgomery County, Maryland, Public Schools; Hai T. Tran, University of Oklahoma; and Rafael Valdivieso, Hispanic Policy Development Project, Washington, D.C., for reading individual chapters and early drafts, making many helpful suggestions that have been incorporated into the text, and encouraging me to continue the effort. I would also like to thank Leslie J. Silverman, formerly of the National Center for

Education Statistics, U.S. Department of Education, who reviewed the work for statistical treatment and supplied invaluable suggestions. The contributions of these individuals are gratefully acknowledged. The mistakes are my own.

The analysis of a large data file such as that presented by the decennial census requires many hours of effort by programmers and other computer experts. In this work, I was fortunate to have the assistance of Judith S. Rowe, manager of Research Services, and Douglas Mills of the Princeton University Computing and Information Technology Center who worked patiently and efficiently to supply my data needs. I would also like to thank Kelly Simmons of the Texas A & M University computer center who was the programmer for the Texas study and spent many hours tirelessly and cheerfully working with me on the original model.

Introduction

This study of young people who are out of school without high school diplomas had its genesis in a study of 1980 census information on high school dropouts in Texas. Its basis is a special analysis applying the model developed for the Texas study to the data for all 50 states and the District of Columbia supplemented with other information from published sources to interpret the findings and to place them in the context of the trends in U.S. educational attainment in the second half of the twentieth century and projected demographic trends through the year 2000.

The Texas study was a contribution to the Texas School Dropout Survey Project of the Intercultural Development Research Association. Its product was *Magnitude of the Problem—Census Analysis,* which constituted the first of a seven-volume report abstracted in *Texas School Dropout Survey Project: A Summary of Findings,* issued on October 31, 1986.[1] In the Texas study, young people were considered to be dropouts if they were not enrolled in school and had not completed 12 years of schooling. Their proportion in a given group was its dropout rate. The data were analyzed for Hispanics, non-Hispanic whites, non-Hispanic blacks, and other non-Hispanics; for 16-to-19-year-olds and 20-to-24-year-olds; for men and women; for native-born and foreign-born youth; and for youth according to whether they had completed fewer than 5 years, 5 to 8 years, or 9 to 11 years of schooling. In addition, since a principal concern was the implication for the labor force of numbers of young people who have failed to obtain an adequate education, data were analyzed by labor force participation and were disaggregated to provide separate information on dropouts in the 20 education service centers established in Texas in connection with the Job Training Partnership Act.

A number of changes have been made in the model for the special analysis. To distinguish them from young people meeting other definitions of dropouts, in this study young people who are out of school and have not completed 12 years of schooling are considered to be undereducated youth. Their proportion in a given group is the undereducation rate, corresponding to the "status" dropout rate of the National Center for Education Statistics.[2] Other differences from the Texas study are the following: (1) the data are analyzed for all racial/ethnic groups separately, including American Indians, Eskimos, and Aleuts and Asians and Pacific Islanders; (2) the data are analyzed for youth with monolingual English-speaking backgrounds and those with non-English language backgrounds (i.e., language minority youth); (3) non-Hispanic white minority youth—non-Hispanic whites with non-English language backgrounds—are considered separately from white majority youth—non-Hispanic whites born in this country and having monolingual English-speaking backgrounds; (4) the data are analyzed for youth from families with incomes above and below the poverty level; and (5) no substate data were produced as a part of the special analysis: the information on the undereducation of young people living in urban and rural areas within the states is from the published volumes of the 1980 census. In addition, while produced in the special analysis, the labor force data are not presented here.

Using the decennial census as the basis for data in a study of this kind offers a number of important advantages. First, the 1980 census provides baseline data that can be used with 1990 census data to determine whether the trends in the numbers and proportions of undereducated youth revealed by interim studies have continued downward, leveled off, or even increased after a decade of unprecedented attention to American education and the implementation of various reforms to enable schools to meet the needs of the twenty-first century. Use of the decennial census makes possible uniform definitions based on data from a single source gathered in a uniform way. The census is the only source of data that yields reliable information based on uniform definitions for all the states, making possible state, as well as regional, comparisons. It is the only national source of data that yields reliable information on all racial/ethnic groups that can be analyzed by characteristic and compared across groups. Because the 1980 and 1990 censuses contained questions on home language usage, use of the census for the data makes it possible to examine the relationship between having a non-English language background and undereducation for the various racial/ethnic groups. As shown in this study, such an examination is critical for an understanding of undereducation, especially among Hispanics, and the results do not necessarily accord with popular opinion. Because of the census language questions, it is possible to identify non-Hispanic white youth born in this country and living in homes in which only English is spoken, that is, white majority youth, to serve as the standard of comparison. Moreover, it is possible to examine for the first time in any research the characteristics of non-Hispanic white minority youth nationally and in the states.

Beyond the census data used for the special analysis, the census offers a quantity of additional information that is available nowhere else. In this study, information from the published volumes of the census on the racial/ethnic groups and their subgroups and on foreign-born and language minority populations in the United States and in the individual states contributed to the understanding of the differences between the undereducation rates of youth belonging to the same racial/ethnic group in different states. Published information on the variations in the distribution of poverty and the racial/ethnic populations in the urban and rural areas of different states confirmed evidence from other sources about the relationship between school districts serving predominantly poor and minority student populations and educational disadvantage as evidenced by high undereducation rates.

There are a number of disadvantages to the approach. As explained in appendix A, the data base for the special analysis was a sample of the 1980 census sample; sampling error, as well as non-sampling error, may have affected the results with implications for the undereducation rates as well as for the numbers of undereducated youth. The census language questions do not provide a basis for determining whether language minority individuals are prepared for school programs offered in the English language or whether they may be limited in English proficiency. Language background, used as an analysis variable in the study, and the published data regarding the self-reported English-speaking ability of various language minority groups, used in the discussion of the variations in the undereducation rates according to language background in chapter 3, can only suggest possible differences in English language proficiency; they do not provide any information on other linguistic or cultural factors that may affect the ability to profit from instruction offered in U.S. schools. The census did not ask foreign-born individuals where they were schooled; thus it is not possible to determine how many of those with low levels of schooling were ever enrolled in U.S. schools or whether their schooling was limited to that received abroad. Since the census data base does not provide information on age at the time of last enrollment for people who are no longer enrolled, it is impossible to determine the extent to which the undereducated youth in the various racial/ethnic groups were overaged when they were in school; the discussion of educational delay in chapter 3 compares the proportions of overaged enrolled students in the various racial/ethnic groups.

As indicated above, the special analysis includes an examination of the poverty status of undereducated youth and the discussion compares the poverty status of the racial/ethnic groups nationally, in the states, and in urban and rural areas within states in relation to the undereducation rates. Family income is only one component of socioeconomic status, a broader concept frequently used in the analysis of educational disadvantage to explain differences among racial/ethnic groups. In this study, no attempt is made to examine other factors, such as parents' occupations and educational levels, or material aspects of the homes of the youth.[3] As a result, there is no way to determine whether or not the differences in undereducation rates between minority youth from families with incomes above the poverty level on the one hand and white majority youth on the other hand would have been less or would have disappeared if a more comprehensive concept of socioeconomic status had been employed. It should also be kept in mind that the average poverty threshold for a family of four used in 1980 was an income of $7,412 or $618 per month to feed, house, and clothe four people. Thus youth from families with incomes above the poverty level may be very poor indeed.

The study is quantitative. The census does not supply any information to make possible an evaluation of the educational content or the quality of the schooling received either by youth who graduate from the system or by those who fail to receive high school diplomas. It does not provide any information on what the youth who, in 1980, were out of school and not high school graduates may have learned when they were in school. For qualitative information about U.S. education and educational attainment in U.S. schools, the reader must turn to other sources, such as the Department of Education's High School and Beyond study and the National Assessment of Educational Progress.

The study does not attempt to determine the reasons why youth are undereducated. When it states that U.S. education is failing all youth, it calls attention to the fact that the majority of undereducated youth are white majority youth from families with incomes above the poverty level. The census provides no information about the characteristics of the schools previously attended by the undereducated youth, the school experiences of these youth, or the societal or personal factors that may influence educational decisions in individual cases. In describing the characteristics of the youth who are more likely to be undereducated, who are more at risk of undereducation than other youth, the study does not intend to assert that certain characteristics either cause or predict undereducation, much less that undereducated youth are somehow deficient in comparison with other youth, except that they lack, at a given time, the minimum formal education deemed necessary for success as productive adult citizens.

The report is divided into nine chapters. Chapter 1 summarizes the findings and presents the principal policy implications of the study. It relates undereducation among youth, aged 16 to 24, in 1980, as revealed by the analysis, (1) to trends since 1940 in the high school graduation rates of adults reported by the Bureau of the Census, (2) to trends in the high school completion rates of students reported by the public schools and used as a comparative measure of how youth are faring in the various states, and (3) to trends in undereducation among youth since 1980 from the Census Bureau's annual October current population surveys of school enrollment. Chapter 1 concludes with a discussion of the projected changes in the demographic composition of the school-age population by the year 2000, the implications of the changes for the numbers of undereducated youth, and the consequences of undereducation for the individual and the nation in the future.

Chapters 2 and 3 present the findings of the special analysis in detail. Chapter 2 discusses the numbers and characteristics of undereducated youth in 1980. White majority youth are the comparison group for the examination of the differences among the racial/ethnic groups by nativity, language background, gender, age, poverty status, years of schooling completed, geographical distribution, and urbanicity. In chapter 3, the subject is undereducation risk. The discussion covers the extent of risk associated with the various characteristics identified in chapter 2. It compares the undereducation rates of minority youth who have those characteristics with those of their majority counterparts. It also contrasts the undereducation risk in the various regions and states and the relationship of the poverty status, nativity, and language background of youth in the states to their state undereducation rates. Chapter 3 concludes with an examination of the relationship of poverty status and urbanicity to the undereducation of members of the racial/ethnic groups in the various regions and states.

The final six chapters take up the racial/ethnic groups individually. They contain discussions of the numbers and characteristics of undereducated white majority youth; African American youth; Hispanic youth; non-Hispanic white minority youth; American Indian, Eskimo, and Aleut youth; and Asian and Pacific Islander youth and the undereducation rates of these groups. These chapters include examinations of the undereducation rates of the various groups, and, in the case of the minorities, their relative educational disadvantage nationally and in the states as measured by undereducation in 1980.

The chapters also include descriptions of the numbers and characteristics of the populations of which the youth were a part in 1980, that is, Hispanic and Asian/Pacific subgroups and American Indian tribes; the major language minority groups to which non-Hispanic white minority people belong; and African American, Hispanic, and non-Hispanic white minority foreign-born populations. The differences in the state populations are related to the likelihood of youth to be undereducated. The chapters on African Americans, Hispanics, non-Hispanic white minority youth, and

Asians and Pacific Islanders also contain an examination of the immigration that has added to these populations since 1980. Each chapter ends with a discussion of the projected (or potential) school-age population of each group and the implications for undereducation in the year 2000.

NOTES

1. San Antonio, Texas: Intercultural Development Research Association.

2. National Center for Education Statistics, U.S. Department of Education, *Dropout Rates in the United States: 1988* (Washington, D.C.: U.S. Government Printing Office, 1989), p. 2.

3. See Center for Education Statistics, U.S. Department of Education, *Who Drops Out of High School? Findings from High School and Beyond* (Washington, D.C.: U.S. Government Printing Office, 1987), pp. 25–29, for a discussion of socioeconomic status (SES) and the composite SES index used in the analysis of the High School and Beyond (HS&B) data base.

UNDEREDUCATION IN AMERICA

1

Undereducation

U.S. education is failing all young people. It is failing minority and poor youth, who are disproportionately out of school without the minimum education needed for entry into the world of work and responsibility as adult citizens. It is also failing middle class white majority youth. Of youth who are out of school without high school diplomas—at least 4.2 million young people at the latest count—more than half are native-born non-Hispanic whites living in homes in which only English is spoken. A large proportion of the undereducated are from families with incomes above the poverty level.

Being a member of a minority group or being poor greatly increases the risk that a young person will be undereducated, and minorities are much more likely to be poor. Minority and poor youth experience to a greater degree than other youth the fundamental inequities between school districts serving predominantly poor and minority populations and those serving more advantaged groups. These differences are underscored by the contrast between the high undereducation rates of young people living in urban ghettoes in the North and in rural areas in the South and the low rates of youth living in other types of environments in their regions. However, even the most advantaged African Americans, Hispanics, and American Indians, Eskimos, and Aleuts are more likely to be undereducated than white majority youth.

Growing up in a home in which a language other than English is spoken is not a handicap for all youth; in particular, it is not a handicap for non-Hispanic whites, for Asians and Pacific Islanders, and for African Americans among whom language minority youth have lower undereducation rates than their English language-background counterparts. However, language background and nativity are associated with higher undereducation rates for Hispanics. Previous studies that have linked educational delay— being older than one's classmates—and other factors with the likelihood of dropping out of school have been unable to explain the high rates of Hispanics in comparison with those of other groups. They have failed to consider the differences between native-born and foreign-born and English language-background and Spanish language-background Hispanics.

Other findings from this study are the following:

On undereducation and minority status:

- American Indians, Eskimos, and Aleuts are the most likely to be undereducated of all native-born youth. In 1980 the rate for this category was 2.2 times that of white majority youth.
- Native-born Hispanics living in homes in which only English is spoken are about as likely as African Americans to be undereducated. Both were 1.6 times more likely to be undereducated than white majority youth in 1980 while native-born Hispanics living in homes in which Spanish is spoken were twice as likely.
- Asians and Pacific Islander youth as a group are the least likely to be undereducated of all youth, but new Southeast Asian immigrants are not faring as well as members of the major Asian American communities in the United States—Japanese Americans, Filipino Americans, and Chinese Americans.

On undereducation and foreign birth:

- Foreign-born youth are twice as likely to be undereducated as native-born youth. The undereducation rate of foreign-born Hispanics is especially high; it contributes to the high rate of Hispanics overall.

On undereducation and poverty:

- Poor youth in all groups are more likely to be undereducated than youth from more economically advantaged backgrounds. However, the undereducation risk associated with poverty is less for native-born African Americans, Hispanics, and American Indians and Alaska Natives, whose overall undereducation rates are already high, than for native-born non-Hispanic whites and Asians and Pacific Islanders, whose overall undereducation rates are low.

On the years of schooling completed by undereducated youth:

- Most youth who discontinue their schooling before completing the twelfth grade stay at least through the ninth grade. In 1980 three-quarters of the youth who were out of school without diplomas had completed at least nine years of schooling.

- There are substantial numbers of mostly native-born youth who leave school, at least for a time, either before the eighth grade or just after completing it. In 1980, 1.1 million young people had completed only five to eight years of schooling and a quarter of a million, fewer than five years. Eight in ten of the former and two-thirds of the latter were born in this country.

- Except among African Americans, undereducated youth from homes in which languages other than English are spoken are less likely to reach high school before discontinuing their education than undereducated youth from homes in which only English is spoken.

- Foreign-born youth are much more likely to have low levels of schooling than native-born youth. In 1980 those who were undereducated were three times more likely than their native-born counterparts to have no more than an eighth grade education.

- Undereducated African American youth are just as likely as undereducated majority whites to complete at least nine years of schooling, and they are more likely to complete the eleventh grade before they discontinue their schooling. Nevertheless, African American students are much more likely than white students to be behind in school and older than most of their classmates.

- As a group, undereducated Hispanics are the least likely of all youth to reach high school before discontinuing their education. Although no more likely than blacks to be behind in school, Hispanics, to a greater extent, leave school when they reach the school-leaving age. The majority of Hispanics who complete no more than eight years of schooling are foreign-born youth.

On undereducation in the various regions and states:

- Youth who live in the South are the most likely to be undereducated and those who live in the North and the Midwest, the least likely.

- Undereducation in the South is associated with poverty in the rural areas, and white and African American youth are equally likely to be undereducated in southern states where many whites and blacks live in rural poverty.

- In the North, undereducation is associated with poverty and the other problems in the inner city ghettoes where most minority and poor youth, but comparatively few white majority youth, live. In northern states, the education gap between whites on the one hand and African Americans and the other minorities on the other hand is wide.

- Undereducation varies widely by state. In 1980 youth living in Kentucky were three times more likely to be out of school and not high school graduates than youth living in Minnesota.

- Minorities constitute the majority of undereducated youth in a number of states, including California, Texas, and New York.

The findings of the this study have a number of important policy implications, including the following:

- Programs to encourage youth to stay in school must begin in the elementary grades when problems, one manifestation of which is grade repetition, first become evident. By the fourth grade, many students are already behind, and by the eighth, many are dropping out.

- To a greater extent than in the past, educational programs must address differences among students who are at risk. The higher undereducation rate of Spanish language-background Hispanics, in comparison with that of English language-background Hispanics, and the fact that native-born, as well as foreign-born, language minority youth of all racial/ethnic groups, except African Americans, complete fewer years of schooling than English language-background youth indicate that linguistic differences must receive more attention in program design.

- More resources must be directed toward the educational needs of the growing numbers of at-risk youth, especially American Indians, Eskimos, and Aleuts, who are the most likely of native-born youth to be undereducated; linguistically different youth; and new immigrants, many of whom arrive in the United States without the requisite schooling for their ages.

- Programs to assist at-risk students to catch up and keep up with their more advantaged classmates must accompany reform efforts. The effects of reforms on minority youth and the poor must be closely monitored to insure educational equity.

- Inequities between school districts serving predominantly minority and poor students and those serving more advantaged students must be eliminated.

- Research to measure educational disadvantage should focus to a greater extent upon the special characteristics of minority populations. In the past, researchers have tended to examine only the variables that correlate closely with the educational risk of white majority students.

When the 1980 census was taken, there were 5.9 million undereducated youth in the United States. They comprised 15.4 percent of all 16-to-24-year-old youth. In October 1980 the Census Bureau counted 5.1 million undereducated civilian young people not living in group quarters—14.1 percent of all youth in that group.[1] By October 1988 the number of undereducated civilian non-institutional youth was estimated to be 4.2 million and the undereducation rate, 12.9 percent.[2] Although 4.2 million youth—one in every eight aged 16 to 24 who was not in the armed forces or living in group quarters—is far too many, the trend, at least through 1988, was clearly downward. The greatest gains were made by African Americans; by 1988 they had almost closed the undereducation gap with whites. Undereducated Hispanics, on the other hand, increased in numbers, and their undereducation rate remained about the same.[3] Information is not available on how native-born Hispanics have been faring in comparison with foreign-born Hispanics on this measure or on whether Spanish language-background Hispanics are continuing to lag behind those from homes in which only English is spoken.

No information is available on the current educational status of American Indians, Eskimos, and Aleuts; Asians and Pacific Islanders; and non-Hispanic white minority youth, although these groups, like Hispanics, have been increasing in numbers from immigration and natural growth. Since Native American youth and many new Asian and non-Hispanic white minority immigrant youth are at greater risk than other youth, the numbers and proportions of American Indians, Eskimos, and Aleuts; Asians and Pacific Islanders; and non-Hispanic white minority youth who are undereducated may be greater now than they were in 1980.

By the end of this century, as a result of the higher growth rate of minority populations, minority children and youth will constitute at least three in ten, and probably more, of the total school-age population. The proportions will be much greater in California, Texas, New York, and a number of other states, where minorities already constitute majorities of the youth who are undereducated. The special needs of at-risk students must be addressed if the favorable overall trends in undereducation in the eighties are to be sustained. Otherwise, the numbers and proportions of undereducated youth will grow, and the gap between youth who are advantaged and those who are disadvantaged will widen with serious social and economic consequences for all.

The following sections of this chapter contain: (1) a discussion of the findings of the study in the context of the trends in educational attainment and undereducation in the United States since 1940, (2) a consideration of the need to use the 1990 census to update the information on undereducation for all groups, and, finally, (3) an examination of the implications of the projected growth in the numbers and proportions of minority populations in the United States during the remaining years of this century for undereducation and the risk of undereducation in the year 2000. The trend information comes from various Bureau of the Census and Department of Education sources.

EDUCATIONAL ATTAINMENT IN THE UNITED STATES SINCE 1940

The proportion of Americans completing 12 years of schooling has risen dramatically over time. In 1940 only a quarter of the population aged 25 and older had graduated from high school. A generation later, in 1970, more than half had. In 1988 more than three-quarters of the adults in the United States had completed at least 12 years of schooling. Among those aged 25 to 29, the proportion rose from 38 percent in 1940 to 86 percent in 1988.[4]

Some of the educational inequities in society have begun to disappear. In 1940 young white adults were more than three times more likely than African Americans in their age group to graduate from high school; their rate was 41 percent in comparison with 12 percent for blacks. By 1988 young African American adults had almost caught up: 82 percent of blacks and 87 percent of whites were high school graduates.[5] Educational attainment information on Hispanics has been published only since 1974. In that year 52 percent of 25-to-29-year-old Hispanics, in comparison with 83 percent of whites and 68 percent of blacks, were high school graduates.[6] By 1988, 62 percent of Hispanics were high school graduates. However, whites and African Americans, aged 25 to 29, were still 1.4 times more likely than Hispanics as a group to graduate from high school.[7]

High school completion data reported by the public schools suggest that the percentage of high school students progressing normally from fifth grade to graduation—that is, taking only eight years—remains relatively constant. Between 1966 and 1980 the number of graduates as a proportion of fifth grade enrollment eight years earlier constituted 73.2 to 74.4 percent.[8] The number of graduates as a proportion of ninth grade enrollment four years earlier constituted 69.5 percent in 1982 and 71.1 percent in 1989.[9] These data, used to infer the dropout rate, have caused one commentator to term the school dropout problem "sticky."[10] However, they do not necessarily contradict other data suggesting that progress is taking place. If the high school completion rates of youth who are being promoted year by year are relatively stable, the rates of the at-risk populations who repeat grades, who leave school for a year or two and return, or who obtain high school diplomas by other means than graduation from the regular high school may be improving. All of these groups are represented in the data from the 1980 decennial census used for this study. All except the latter are represented in the Census Bureau's current population survey (CPS) samples of the civilian non-institutional population, which obtain information on educational attainment each March and on school enrollment each October.[11] They are not represented in the data reported by the public schools.

THE UNDEREDUCATION RATE

The undereducation rate of young people, aged 16 to 24, in this study is the reverse of the high school completion rate. It is the proportion of youth at a given time who have discontinued their education before completing 12 years of schooling and graduating from high school. Some of these youth will return to school or will complete their education by alternate methods, those with more schooling probably to a greater extent than those with less.[12] Conversely, some, who are not included among the undereducated because they are still enrolled in school, will not complete 12 years and will become part of the population, aged 25 and older, who are not high school graduates.

The undereducation rate is the "status" dropout rate, as defined by the

National Center for Education Statistics (NCES).[13] It differs from the "event" rate, which is a measure of the extent to which young people are dropping out of school annually,[14] and the "cohort" rate, which is a measure of the extent to which a given group of young people—for example, 1980 sophomores in NCES's High School and Beyond study—have dropped out within a particular period.[15]

UNDEREDUCATED YOUTH IN THE EIGHTIES

The numbers of undereducated youth have been decreasing during the 1980s, and they have been decreasing more, proportionally, than the total numbers of youth have decreased with the changing demographics of the U.S. population. Thus, consistent with the rise in the educational attainment of adults, youth who are out of school without high school diplomas not only are fewer, but also constitute a smaller proportion of their age group now than they did in 1980. Moreover, consistent with the findings for adults, African American youth are continuing to close the undereducation gap that separates them from whites. Unfortunately, the same cannot be said for Hispanics as a group. After seeming to dip briefly in the intervening years, the Hispanic undereducation rate near the end of the decade was about at its level at the beginning. As a group, Hispanics are still more than two and a half times more likely to be undereducated than the total population of whites. The comparative trends in the undereducation rates of whites, African Americans, and Hispanics between 1980 and 1988 are illustrated in figure 1.1.

When the decennial census was taken on April 1, 1980, 5.9 million young people, aged 16 to 24, were not enrolled in school and had not completed 12 years of schooling. They constituted 15.4 percent of all young people in their age group in spring 1980. In October, as shown in table 1.1, the current population survey identified 5.1 million undereducated civilian youth, aged 16 to 24, not living in group quarters, and the undereducation rate of that population was 14.1 percent.[16] By October 1988 the number had fallen to 4.2 million, and the rate was 12.9 percent.[17] Whites, including Hispanics, continued to be the least likely to be undereducated between 1980 and 1988, but they made little progress.[18] African Americans in 1988, in contrast, were 1.3 times less likely to be undereducated than their counterparts in 1980, and their 1988 rate was close to that of whites.[19] Hispanics as a group ended about where they started with more than 35 percent undereducated.[20]

In addition to having high undereducation rates, as demonstrated in this study, Hispanics as a group are less likely than other youth to reach the high school years before discontinuing their education. Among undereducated civilian Hispanics, aged 14 to 24, not living in group quarters in October 1980, about half had completed fewer than nine years of

Figure 1.1
Undereducation Rates, October 1980 to October 1988

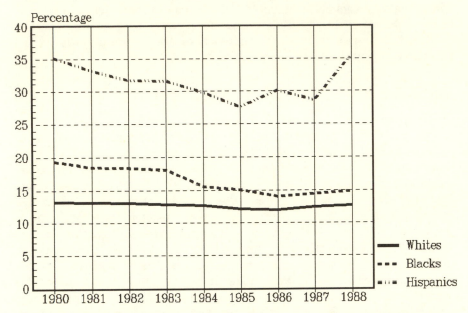

schooling. In comparison, only about one in five African Americans and a quarter of whites, including Hispanics, in this group had failed to reach the high school years before discontinuing their education.[21] In 1986 the proportion of undereducated Hispanics, aged 14 to 24, completing fewer than nine years was 44.0 percent while those of blacks and whites were 19.2 percent and 28.5 percent, respectively.[22] These trends are depicted in figure 1.2, and the data are shown in table 1.2. In 1988 the Hispanic proportion of undereducated youth, aged 16 to 24, who had reached at least the high school years was about half; that of non-Hispanic youth in this age group was 20.6 percent.[23] In comparison with undereducated Hispanics indentified in the decennial census for this study, 55.6 percent of whom had completed more than eight years of schooling, Hispanics in 1988 had retrogressed.

As shown in this study, the level of schooling of undereducated African American youth is equal to that of white majority youth. They also have the highest level of schooling among the three groups for which information since 1980 is available. In comparison with all white youth, aged 14 to 24, including Hispanics, blacks are more likely to reach the high school years and to stay in school through the eleventh grade. The proportions of African Americans reaching high school, shown in table 1.2, did not change between 1980 and 1986, but somewhat more of them had completed the eleventh grade in 1986 than in 1980—33.8 percent in compari-

Table 1.1
Estimated Numbers of Young People, Aged 16 to 24, and Numbers and Proportions of Undereducated Youth, by Race, Hispanic Ethnicity, and Year: United States, October 1980 to October 1988 (Civilian non-institutional population)

Year	Total	Whites	Blacks	Hispanics[1]
October 1980				
Total population	36,143,000	30,675,000	4,711,000	2,517,000
Undereducated youth	5,085,000	4,067,000	912,000	885,000
Proportion	14.1	13.3	19.4	35.2
October 1981				
Total population	36,945,000	31,109,000	4,932,000	2,684,000
Undereducated youth	5,141,000	4,107,000	913,000	890,000
Proportion	13.9	13.2	18.5	33.2
October 1982				
Total population	36,452,000	30,491,000	4,984,000	2,599,000
Undereducated youth	5,056,000	4,001,000	917,000	823,000
Proportion	13.9	13.1	18.4	31.7
October 1983				
Total population	35,884,000	29,906,000	4,947,000	2,586,000
Undereducated youth	4,904,000	3,852,000	894,000	817,000
Proportion	13.7	12.9	18.1	31.6
October 1984				
Total population	35,204,000	29,256,000	4,923,000	2,558,000
Undereducated youth	4,627,000	3,702,000	767,000	762,000
Proportion	13.1	12.7	15.6	29.8
October 1985				
Total population	34,382,000	28,578,000	4,800,000	2,886,000
Undereducated youth	4,324,000	3,474,000	725,000	797,000
Proportion	12.6	12.2	15.1	27.6
October 1986				
Total population	33,945,000	28,080,000	4,755,000	3,206,000
Undereducated youth	4,142,000	3,368,000	669,000	966,000
Proportion	12.2	12.0	14.1	30.1
October 1987				
Total population	33,452,000	27,589,000	4,733,000	3,234,000
Undereducated youth	4,251,000	3,443,000	688,000	925,000
Proportion	12.7	12.5	14.5	28.6
October 1988				
Total population	32,893,000	27,043,000	4,693,000	3,267,000
Undereducated youth	4,231,000	3,423,000	698,000	1,169,000
Proportion	12.9	12.7	14.9	35.8

Source: Derived from Bureau of the Census, *School Enrollment—Social and Economic Characteristics of Students: October 1981 and 1980*, pp. 6–7 and 60–61; *October 1982*, pp. 7–8; *October 1983*, pp. 9–10; *October 1985 and 1984*, pp. 9–10 and 59–60; *October 1986*, pp. 5–7; and *October 1988 and 1987*, pp. 5–6 and 78–79.

[1]May be of any race.

son with 31.7 percent at the beginning of the decade. Whites appear to have lost some ground between 1980 and 1986 both in the proportion reaching high school and in the proportion completing the eleventh

Figure 1.2
Percentages of Undereducated Youth Completing Fewer Than Nine Years of Schooling, October 1980 to October 1986

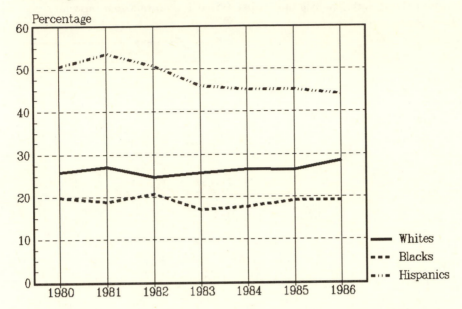

grade.[24] Figure 1.3 illustrates the 1980–86 trends in the proportions of white, African American, and Hispanic youth, aged 14 to 24, completing the eleventh grade before discontinuing their education.

The numbers of undereducated Hispanic youth now surpass those of African American youth; Hispanics constitute the largest minority group among youth who are out of school and have not completed the twelfth grade. Their proportion of undereducated youth is increasing. In October 1988, 3.4 million or 81 percent of undereducated youth, including Hispanics, were white, and 698,000 or 16 percent were African American. There were 1.2 million undereducated Hispanic young people, and they constituted 28 percent of all civilian undereducated youth not living in group quarters. This figure represents an increase of at least 10 percent over their proportion of the group sampled by the October 1980 current population survey.[25]

UNDEREDUCATED YOUTH IN THE REMAINDER OF THIS CENTURY

The annual school enrollment surveys of the Bureau of the Census used to estimate the trends in the undereducation of youth, aged 16 to 24, between October 1980 and October 1988 discussed above furnish informa-

Table 1.2
Estimated Numbers of Undereducated Youth, Aged 14 to 24, and Proportions by Years of Schooling Completed, by Race, Hispanic Ethnicity, and Year: United States, October 1980 to October 1986 (Civilian non-institutional population)

Year	Total	Whites	Blacks	Hispanics[1]
October 1980				
Number	5,212,000	4,166,000	935,000	919,000
Eight years or fewer	24.8	25.9	19.8	50.6
Nine years	19.7	20.0	18.3	15.8
Ten years	29.1	28.9	30.3	15.9
Eleven years	26.3	25.2	31.7	17.7
October 1981				
Number	5,288,000	4,216,000	943,000	926,000
Eight years or fewer	25.7	27.1	18.8	53.6
Nine years	18.6	18.5	19.4	14.3
Ten years	29.5	29.6	29.5	16.1
Eleven years	26.2	24.8	32.3	16.1
October 1982				
Number	5,160,000	4,080,000	939,000	840,000
Eight years or fewer	24.0	24.7	20.7	50.7
Nine years	20.8	20.5	21.6	15.5
Ten years	28.3	28.6	26.8	15.4
Eleven years	27.0	26.3	30.9	18.5
October 1983				
Number	5,026,000	3,952,000	917,000	841,000
Eight years or fewer	24.3	25.7	16.9	46.0
Nine years	19.4	19.6	18.6	17.4
Ten years	28.2	28.0	29.6	18.8
Eleven years	28.1	26.7	34.9	17.8
October 1984				
Number	4,783,000	3,831,000	789,000	789,000
Eight years or fewer	25.2	26.5	17.6	45.1
Nine years	21.5	21.8	20.7	19.1
Ten years	26.8	26.4	29.0	20.7
Eleven years	26.6	25.3	32.7	15.1
October 1985				
Number	4,456,000	3,583,000	750,000	820,000
Eight years or fewer	25.5	26.4	19.1	45.1
Nine years	20.8	21.9	16.7	17.7
Ten years	27.2	26.4	32.8	18.8
Eleven years	26.5	25.4	31.5	18.4
October 1986				
Number	4,319,000	3,497,000	707,000	989,000
Eight years or fewer	27.4	28.5	19.2	44.0
Nine years	21.6	21.5	23.2	20.7
Ten years	24.8	25.1	23.8	18.6
Eleven years	26.3	24.9	33.8	16.7

Source: Derived from Bureau of the Census, *School Enrollment—Social and Economic Characteristics of Students: October 1981 and 1980*, pp. 22–24 and 73–75; *October 1982*, pp. 21–23; *October 1983*, pp. 24–26; *October 1985 and 1984*, pp. 22–24 and 66–68; *October 1986*, pp. 23–26.

Note: Detail may not add to 100.0 percent because of rounding.

[1]May be of any race.

Figure 1.3
**Percentages of Undereducated Youth Completing Eleven Years of
Schooling, October 1980 to October 1986**

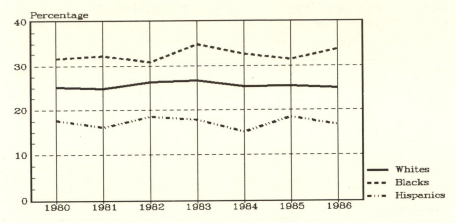

tion only about civilian non-institutional whites, African Americans, and Hispanics in the aggregate. They do not provide information about the other racial/ethnic groups or information on undereducation in individual states. The 1990 decennial census will yield a new comprehensive measure of the total number of young people in the age group 16 to 24 who are not enrolled in school and have not completed 12 years of schooling, how much education they received before discontinuing schooling, and their proportion in the general population of their age group for comparison with the 1980 census data in this study. It will furnish a gauge of what has happened to at-risk youth during a decade of school reform, including the implementation of minimum competency testing for graduation in a number of the largest states.[26]

Like the 1980 census, the 1990 census will make it possible to examine the undereducation rates and educational attainment of mutually exclusive racial/ethnic groups, including American Indians, Eskimos, and Aleuts; Asians and Pacific Islanders; and non-Hispanic white minority youth, to compare their characteristics, and to estimate the differences in numbers, rates, and characteristics in the various states and regions where these groups are found in sufficient numbers. With the 1990 data, it will be possible to study foreign-born and native-born youth and language minority and English language-background youth separately; thus, as in this study, it will be possible to construct a comparison group consisting of white majority youth—youth who were born in this country and who live in families in which only English is spoken. As shown in this study, but frequently overlooked in studies using smaller data bases, American Indians, Eskimos, and Aleuts have the highest undereducation rate of native-born youth. Asians and Pacific Islanders in the aggregate have the lowest rate of all, but there are wide differences among groups with different national and ethnic origins that are only apparent in a large data base such as that of the decennial census. Language background and nativity are especially important in the interpretation of the undereducation rates of Hispanic youth, the numbers of those who are undereducated, and their educational attainment, as also shown in this study. Consideration of these factors is important in the identification of at-risk populations, in the planning and implementation of appropriate educational programs, and in the evaluation of the impact of the school reform movement.

The changes in the composition of the population of undereducated youth between 1980 and 1988 reflect the changing composition of the U.S. population in general as well as the continued disadvantage of Hispanic youth in comparison with whites and African Americans that the 1990 census will confirm or refute. The demographic changes have profound implications for the composition of the school-age population and for the numbers and proportions of youth who are potentially at risk of undereducation in the remaining years of this century. Assuming moderate rates of fertility and mortality and moderate net immigration, the population of the United States is projected to grow from 238.6 million in 1985 to 268.0 million in the year 2000. Only 41.4 percent of the increase will consist of non-Hispanic whites.[27] However, because the minority populations are younger and have higher birth rates than whites for the most part, the differential growth will especially affect the school-age population. If the projections prove to be accurate, the population aged 5 to 17 will increase from 44.4 million in 1985 to 48.8 million by the year 2000, as shown in table 1.3. Only 1.5 million of the 4.4 million increase—34.3 percent—will consist of non-Hispanic white children and youth. Hispanics will contribute 1.9 million, or 44.0 percent; African Americans will contribute 1.7 million, or 39.4 percent; and other races, 362,000, or 8.4 percent. By the year 2000, if these projections hold, the proportion of Hispanics will increase from 9.6 percent to 12.7 percent of the school-age population and that of blacks from 14.9 percent to 17.1 percent, while that of non-Hispanic whites will decrease from 72.8 percent to 69.4 percent.[28]

The projected numbers of minority school-age children and youth by the year 2000 should be understood as minimum numbers; the numbers and the increases in their proportions vis-à-vis the proportion of non-Hispanic white children and youth will very likely be greater because actual immigration since 1980 has outpaced the moderate annual net immigration assumptions for all the minorities. Moreover, for Asians, and possibly for other groups, the assumed moderate fertility and mortality rates based upon the characteristics of the Asians and others who have traditionally predominated in these populations in the United States may not be valid for the new immigrants. (See table 9.10 in chapter 9.)

Table 1.3
Projected Numbers and Distribution of School-Age Children and Youth, by Hispanic Ethnicity and Race: United States, 1985–2000

Year	Total	Hispanics	Non-Hispanic whites	Blacks	Other races
1985	44,385,000	4,279,000	32,330,000	6,597,000	1,413,000
	100.0%	9.6%	72.8%	14.9%	3.2%
1990	45,139,000	4,825,000	31,971,000	7,042,000	1,573,000
	100.0%	10.7%	70.8%	15.6%	3.5%
1995	48,518,000	5,555,000	33,712,000	7,871,000	1,705,000
	100.0%	11.4%	69.5%	16.2%	3.5%
2000	48,763,000	6,207,000	33,830,000	8,321,000	1,775,000
	100.0%	12.7%	69.4%	17.1%	3.6%

Source: Derived from Bureau of the Census, *Projections of the Hispanic Population: 1983 to 2080*, p. 14.

Note: Moderate rates of fertility, mortality, and net immigration assumed.

The proportions of minorities will be much greater in many states. Already in 1980 there were eight states in which minority youth outnumbered majority youth among youth who were out of school and had not completed the twelfth grade and two others in which the number of undereducated majority and minority youth were about the same. These states included California, Texas, and New York—states that, since 1980, have received large numbers of new Hispanic, Asian, and other minority immigrants. The 1990 census will provide definitive information on the growth of minority and new immigrant populations and its effect on the numbers and proportions of undereducated youth in the nation and in the individual states during the 1980s.

The consequences of undereducation are extremely serious, both for the disadvantaged individual and for the nation that is already challenged on both the domestic and international economic fronts. For the individual, dropping out of high school is, as one commentator put it, a step in the process of disengagement, "a downward spiral that might include unemployment, crime, extreme apathy, abuse of drugs or alcohol, and teenage pregnancy."[29] If not actually "tantamount to a denial of employment,"[30] the failure to obtain a diploma effectively curtails the opportunities for postsecondary education—education that will be required to qualify for a majority of new jobs in the twenty-first century.[31] For the nation, dropouts represent lost tax revenues and increased spending for welfare, crime and incarceration, unemployment insurance and placement services, adult job training, and health care. They represent incalculable losses in productivity and in citizen participation. Their numbers further reduce the potential pool of internationally competitive new workers.

In 1972 the differential in lifetime earnings between males, aged 25 to 34, with and without diplomas was estimated to be $237 billion; the resulting loss to the nation in taxes was $71 billion, and the costs of welfare and crime associated with undereducation amounted to $6 billion.[32] The Intercultural Development Research Association calculated in 1986 that each cohort of dropouts in Texas forgoes $11.8 billion in lifetime earnings after taxes and costs the public $5.1 billion in unrealized tax revenues and $17.6 million in payments for welfare and all the other consequences of inadequate education.[33] Extrapolating from IDRA's estimates, the 4.2 million undereducated youth in 1988, during their lifetimes, will fail to earn $577.5 billion after taxes, and the public will lose $247.5 billion in tax revenues and expend $31.8 billion that would otherwise be unnecessary. Since the early 1970s the mean annual earnings of young adult males have fallen, and they have fallen more for those with less education than for those with more.[34] Thus the gap between those who have completed high school and those who have not is greater than ever.

The extent to which demographic trends will determine the future numbers and composition of the population of undereducated youth in the United States through the end of this century depends on the extent to which genuine efforts are made to restructure schools and to help the at-risk groups—minorities and the poor—to overtake their more advantaged classmates. It depends on the extent to which programs and additional resources are directed toward the populations with special needs, such as American Indians, Eskimos, and Aleuts; the linguistically different; and new immigrants. It depends on the seriousness of the effort to eliminate inequities between rich and poor school districts and to take other steps to insure that all students truly have an equal chance. Ernest L. Boyer, a former U.S. commissioner of education, calls serving disadvantaged students "the urgent unfinished business for American education." He states, "Unless we find ways to overcome the problem of failure in the schools, generations of students will continue to be doomed to frustrating, unproductive lives. This nation cannot afford to pay the price of wasted youth."[35]

NOTES

1. Bureau of the Census, U.S. Department of Commerce, *School Enrollment—Social and Economic Characteristics of Students: October 1981 and 1980* (Washington, D.C.: U.S. Government Printing Office, 1985), p. 60.

2. Bureau of the Census, U.S. Department of Commerce, *School Enrollment—Social and Economic Characteristics of Students: October 1988 and 1987* (Washington, D.C.: U.S. Government Printing Office, 1990), p. 5.

3. Ibid., pp. 5–6.

4. National Center for Education Statistics, U.S. Department of Education, *Digest of Educational Statistics, 1989* (Washington, D.C.: U.S. Government Printing Office, 1989), p. 15.

5. Ibid.

6. Bureau of the Census, U.S. Department of Commerce, *Educational Attainment in the United States: March 1982 to 1985* (Washington, D.C.: U.S. Government Printing Office, 1987), pp. 106–107.

7. National Center for Education Statistics, *Digest,* p. 16.

8. National Center for Education Statistics, U.S. Department of Education, *Digest of Education Statistics, 1982* (Washington, D.C.: U.S. Government Printing Office, 1982), p. 15.

9. U.S. Department of Education, "State Education Performance Chart, 1982 and 1989," reprinted in *Education Week* (Washington, D.C.), May 9, 1990, p. 29.

10. Dale Mann, "Can We Help Dropouts? Thinking about the Undoable," in *School Dropouts: Patterns and Policies,* ed. Gary Natriello (New York: Teachers College Press, 1987), p. 7.

11. See Bureau of the Census, *School Enrollment: October 1988 and 1987,* p. 191, and idem, *Educational Attainment: March 1982 to 1985,* p. 109.

12. The 1980 sophomores in the HS&B study who dropped out as sophomores were less likely than those who dropped out as juniors, and those who dropped out as juniors less likely than those who dropped out as seniors, to return to graduate by 1984. Andrew J. Kolstad and Jeffrey A. Owings, "High School Dropouts Who Change Their Minds about School" (Paper presented at the annual meeting of the American Educational Research Association, San Francisco, April 16, 1986), pp. 12–13.

13. National Center for Education Statistics, U.S. Department of Education, *Dropout Rates in the United States: 1988* (Washington, D.C.: U.S. Government Printing Office, 1989), p. ix.

14. Ibid. See also Robert Kominski, "Estimating the National High School Dropout Rate," *Demography* 27 (May 1990): 303–311.

15. National Center for Education Statistics, *Dropout Rates,* p. x.

16. Bureau of the Census, *School Enrollment: October 1981 and 1980,* p. 60. In April 1980, excluding youth in military quarters, there were 2.4 million youth, aged 15 to 24, living in group quarters. Bureau of the Census, U.S. Department of Commerce, *1980 Census of Population, Detailed Population Characteristics, Part 1, United States Summary* (Washington, D.C.: U.S. Government Printing Office, 1984), p. 88. There were 841,000 youth, aged 16 to 24, in the armed forces identified in the present study. There is no way to determine how many of the former were undereducated; 142,000 of the latter were. Neither of these groups is included in the October CPS samples, which, of course, represent different points in time and different points in the educational cycle.

17. Bureau of the Census, *School Enrollment: October 1988 and 1987,* p. 5. The population controls for the October 1980 CPS were based on data from the 1970 census. Beginning in October 1981, the population controls were based on data from the 1980 census, and in 1985 a new sample design was implemented with revised weighting procedures for Hispanics based on independent population controls for that group. Bureau of the Census, U.S. Department of Commerce, *School*

Enrollment—Social and Economic Characteristics of Students: October 1982 (Washington, D.C.: U.S. Government Printing Office, 1986), p. 87; and idem, *School Enrollment—Social and Economic Characteristics of Students: October 1985 and 1984* (Washington, D.C.: U.S. Government Printing Office, 1988), pp. 125 and 127. These changes may have affected the absolute numbers shown in table 1.1.

18. Bureau of the Census, *School Enrollment: October 1981 and 1980,* p. 61; and *October 1988 and 1987,* p. 5. The difference between 13.3 percent and 12.7 percent, each with a standard error of ± 0.3 percent, is barely significant at the 68 percent confidence level.

19. Ibid., p. 6. The difference between the 1988 rate of whites and that of blacks is significant at the 68 percent confidence level.

20. Bureau of the Census, *School Enrollment: October 1981 and 1980,* p. 61; *October 1985 and 1984,* pp. 10 and 60; idem, *School Enrollment—Social and Economic Characteristics of Students: October 1986* (Washington, D.C.: U.S. Government Printing Office, 1988), p. 7; and *October 1988 and 1987,* p. 6. As a result of the changes in the sample noted in fn 17, above, the Census Bureau warns that comparisons of Hispanic data over time should be made cautiously. Ibid., p. 196.

21. Bureau of the Census, *School Enrollment: October 1981 and 1980,* pp. 60–61.

22. Bureau of the Census, *School Enrollment: October 1986,* pp. 23–26.

23. National Center for Education Statistics, *Dropout Rates,* p. 22.

24. Bureau of the Census, *School Enrollment: October 1981 and 1980,* pp. 73–74; and *October 1986,* pp. 24–25.

25. Bureau of the Census, *School Enrollment: October 1988 and 1987,* pp. 5–6; and *October 1981 and 1980,* pp. 60–61.

26. Eighteen states and the District of Columbia had minimum competency tests for graduation as of 1988; they included California, New York, and Texas. U.S. Department of Education, "State Education Performance Chart."

27. Bureau of the Census, U.S. Department of Commerce, *Projections of the Hispanic Population: 1983 to 2080* (Washington, D.C.: U.S. Government Printing Office, 1986), p. 14.

28. Ibid.

29. Michael W. Sherraden, "School Dropouts in Perspective," *The Educational Forum 51* (Fall 1986): 28.

30. Gary G. Wehlage and Robert A. Rutter, "Dropping Out: How Much Do Schools Contribute to the Problem?" in *School Dropouts: Patterns and Policies,* ed. Gary Natriello (New York: Teachers College Press, 1987), p. 71.

31. William B. Johnston, *Workforce 2000: Work and Workers for the 21st Century* (Indianapolis: Hudson Institute, 1987), p. xxvii.

32. Henry M. Levin, *The Costs to the Nation of Inadequate Education: A Report Prepared for the Select Committee on Equal Educational Opportunity of the United States Senate,* January 1972 (Washington, D.C.: U.S. Government Printing Office, 1972), p. vi.

33. Intercultural Development Research Association, *Texas School Dropout Survey Project: A Summary of Findings* (San Antonio: 1986), pp. 34–45.

34. The William T. Grant Foundation Commission on Work, Family and Citi-

zenship, *The Forgotten Half: Pathways to Success for America's Youth and Young Families* (Washington, D.C., 1988), pp. 26–27.

35. Ernest L. Boyer, *High School: A Report on Secondary Education in America* (New York: Harper and Row, 1983), pp. 246–247.

2

Who Are the Undereducated Youth?

The average youth who is not enrolled in school and is not a high school graduate is a majority white male who was born in the United States into a monolingual English-speaking family with an income above the poverty level. Before discontinuing his education, he completed at least the ninth grade. He lives in an urban area.

In 1980 there were 5.9 million undereducated youth, aged 16 to 24, in the United States. Fifty-eight percent of them—3.4 million—were white majority youth. Only 1.5 million, or a quarter of undereducated youth in 1980, were from the poorest levels of society. The risk of undereducation in the United States is pervasive. U.S. schools are failing to retain advantaged as well as disadvantaged youth through 12 years of education.

The undereducated white majority young people in 1980 were part of the nearly eight in ten undereducated youth—4.6 million—with English language backgrounds and the nine in ten—5.3 million—who were born in one of the 50 states, the District of Columbia, Puerto Rico, or another outlying U.S. area. After white majority youth, the largest groups of undereducated youth in 1980 consisted of more than a million African Americans—17 percent of the total—and nearly a million Hispanics—16 percent of the total. In addition, there were 337,000 undereducated non-Hispanic whites with non-English language backgrounds; 82,000 undereducated American Indians, Eskimos, and Aleuts; and 55,000 undereducated Asians and Pacific Islanders.

Undereducated youth are more likely to be male than female, and because so many teenagers who are potentially undereducated are nevertheless still in school, undereducated youth at any given time are more likely to be young adults than teenagers. In 1980, 3.2 million young men were undereducated in comparison with 2.7 million young women. Undereducated youth, aged 20 to 24, outnumbered those aged 16 to 19 by a factor of 1.2 per year of age; there were 3.6 million of the former and 2.3 million of the latter.

Most undereducated youth continue in school at least through the ninth grade. In 1980 three-quarters—4.5 million—had completed 9 to 11 years of schooling. However, 1.1 million had completed only 5 to 8 years of schooling, and there were a quarter of a million youth with fewer than 5 years of schooling.

Foreign-born youth are much more likely to have low levels of schooling than native-born youth. In 1980 native-born youth were nearly twice as likely to have completed at least the ninth grade as foreign-born youth; the latter were more than five times as likely not to have gone beyond the fourth grade as the former. On the other hand, two-thirds of the youth with very low levels of schooling, and eight in ten of those who had completed five to eight years of schooling, were born in the United States or its outlying areas. Among these youth, excluding African Americans, those who live in households in which non-English languages are spoken are less likely to reach high school before discontinuing their education than those from monolingual English-speaking homes.

The majority of undereducated youth in the United States live in urban areas, and the largest group lives in the central cities of metropolitan areas. Rural undereducated youth outnumber those who live in the suburbs of metropolitan areas and those who live in smaller urban places. In 1980 about a third of the 16-to-19-year-old civilian youth who were out of school without high school diplomas lived in the central cities; a quarter lived in the suburbs, and one in eight lived in smaller cities. Nearly three in ten undereducated youth lived in rural areas;[1] they lived in places with fewer than 2,500 inhabitants.

The following sections of this chapter contain a discussion of these and other characteristics of the youth who are out of school and have not completed 12 years of school, using white majority youth as the comparison group. They also contain an examination of the geographical distribution of undereducated youth in general and of undereducated minority youth in the various states. The distribution of the racial/ethnic populations and of undereducated youth, aged 16 to 19, in these populations in urban and rural areas within the states is considered in the final section. Data to study the latter come from the published volumes of the 1980 census.

THE RACIAL/ETHNIC AFFILIATION OF UNDEREDUCATED YOUTH

White majority youth constitute the largest proportion of undereducated youth in the United States. Nearly three out of five of the young people, aged 16 to 24, who were not enrolled in school and had not completed the twelfth grade in 1980 were non-Hispanic whites born in the United States, Puerto Rico, or another outlying U.S. area and living in households in which only English is spoken. There were 3.4 million such youth. In all, 2.4 million were minority youth: 1,023,000 African Americans; 923,000 Hispanics; 337,000 non-Hispanic whites living in households in which one or more persons speak a language other than English; 82,000 American Indians, Eskimos, and Aleuts; and 55,000 Asians and Pacific Islanders. In addition, there were 38,000 non-Hispanics consisting of white foreign-born English language-background young people and young people not identified with any of the racial groups who were not enrolled and had not completed 12 years of schooling. Figure 2.1 illustrates the percentages of the 1980 undereducated youth who belonged to the various racial/ethnic groups. The numbers and proportions of these groups and the numbers and proportions with various characteristics discussed in the following sections are shown in table 2.1.

Figure 2.1
Racial/Ethnic Affiliation of Undereducated Youth, 1980

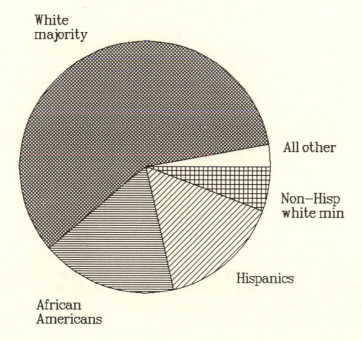

Table 2.1

Estimated Numbers and Distribution of Undereducated Youth, by Nativity and Selected Characteristic: United States, 1980

Characteristic	Total Number	Total Percent	Native born Number	Native born Percent	Foreign born Number	Foreign born Percent
Total	5,883,000	100.0	5,340,000	100.0	543,000	100.0
Racial/ethnic group						
African Americans	1,023,000	17.4	1,000,000	18.7	22,000	4.0
American Indians, Eskimos, and Aleuts	82,000	1.4	81,000	1.5	1,000	0.3
Asians and Pacific Islanders	55,000	0.9	15,000	0.3	40,000	7.3
Hispanics	923,000	15.7	535,000	10.0	387,000	71.3
Non-Hispanic white minority	337,000	5.7	277,000	5.2	60,000	11.0
White majority	3,426,000	58.2	3,426,000	64.2	NA	
Other non-Hispanics	38,000	0.6	5,000	0.1	33,000	6.0
Language background						
English only	4,576,000	77.8	4,523,000	84.7	53,000	9.7
Non-English	1,307,000	22.2	817,000	15.3	490,000	90.3
Gender						
Males	3,163,000	53.8	2,870,000	53.7	293,000	53.9
Females	2,720,000	46.2	2,470,000	46.3	250,000	46.1
Age						
16 to 19	2,327,000	39.6	2,161,000	40.5	166,000	30.5
20 to 24	3,556,000	60.4	3,179,000	59.5	377,000	69.5
Poverty status in 1979[1]						
Above poverty level	4,097,000	69.6	3,718,000	69.6	379,000	69.9
Below poverty level	1,498,000	25.5	1,345,000	25.2	153,000	28.2
Years of schooling completed						
Fewer than 5	251,000	4.3	160,000	3.0	91,000	16.8
5 to 8	1,140,000	19.4	916,000	17.2	223,000	41.1
9 to 11	4,492,000	76.4	4,264,000	79.8	228,000	42.0

Note: Percentages calculated on unrounded numbers. Detail may not add to total number or to 100.0 percent because of rounding. NA = not applicable.

[1]Not determined for people living in group quarters.

NATIVE-BORN AND FOREIGN-BORN UNDEREDUCATED YOUTH

Undereducated youth are predominantly native born. Among minority youth, only Asians and Pacific Islanders are largely foreign born, as illustrated in figure 2.2. In 1980, 91 percent of all undereducated youth—5.3 million—were born in one of the states, the District of Columbia, Puerto Rico, or another outlying area. They included all of the white majority

Figure 2.2
Nativity and Language Background of Undereducated Youth, 1980

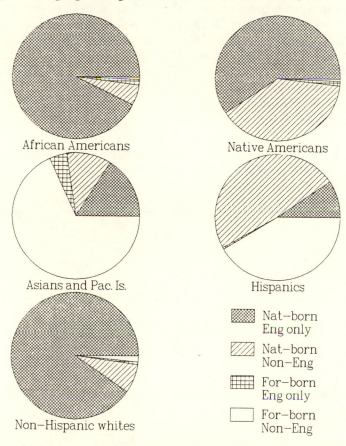

African Americans

Native Americans

Asians and Pac. Is.

Hispanics

Non-Hispanic whites

	Nat–born Eng only
	Nat–born Non–Eng
	For–born Eng only
	For–born Non–Eng

youth by definition and almost all of the American Indians, Eskimos, and Aleuts, and almost all African Americans. They included 82 percent of non-Hispanic white minority youth and 58 percent of the Hispanics. In contrast, nearly three-quarters of undereducated Asians and Pacific Islanders were born in foreign countries.

Hispanics constitute the largest proportion of foreign-born undereducated youth. In 1980 71 percent were Hispanics, 11 percent were non-Hispanic whites, and 7 percent were Asians and Pacific Islanders.

ENGLISH LANGUAGE-BACKGROUND AND NON-ENGLISH LANGUAGE-BACKGROUND UNDEREDUCATED YOUTH

Except for Hispanics, native-born undereducated youth overwhelmingly live in households in which only English is spoken, as also illustrated in figure 2.2. In 1980, 85 percent, or 4.5 million young people, lived in such households. In all, 3.4 million of these youth were majority whites and 1.1 million were native-born minority youth. Among native-born undereducated African Americans, 95 percent lived in monolingual English-speaking households; among whites, 93 percent; and among native-born undereducated American Indians, Eskimos, and Aleuts and Asians and Pacific Islanders, about 60 percent did so. In contrast, all but 17 percent of native-born undereducated Hispanics lived in Spanish-speaking households. These data are shown in table 2.2.

Table 2.2
Estimated Proportions of Undereducated Youth, by Language Background, Nativity, and Racial/Ethnic Group: United States, 1980

Nativity and racial/ethnic group	Number	English only	Non-English
Total	5,883,000	77.8	22.2
African Americans	1,023,000	94.1	5.9
American Indians, Eskimos, and Aleuts	82,000	60.7	39.3
Asians and Pacific Islanders	55,000	20.8	79.2
Hispanics	923,000	10.2	89.8
Non-Hispanic whites	3,791,000	91.1	8.9
Native born	5,340,000	84.7	15.3
African Americans	1,001,000	94.6	5.4
American Indians, Eskimos, and Aleuts	81,000	60.6	39.4
Asians and Pacific Islanders	15,000	59.2	40.8
Hispanics	535,000	16.7	83.3
Non-Hispanic whites	3,703,000	92.5	7.5
Foreign born	543,000	9.7	90.3
African Americans	22,000	71.2	28.8
American Indians, Eskimos, and Aleuts	1,000	67.6	32.4
Asians and Pacific Islanders	40,000	6.2	93.8
Hispanics	387,000	1.2	98.8
Non-Hispanic whites	88,000	32.1	67.9

Most foreign-born undereducated Hispanics, Asians, Pacific Islanders, and non-Hispanic whites live in households in which languages other than English are spoken. Of all foreign-born undereducated youth in 1980, nine out of ten lived in such households. They included almost all of the Hispanics and 95 percent of the Asians and Pacific Islanders, as shown in table 2.2. They included nearly seven out of ten of the non-Hispanic whites. Among foreign-born blacks in contrast, 71 percent lived in monolingual English-speaking households, reflecting their probable origins in Caribbean and African countries that were once British colonies.

UNDEREDUCATED MEN AND WOMEN

Undereducated men outnumber undereducated women. In 1980, 54 percent, or 3.2 million, of the undereducated youth were males, in comparison with 46 percent, or 2.7 million, who were females. Men outnumber women in similar proportions in both the native-born and foreign-born populations as a whole. Among undereducated foreign-born Asian/Pacific youth, however, women are the majority, and among undereducated foreign-born white minority youth, men and women are about evenly represented, as shown in table 2.3.

Table 2.3
Estimated Proportions of Undereducated Youth, by Gender, Nativity, and Racial/Ethnic Group: United States, 1980

Nativity and racial/ethnic group	Number	Men	Women
Total	5,883,000	53.8	46.2
African Americans	1,023,000	54.4	45.6
American Indians, Eskimos, and Aleuts	82,000	52.2	47.8
Asians and Pacific Islanders	55,000	46.4	53.6
Hispanics	923,000	53.0	47.0
Non-Hispanic white minority	337,000	52.6	47.4
White majority	3,426,000	54.1	45.9
Native born	5,340,000	53.7	46.3
African Americans	1,001,000	54.4	45.6
American Indians, Eskimos, and Aleuts	81,000	52.3	47.7
Asians and Pacific Islanders	15,000	53.4	46.6
Hispanics	535,000	50.8	49.2
Non-Hispanic white minority	277,000	53.4	46.6
White majority	3,426,000	54.1	45.9
Foreign born	543,000	53.9	46.1
African Americans	22,000	52.5	47.5
American Indians, Eskimos, and Aleuts	1,000	44.6	55.4
Asians and Pacific Islanders	40,000	43.7	56.3
Hispanics	387,000	56.0	44.0
Non-Hispanic white minority	60,000	48.5	51.5

UNDEREDUCATED TEENAGERS AND YOUNG ADULTS

At any given time, many teenagers, because of delayed entry in school, grade repetition, or discontinuous attendance, are enrolled at grade levels a year or more behind those appropriate for their ages. Some of these youth will leave school without graduating; they will become a part of the undereducated 20-to-24-year-old population. It is, therefore, not surprising to find that the undereducated young adults, aged 20 to 24, in this study outnumbered the undereducated teenagers. In 1980, 2.3 million undereducated youth were aged 16 to 19 and 3.6 million were aged 20 to 24. Among native-born youth, 40 percent were teenagers and 60 percent were young adults. There are proportionally many more young adults than teenagers in the foreign-born population in general;[2] thus, the distribution was even more uneven among foreign-born undereducated youth. As shown in table 2.4, young undereducated adults outnumbered teenagers by a factor of 1.2 per year of age among native-born youth and by a factor of 1.8 among foreign-born youth. African Americans are the most likely native-born group to be older. Among the foreign-born youth, Asians and Pacific Islanders are especially likely to be older.

Table 2.4
Factors Representing the Excess of Average Numbers per Year of Age of Undereducated Youth, Aged 20 to 24, Over Those of Undereducated Youth, Aged 16 to 19, by Nativity and Racial/Ethnic Group: United States, 1980

Racial/ethnic group	Total	Native born	Foreign born
Total	1.2	1.2	1.8
African Americans	1.4	1.4	1.6
American Indians, Eskimos, and Aleuts	1.0	1.0	*
Asians and Pacific Islanders	1.7	1.1	2.1
Hispanics	1.4	1.2	1.9
Non-Hispanic white minority	1.1	1.0	1.8
White majority	1.2	1.2	NA

NA = not applicable.
*Fewer than an estimated 1,000 young people per year of age.

THE POVERTY STATUS OF UNDEREDUCATED YOUTH

The majority of undereducated youth, foreign-born as well as native-born, are not from the poorest sectors of society. In 1980, 4.1 million, or 70 percent of all undereducated youth, were from families with 1979 incomes above the poverty level, and the proportions were similar among native-born and foreign-born youth. There were 3.7 million native-born youth and 379,000 foreign-born youth from such families. However, foreign-born youth, and therefore foreign-born undereducated youth, are more likely to be from poor families than native-born youth. Twenty-eight percent of undereducated foreign-born youth in comparison with a quarter of undereducated native-born youth were from families with incomes below the 1979 poverty level in 1980. There were 288,000 undereducated young people whose poverty status was not determined in 1980 because they were living in military barracks, institutions, or other types of group quarters.

The likelihood of undereducated youth to be poor differs considerably according to their racial/ethnic affiliation. As shown in table 2.5, the proportions from families with incomes below the poverty level ranged from fewer than one out of five non-Hispanic whites to two out of five African Americans in 1980. The differences in the proportions of undereducated members of the various racial/ethnic groups who are poor parallel the differences in the poverty status of these groups as a whole. These differences are discussed as undereducation risk factors in the following chapter.

Table 2.5
Estimated Proportions of Undereducated Youth, by Poverty Status, Nativity, and Racial/Ethnic Group: United States, 1980

Nativity and racial/ethnic group	Number	Above poverty	Below poverty
Total	5,883,000	69.6	25.5
African Americans	1,023,000	51.2	40.7
American Indians, Eskimos, and Aleuts	82,000	56.2	38.4
Asians and Pacific Islanders	55,000	64.0	32.0
Hispanics	923,000	65.6	31.5
Non-Hispanic white minority	337,000	79.1	19.1
White majority	3,426,000	75.7	19.5
Native born	5,340,000	69.6	25.2
African Americans	1,001,000	51.0	40.8
American Indians, Eskimos, and Aleuts	81,000	56.5	38.2
Asians and Pacific Islanders	15,000	68.8	22.5
Hispanics	535,000	62.9	33.1
Non-Hispanic white minority	277,000	78.6	19.6
White majority	3,426,000	75.7	19.5
Foreign born	543,000	69.9	28.2
African Americans	22,000	60.2	33.8
American Indians, Eskimos, and Aleuts	1,000	40.5	50.0
Asians and Pacific Islanders	40,000	62.1	35.6
Hispanics	387,000	69.4	29.3
Non-Hispanic white minority	60,000	81.7	17.0

Note: Poverty status not determined for people living in group quarters.

THE YEARS OF SCHOOLING COMPLETED BY UNDEREDUCATED YOUTH

Most youth who are out of school without high school diplomas have completed at least nine years of schooling. However, most of those who reach high school are native-born youth. Foreign-born youth, proportionally, have much less education. In 1980, 4.5 million or three-quarters of all undereducated youth, aged 16 to 24, had finished the ninth, tenth, or eleventh grades before discontinuing their education. Among native-born youth, eight in ten had done so, and they represented 95 percent of the youth with at least a ninth grade education in 1980. In contrast, only 42 percent of foreign-born undereducated youth had completed nine or more years of schooling, and about the same proportion had completed from five to eight years. Seventeen percent of foreign-born youth but only 3 percent of native-born youth had completed fewer than five years.

The 1980 census did not ask where individuals were schooled, and the study did not attempt to separate youth who were recent arrivals—those who had arrived between 1975 and 1980—from those who were clearly young enough at the time they immigrated to have enrolled in school in the United States. Thus it is impossible to generalize about the relationship of undereducation among foreign-born young people to their experiences in U.S. schools or to the level of schooling they brought with them to this country. This caveat will become more relevant in the next chapter, which considers the differences in the extent of risk of undereducation among native-born and foreign-born members of the various racial/ethnic groups.

Undereducated youth from the various racial/ethnic groups differ in the number of years of schooling they are likely to have completed. As illustrated in figure 2.3, the 1980 proportions of those with at least a ninth grade education ranged from 81 percent of African Americans to 56 percent of Hispanics, and those with fewer than five years, from 16 percent of Asians and Pacific Islanders to 3 percent of white majority youth, African Americans, and American Indians, Eskimos, and Aleuts.

The differences in the extent of schooling among the racial/ethnic groups are related not only to differences in nativity among the groups but also to differences in language background, as shown in table 2.6. Not only do foreign-born members of each group have lower levels of education than their native-born counterparts, but within each nativity group, except for African Americans, the members of each group who live in households in which languages other than English are spoken have lower levels of education than their counterparts in monolingual English-speaking households. In all groups, more than four out of five native-born youth with English language backgrounds had completed at least nine years of schooling in 1980. A similar proportion of native-born non-English language-background African Americans had completed at least nine years; the proportions of the other native-born groups with non-English language backgrounds ranged from 77 percent of non-Hispanic white minority youth to 69 percent of Hispanics. Among foreign-born language minority youth, the proportions of youth with at least nine years of schooling ranged from 64 percent of African Americans to 33 percent of

Figure 2.3
Years of Schooling Completed by Undereducated Youth, 1980

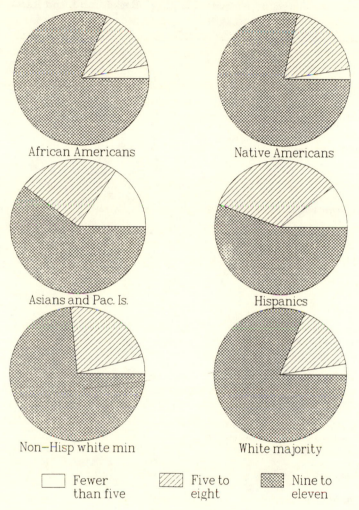

African Americans   Native Americans

Asians and Pac. Is.   Hispanics

Non—Hisp white min   White majority

☐ Fewer   ▨ Five to   ▩ Nine to
  than five   eight   eleven

Hispanics, much lower than the proportions of any of the native-born groups.

Native-born Asians and Pacific Islanders are the most likely among native-born youth to have very low levels of schooling. Six percent of those with English language backgrounds and 10 percent of those with language minority backgrounds had fewer than five years of schooling in 1980. In comparison, no more than 4 percent of any of the other native-born groups had failed to continue at least through the fifth grade. Among foreign-born language minority youth, Hispanics and Asians and Pacific Is-

Table 2.6
Estimated Numbers of Undereducated Youth and Distribution by Years of Schooling Completed, by Nativity, Language Background, and Racial/ Ethnic Group: United States, 1980

Nativity, language background, and racial/ethnic group	Number	Percent by years completed		
		<5	5 to 8	9 to 11
Total	5,883,000	4.3	19.4	76.4
African Americans	1,023,000	3.3	15.6	81.1
American Indians, Eskimos, and Aleuts	82,000	2.6	19.1	78.4
Asians and Pacific Islanders	55,000	15.7	24.1	60.2
Hispanics	923,000	10.5	34.0	55.6
Non-Hispanic white minority	337,000	4.2	22.5	73.3
White majority	3,426,000	2.7	16.2	81.0
Native born, English only	4,523,000	2.9	16.0	81.1
African Americans	947,000	3.2	15.7	81.2
American Indians, Eskimos, and Aleuts	49,000	1.7	16.3	82.0
Asians and Pacific Islanders	9,000	6.1	10.5	83.4
Hispanics	90,000	3.9	13.9	82.3
White majority	3,426,000	2.7	16.2	81.0
Native born, non-English	817,000	3.7	23.3	73.0
African Americans	54,000	3.4	14.5	82.1
American Indians, Eskimos, and Aleuts	32,000	3.8	23.2	72.9
Asians and Pacific Islanders	6,000	10.1	16.2	73.7
Hispanics	446,000	4.3	26.2	69.5
Non-Hispanic white minority	277,000	2.8	20.4	76.8
Foreign born, English only	53,000	4.9	14.8	80.4
African Americans	16,000	4.8	15.7	79.6
American Indians, Eskimos, and Aleuts	1,000	6.0	12.0	82.0
Asians and Pacific Islanders	2,000	9.7	15.3	75.0
Hispanics	5,000	12.4	24.9	62.7
Non-Hispanic whites	28,000	3.0	12.2	84.7
Foreign born, non-English	490,000	18.1	44.0	37.9
African Americans	6,000	14.6	21.0	64.4
Asians and Pacific Islanders	37,000	19.3	29.2	51.4
Hispanics	383,000	19.2	47.8	33.1
Non-Hispanic white minority	60,000	10.8	32.0	57.2

Note: Detail may not add to 100.0 percent because of rounding.

landers were equally likely to have completed fewer than five years of schooling in 1980. These differences should be kept in mind in connection with the discussion of the risks of undereducation for the various racial/ ethnic groups in the next chapter.

Although foreign-born youth are the most likely to have low levels of education, a substantial majority of youth who have completed fewer than five years of schooling, and an even greater proportion of those with five to eight years of schooling, are native born. The largest number of them are white majority youth. In 1980, as shown in table 2.7, two-thirds of those with less than a fifth grade education and four-fifths of those who had completed five to eight years were born in this country. Thirty-seven percent of those with the least schooling and almost half of those with five to eight years of schooling—650,000 young people altogether—were members of the majority.

Table 2.7
Estimated Numbers and Distribution of Undereducated Youth Who Have Completed Fewer Than Five Years, Five to Eight Years, and Nine to Eleven Years of Schooling, by Nativity and Racial/Ethnic Group: United States, 1980

	Years completed					
	Fewer than 5		5 to 8		9 to 11	
Nativity and racial/ethnic group	Number	Percent	Number	Percent	Number	Percent
Total	251,000	100.0	1,140,000	100.0	4,492,000	100.0
Native born	160,000	63.6	916,000	80.4	4,264,000	94.9
African Americans	32,000	12.7	156,000	13.7	813,000	18.1
American Indians, Eskimos, and Aleuts	2,000	0.8	15,000	1.3	63,000	1.4
Asians and Pacific Islanders	1,000	0.5	2,000	0.2	12,000	0.3
Hispanics	23,000	9.0	129,000	11.4	383,000	8.5
Non-Hispanic white minority	8,000	3.1	57,000	5.0	213,000	4.7
White majority	94,000	37.5	556,000	48.8	2,776,000	61.8
Foreign born	91,000	36.4	223,000	19.6	228,000	5.1
African Americans	2,000	0.7	4,000	0.3	16,000	0.4
American Indians, Eskimos, and Aleuts	*	†	*	†	1,000	†
Asians and Pacific Islanders	7,000	3.0	11,000	1.0	21,000	0.5
Hispanics	74,000	29.4	184,000	16.1	129,000	2.9
Non-Hispanic white minority	6,000	2.6	19,000	1.7	34,000	0.8

Note: Percentages calculated on unrounded numbers.

*Fewer than an estimated 1,000 young people.

†Less than an estimated 0.1 of a percent.

Among the foreign born, Hispanics constitute the largest group with an eighth grade education or less. There were 74,000 Hispanic youth who had completed fewer than five years and 184,000 who had completed from five to eight years of schooling in 1980.

UNDEREDUCATED YOUTH IN THE STATES

Undereducated youth are found in all states and in 1980 only Vermont had fewer than 10,000. Not surprisingly, the largest numbers are found in the states with the largest overall populations. There were 704,000 young people in California in 1980 who were not enrolled in school and had not completed the twelfth grade. Texas was home to 497,000 undereducated youth and New York, to 363,000. There were 296,000 undereducated youth in Illinois and 257,000 in Florida. In addition, there were 15 other states in the eastern and central parts of the country in which at least 100,000 undereducated youth lived in 1980. The geographical distribution of these youth is displayed in figure 2.4; table 2.8 shows the numbers for each state and the District of Columbia.

As will be noted from table 2.8, minorities are concentrated in certain states. In 1980 three-quarters of undereducated Hispanics lived in four states: California with 336,000, Texas with 197,000, New York with 95,000, and Illinois with 55,000. Fifty-three percent of undereducated Asians and Pacific Islanders lived in the states of California, Hawaii, and New York, with 17,000, 8,000, and 4,000 members of this group, respectively. Forty-one percent of undereducated American Indians, Eskimos, and Aleuts lived in four states: 10,000 in Arizona, 9,000 in California, 8,000 in Oklahoma, and 7,000 in New Mexico.

It has already been observed that the majority of undereducated youth in the United States are white youth, born in the United States and living in monolingual English-speaking families. However, this is not the case in all states. As shown in table 2.9, there were eight states in 1980 in which white majority youth were the minority among undereducated youth—Arizona, California, Hawaii, Louisiana, New Jersey, New Mexico, New York, and Texas—and two states in which they constituted only about half of the undereducated youth—Illinois and Mississippi. Only a quarter of undereducated youth in New Mexico were members of the white majority; most were Hispanics. White majority youth constituted about a third of undereducated youth in Hawaii where the largest group—45 percent—consisted of Asians and Pacific Islanders. Asians and Pacific Islanders constituted 36 percent in California where Hispanics made up nearly half the total. In contrast to these states, at least 85 percent of undereducated youth in five states—Iowa, Kentucky, New Hampshire, Vermont, and West Virginia—consisted of white majority youth. The District of Columbia is a special case: it is a central city whose suburbs are in Maryland and Virginia. In 1980 the population of the District was 70 percent African American;[3] more than nine out of ten undereducated young people were African Americans.

Figure 2.4
Undereducated Youth in the United States, 1980

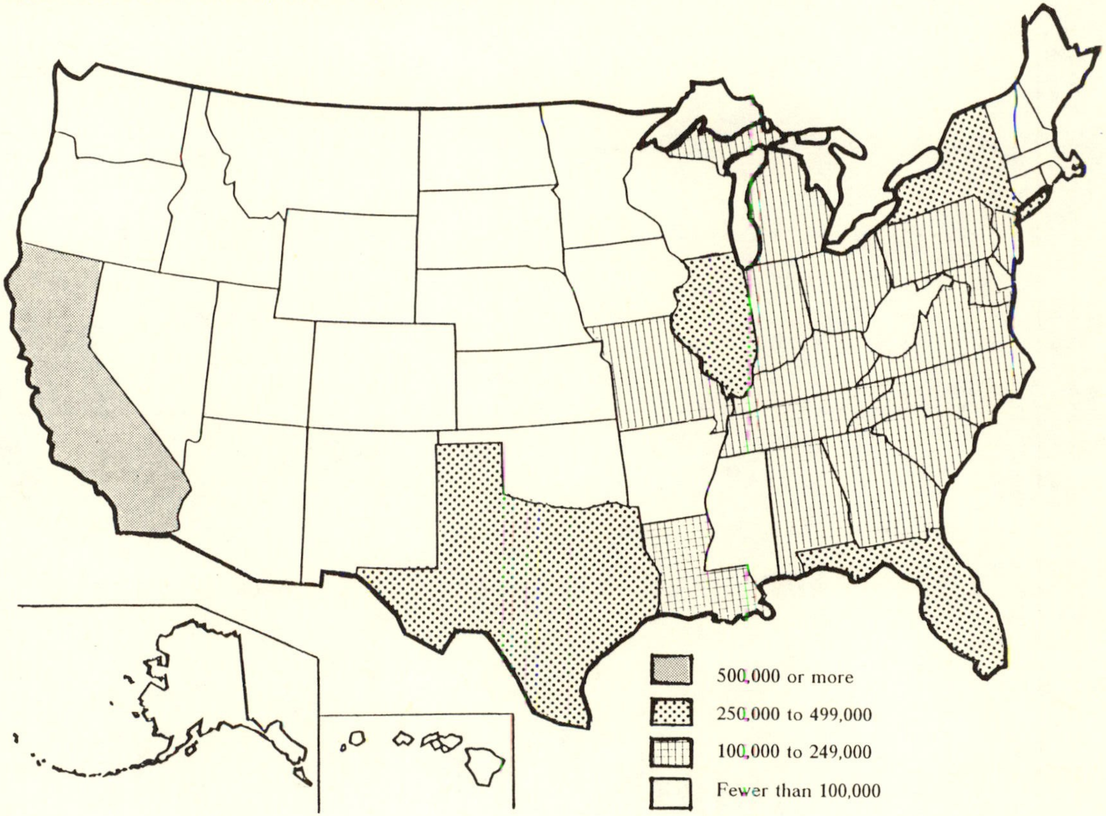

500,000 or more
250,000 to 499,000
100,000 to 249,000
Fewer than 100,000

Table 2.8
Estimated Numbers of Undereducated Youth, by Racial/Ethnic Group and State: United States, 1980 (Numbers in thousands)

State	Total	African Americans	Amer. Indians, Eskimos, & Aleuts	Asians & Pacific Islanders	His-panics	Non-Hispanic white minority	White majority	Other non-His-panics
Total	5,883	1,023	82	55	923	337	3,426	38
Alabama	129	39	1	*	2	3	84	*
Alaska	10	*	3	*	*	1	5	*
Arizona	83	3	10	*	28	4	37	1
Arkansas	69	14	1	*	1	2	52	*
California	704	50	9	17	336	35	251	7
Colorado	69	3	1	1	20	4	39	1
Connecticut	60	8	*	1	9	7	34	1
Delaware	13	4	*	*	*	1	8	*
District of Columbia	19	17	*	*	1	*	1	*
Florida	257	57	2	1	29	13	153	2
Georgia	195	64	1	1	4	5	120	1
Hawaii	17	1	*	8	2	1	6	*
Idaho	26	*	1	*	4	1	19	*
Illinois	296	74	1	2	55	18	146	2
Indiana	143	15	*	*	4	8	115	1
Iowa	48	1	*	*	1	3	42	*
Kansas	52	5	1	1	4	3	38	*
Kentucky	150	13	*	*	2	4	129	1
Louisiana	148	56	1	1	4	15	69	*
Maine	22	*	*	*	*	3	18	*
Maryland	102	37	1	1	2	4	57	1
Massachusetts	97	6	*	1	9	19	61	1
Michigan	217	46	2	1	7	14	146	1
Minnesota	56	1	2	1	1	4	46	*
Mississippi	94	43	*	*	1	2	47	*
Missouri	128	23	1	*	2	5	96	1
Montana	14	*	2	*	*	1	10	*
Nebraska	24	2	*	*	1	1	19	*
Nevada	24	2	1	*	3	2	16	*
New Hampshire	19	*	*	*	*	3	16	*
New Jersey	139	34	1	1	24	14	65	1
New Mexico	43	*	7	*	22	2	10	*
New York	363	82	2	4	95	34	144	2
North Carolina	195	53	4	*	3	5	128	1
North Dakota	11	*	1	*	*	1	8	*
Ohio	239	37	1	*	5	14	181	1
Oklahoma	83	7	8	1	4	4	59	*
Oregon	65	1	2	1	4	4	53	*
Pennsylvania	217	38	1	1	10	17	150	1
Rhode Island	24	2	*	*	1	6	14	*
South Carolina	103	34	1	*	2	3	63	1
South Dakota	13	*	3	*	*	1	8	*
Tennessee	148	26	*	*	2	4	115	*
Texas	497	64	2	3	197	22	206	4
Utah	34	1	1	1	4	2	25	1
Vermont	9	*	*	*	*	1	8	*
Virginia	154	43	1	1	3	5	101	1
Washington	97	4	4	2	8	6	73	1
West Virginia	58	2	*	*	1	2	54	*
Wisconsin	89	9	2	1	4	6	67	*
Wyoming	13	*	*	*	2	1	10	*

Note: Detail may not add to total because of rounding.

*Fewer than an estimated 1,000 young people.

Table 2.9
Percentage Distribution of Undereducated Youth, by Racial/Ethnic Group and State: United States, 1980 (Numbers in thousands)

State	Total	African Americans	Amer. Indians, Eskimos, & Aleuts	Asians & Pacific Islanders	His-panics	Non-Hispanic white minority	White majority	Other non-His-panics
Total	100.0	17.4	1.4	0.9	15.7	5.7	58.2	0.6
Alabama	100.0	30.5	0.4	0.2	1.3	2.7	64.7	0.2
Alaska	100.0	2.2	32.8	2.6	3.2	5.3	53.0	0.8
Arizona	100.0	3.5	11.5	0.5	33.7	5.3	44.9	0.7
Arkansas	100.0	19.8	1.1	0.3	1.2	2.7	74.6	0.3
California	100.0	7.1	1.3	2.4	47.7	4.9	35.6	0.9
Colorado	100.0	4.6	1.5	1.5	28.8	5.3	57.2	1.1
Connecticut	100.0	13.0	0.2	0.9	14.9	12.5	57.6	0.9
Delaware	100.0	28.7	0.3	0.3	2.7	5.1	62.7	0.2
District of Columbia	100.0	92.3	*	0.2	3.3	0.3	3.8	0.1
Florida	100.0	22.3	0.6	0.4	11.5	5.1	59.3	0.8
Georgia	100.0	32.9	0.5	0.3	1.8	2.5	61.6	0.5
Hawaii	100.0	4.2	0.9	45.1	12.4	3.2	32.3	1.8
Idaho	100.0	0.4	2.3	0.5	16.4	4.5	75.2	1.3
Illinois	100.0	24.8	0.3	0.6	18.4	6.0	49.3	0.5
Indiana	100.0	10.4	0.2	0.3	2.7	5.5	80.6	0.4
Iowa	100.0	2.8	0.6	0.6	2.1	5.7	87.3	0.9
Kansas	100.0	10.3	1.5	1.2	7.0	5.6	73.7	0.7
Kentucky	100.0	8.8	0.3	0.2	1.6	2.7	86.0	0.4
Louisiana	100.0	38.1	0.7	0.5	2.9	10.4	47.0	0.3
Maine	100.0	0.4	0.7	0.2	0.4	13.8	83.4	1.1
Maryland	100.0	36.4	0.6	0.7	1.6	4.1	55.9	0.7
Massachusetts	100.0	6.3	0.3	0.8	9.3	18.4	63.6	1.3
Michigan	100.0	21.0	1.1	0.3	3.4	6.6	67.0	0.6
Minnesota	100.0	2.3	4.2	1.5	2.3	6.7	82.2	0.9
Mississippi	100.0	45.6	0.4	0.1	1.2	2.2	50.1	0.4
Missouri	100.0	18.1	0.7	0.3	1.6	3.7	75.0	0.6
Montana	100.0	0.4	14.3	0.7	3.2	8.4	72.7	0.3
Nebraska	100.0	6.6	1.8	0.8	6.0	4.8	79.4	0.6
Nevada	100.0	8.4	3.3	1.4	13.0	6.7	66.2	1.0
New Hampshire	100.0	0.3	0.2	0.3	0.2	14.6	83.2	1.1
New Jersey	100.0	24.5	0.4	0.6	17.4	9.9	46.6	0.5
New Mexico	100.0	1.1	17.0	0.6	51.9	4.7	24.2	0.5
New York	100.0	22.5	0.5	1.2	26.0	9.5	39.7	0.7
North Carolina	100.0	27.4	2.2	0.2	1.7	2.4	65.6	0.5
North Dakota	100.0	0.5	10.0	0.2	1.5	14.0	73.3	0.8
Ohio	100.0	15.4	0.4	0.2	2.1	6.0	75.6	0.3
Oklahoma	100.0	8.1	9.5	0.8	5.1	4.4	71.6	0.6
Oregon	100.0	1.9	3.1	1.0	6.4	6.4	80.6	0.6
Pennsylvania	100.0	17.4	0.3	0.5	4.4	7.9	69.2	0.3
Rhode Island	100.0	6.8	0.4	1.8	4.9	24.4	60.0	1.7
South Carolina	100.0	33.3	0.6	0.3	1.7	2.6	60.9	0.5
South Dakota	100.0	0.1	24.2	0.4	2.2	9.7	63.0	0.3
Tennessee	100.0	17.5	0.3	0.2	1.1	2.8	77.9	0.3
Texas	100.0	12.9	0.4	0.7	39.5	4.3	41.4	0.7
Utah	100.0	2.4	3.8	2.4	11.8	4.7	73.3	1.6
Vermont	100.0	0.9	1.1	0.2	0.2	11.3	86.0	0.2
Virginia	100.0	27.8	0.3	0.6	1.6	3.4	65.6	0.7
Washington	100.0	3.8	3.6	2.0	8.5	5.9	75.0	1.3
West Virginia	100.0	3.1	0.2	*	0.9	3.0	92.4	0.3
Wisconsin	100.0	10.6	1.8	0.7	4.4	6.9	75.2	0.4
Wyoming	100.0	0.3	3.8	0.2	12.2	5.0	77.3	1.2

Note: Detail may not add to 100.0 percent because of rounding.

*Less than an estimated 0.1 of a percent.

35

POOR, FOREIGN-BORN, AND LANGUAGE MINORITY UNDEREDUCATED YOUTH IN THE STATES

Of the three groups of young people who, as discussed in the next chapter, are especially at risk of undereducation, those from families with incomes below the poverty level are the most widely distributed among the states. In no state in 1980 were there fewer than 2,000 poor undereducated youth, as shown in table 2.10. The largest numbers were in California, Texas, and New York. Hispanics constituted the largest proportion of these youth in each case. The largest number of poor undereducated African American youth lived in New York and the second largest number in Illinois; other groups of at least 20,000 poor African American youth lived in six southern states. The largest groups of poor undereducated non-Hispanic white youth lived in California, Ohio, and Kentucky.

As shown in table 2.11, foreign-born undereducated youth are highly concentrated: in 1980, 44 percent lived in California and 88 percent of them were Hispanic. California also led in the number of undereducated youth from language minority homes, as shown in table 2.12. Three-quarters of Spanish language-background undereducated Hispanic youth lived in California, Texas, New York, or Illinois. The proportions of youth who are poor, foreign born, or members of language minorities in the various racial/ethnic groups in the states are discussed in relation to the risk of undereducation in the following chapter and in connection with the different state populations in the chapters treating each racial/ethnic group separately.

URBAN AND RURAL UNDEREDUCATED YOUTH

The population of the United States as a whole is highly urbanized, but the racial/ethnic groups differ in the extent to which they live in certain types of urban and rural environments. As will be demonstrated in the following chapters, the risk of undereducation varies according to where youth live, and it reflects inequities between school districts serving predominantly poor and minority students and those serving more advantaged students. Not surprisingly, the largest group of undereducated youth, among whom minority youth are disproportionately represented, is found in the inner cities of large metropolitan areas where poverty and other ills exacerbate their problems. Second only to them are the numbers of undereducated youth living in rural areas where poverty was also prevalent, especially in some regions of the country, in 1980.[4] Among undereducated civilian youth, aged 16 to 19, in 1980, as shown in table 2.13, 71.9 percent lived in urban areas: 33.8 percent in the central cities of metropolitan areas, a quarter in the suburbs, and 13.3 percent in smaller cities outside the metropolitan areas. The remainder, 28.1 percent, lived in places with fewer than 2,500 inhabitants.[5]

Table 2.10
Estimated Numbers of Undereducated Youth from Families with Incomes Below the Poverty Level, by Racial/Ethnic Group and State: United States, 1980 (Numbers in thousands)

State	Total	African Americans	Amer. Indians, Eskimos, & Aleuts	Asians & Pacific Islanders	His-panics	Non-Hispanic whites
Total	1,498	416	32	18	291	740
Alabama	39	20	*	*	1	19
Alaska	2	*	1	*	*	1
Arizona	23	1	5	*	8	8
Arkansas	21	7	*	*	*	13
California	168	17	2	5	90	52
Colorado	16	1	*	*	6	7
Connecticut	13	3	*	*	4	6
Delaware	3	1	*	*	*	2
District of Columbia	6	6	*	*	*	*
Florida	66	26	*	*	9	31
Georgia	51	28	*	*	1	22
Hawaii	4	*	*	2	*	1
Idaho	7	*	*	*	2	5
Illinois	74	30	1	*	15	28
Indiana	32	5	*	*	1	25
Iowa	10	1	*	*	*	9
Kansas	10	2	*	*	1	7
Kentucky	48	7	*	*	1	41
Louisiana	42	25	*	*	1	15
Maine	6	*	*	*	*	5
Maryland	24	13	*	*	*	10
Massachusetts	22	2	*	*	4	15
Michigan	51	16	1	*	2	31
Minnesota	12	1	1	*	*	9
Mississippi	32	21	*	*	*	10
Missouri	30	9	*	*	*	20
Montana	5	*	1	*	*	3
Nebraska	5	1	*	*	*	4
Nevada	4	*	*	*	1	3
New Hampshire	4	*	*	*	*	3
New Jersey	34	14	*	*	9	11
New Mexico	14	*	4	*	7	2
New York	117	35	1	1	42	37
North Carolina	43	19	1	*	1	22
North Dakota	2	*	1	*	*	2
Ohio	63	16	*	*	2	45
Oklahoma	19	2	3	*	1	12
Oregon	16	1	1	*	2	13
Pennsylvania	56	17	*	*	4	34
Rhode Island	5	1	*	*	*	4
South Carolina	24	13	*	*	*	10
South Dakota	5	*	2	*	*	3
Tennessee	41	12	*	*	1	28
Texas	125	24	*	1	65	35
Utah	7	1	*	*	1	4
Vermont	2	*	*	*	*	2
Virginia	34	14	*	*	*	18
Washington	24	1	1	1	3	19
West Virginia	17	1	*	*	*	16
Wisconsin	19	4	1	*	1	13
Wyoming	2	*	*	*	*	1

Note: Poverty status not determined for people living in group quarters. Detail may not add to total because of rounding.

*Fewer than an estimated 1,000 young people.

Table 2.11
Estimated Numbers of Undereducated Foreign-Born Youth, by Racial/ Ethnic Group and State: United States, 1980 (Numbers in thousands)

State	Total	African Americans	Amer. Indians, Eskimos, & Aleuts	Asians & Pacific Islanders	Hispanics	Non-Hispanic white minority
Total, all states	543	22	1	40	387	60
Alabama	1	*	*	*	*	*
Arizona	8	*	*	*	7	*
Arkansas	1	*	*	*	*	*
California	239	1	*	13	211	8
Colorado	4	*	*	1	3	*
Connecticut	5	*	*	*	1	2
District of Columbia	1	*	*	*	*	*
Florida	23	3	*	1	15	1
Georgia	3	*	*	*	*	*
Hawaii	3	*	*	2	*	*
Idaho	2	*	*	*	2	*
Illinois	39	1	*	1	30	5
Indiana	2	*	*	*	1	*
Iowa	1	*	*	*	*	*
Kansas	2	*	*	1	1	*
Kentucky	1	*	*	*	*	*
Louisiana	3	1	*	1	1	*
Maryland	3	1	*	1	1	1
Massachusetts	13	1	*	1	2	8
Michigan	7	*	*	1	1	4
Minnesota	2	*	*	1	*	*
Mississippi	1	*	*	*	*	*
Missouri	2	*	*	*	*	*
Nebraska	1	*	*	*	*	*
Nevada	2	*	*	*	*	*
New Hampshire	1	*	*	*	*	*
New Jersey	13	1	*	1	6	4
New Mexico	4	*	*	*	3	*
New York	51	9	*	4	24	11
North Carolina	2	*	*	*	*	*
Ohio	3	*	*	*	*	1
Oklahoma	3	*	*	1	1	*
Oregon	3	*	*	*	2	1
Pennsylvania	4	*	*	1	1	1
Rhode Island	4	*	*	*	1	3
South Carolina	1	*	*	*	*	*
Tennessee	1	*	*	*	*	*
Texas	70	1	*	3	62	2
Utah	2	*	*	1	1	*
Virginia	3	*	*	1	1	1
Washington	7	1	*	1	4	1
Wisconsin	2	*	*	1	1	*
Wyoming	1	*	*	*	*	*

Note: Detail may not add to total because of rounding. Totals include non-Hispanic white youth with English language backgrounds.

*Fewer than an estimated 1,000 young people.

Table 2.12
Estimated Numbers of Undereducated Youth with Non-English Language Backgrounds, by Racial/Ethnic Group and State: United States, 1980 (Numbers in thousands)

State	Total	African Americans	Amer. Indians, Eskimos, & Aleuts	Asians & Pacific Islanders	His-panics	Non-Hispanic white minority
Total	1,307	60	32	44	828	337
Alabama	6	2	*	*	1	3
Alaska	3	*	2	*	*	1
Arizona	39	*	8	*	25	4
Arkansas	3	1	*	*	*	2
California	363	3	2	14	307	35
Colorado	19	*	*	1	14	4
Connecticut	17	1	*	*	8	7
Delaware	1	*	*	*	*	1
District of Columbia	2	1	*	*	1	*
Florida	45	5	*	1	26	13
Georgia	9	2	*	*	2	5
Hawaii	6	*	*	4	1	1
Idaho	5	*	*	*	4	1
Illinois	75	4	*	2	51	18
Indiana	12	1	*	*	3	8
Iowa	4	*	*	*	1	3
Kansas	7	*	*	*	3	3
Kentucky	6	*	*	*	1	4
Louisiana	25	6	1	1	2	15
Maine	3	*	*	*	*	3
Maryland	8	2	*	1	1	4
Massachusetts	28	*	*	1	9	18
Michigan	23	2	*	1	5	14
Minnesota	6	*	1	1	1	4
Mississippi	4	1	*	*	*	2
Missouri	7	1	*	*	1	5
Montana	2	*	1	*	*	1
Nebraska	3	*	*	*	1	1
Nevada	5	*	*	*	3	2
New Hampshire	3	*	*	*	*	3
New Jersey	40	2	*	1	23	14
New Mexico	30	*	7	*	21	2
New York	137	8	1	4	90	34
North Carolina	9	2	*	*	2	5
North Dakota	2	*	1	*	*	1
Ohio	20	2	*	*	3	14
Oklahoma	9	*	2	*	3	4
Oregon	8	*	*	*	3	4
Pennsylvania	28	2	*	1	8	17
Rhode Island	8	*	*	*	1	6
South Carolina	5	2	*	*	1	3
South Dakota	3	*	2	*	*	1
Tennessee	6	1	*	*	*	4
Texas	219	4	*	3	188	22
Utah	6	*	1	1	3	1
Vermont	1	*	*	*	*	1
Virginia	9	2	*	1	1	5
Washington	15	*	1	1	7	6
West Virginia	2	*	*	*	*	2
Wisconsin	10	*	*	1	3	6
Wyoming	2	*	*	*	1	1

Note: Detail may not add to total because of rounding.

*Fewer than an estimated 1,000 young people.

Table 2.13
Percentage Distribution of Undereducated Civilian Youth, Aged 16 to 19, by
Urbanicity, Race, and Hispanic Ethnicity: United States, 1980

Race and Hispanic ethnicity	Total	Urban				Rural	
		Total	Central cities	Urban fringe	Places of 2,500+	Total	Rural farm
Total	100.0	71.9	33.8	24.8	13.3	28.1	1.7
American Indians, Eskimos, and Aleuts	100.0	51.2	21.1	15.4	14.7	48.8	1.4
Asians and Pacific Islanders	100.0	92.4	51.8	31.6	9.0	7.6	0.2
Blacks	100.0	81.9	57.2	14.2	10.5	18.1	0.4
Hispanics[1]	100.0	89.1	51.5	25.7	11.9	10.9	0.6
Whites	100.0	68.2	26.7	27.4	14.4	31.8	2.1

Source: Derived from Bureau of the Census, *1980 Census of Population, General Social and Economic Characteristics, Part 1, United States Summary*, pp. 71, 97–98, and 118.

[1]May be of any race.

Among the racial/ethnic groups, Asians and Pacific Islanders are the most urbanized group in the United States, but more of them, proportionally, live in the suburbs of metropolitan areas than members of other groups. In 1980, 92.4 percent of undereducated civilian Asian/Pacific youth, aged 16 to 19, lived in urban areas; 51.8 percent in central cities; and 31.6 percent in urban fringe areas. The second most urbanized group consists of Hispanics. About as many undereducated Hispanic teenagers, proportionally, lived in central cities as Asians and Pacific Islanders in 1980, but fewer lived in the suburbs. African Americans are the most likely of all groups to live in central cities, which were home to 57.2 percent of undereducated black teenagers in 1980. American Indians, Eskimos, and Aleuts are the least urbanized group: in 1980 about half of the undereducated Native American youth lived in urban areas and half in rural areas. Among non-Hispanic whites as a whole, seven in ten, and among undereducated white teenagers, including Hispanics, 68.2 percent, lived in urban areas; the latter, but not the non-Hispanic white population as a whole, were nearly evenly divided between central cities and fringe areas. In the total population, a third live in the suburbs, but only a quarter, in the inner cities. The rural farm population is almost entirely non-Hispanic white: in 1980 only 2.1 percent of undereducated white youth, aged 16 to 19, lived there, but they constituted 91.6 percent of all undereducated rural farm teenagers.[6]

Certain states are more urbanized than others, and undereducated youth are much more likely to be urban dwellers in some states than in others. In 1980, as shown in table 2.14, the proportions living in central

Table 2.14
Percentage Distribution of Undereducated Civilian Youth, Aged 16 to 19, by Urbanicity and State: United States, 1980

State	Total	Urban					Rural	
		Total	Central cities	Urban fringe	Places of 10,000+	Places of 2,500-10,000	Total	Rural farm
Total	100.0	71.9	33.8	24.8	6.4	6.9	28.1	1.7
Alabama	100.0	53.5	25.0	13.7	5.9	8.9	46.5	1.1
Alaska	100.0	59.3	40.7	*	7.8	10.7	40.7	*
Arizona	100.0	79.4	46.7	19.9	4.6	8.1	20.6	0.5
Arkansas	100.0	48.6	15.6	6.3	12.6	14.0	51.4	3.0
California	100.0	91.0	36.1	46.1	4.3	4.6	9.0	0.7
Colorado	100.0	83.1	38.6	33.4	4.4	6.6	16.9	0.8
Connecticut	100.0	85.2	51.5	28.0	2.2	3.5	14.8	*
Delaware	100.0	61.4	17.3	37.2	2.6	4.3	38.6	2.8
District of Columbia	100.0	100.0	100.0	NA	NA	NA	NA	NA
Florida	100.0	79.7	26.7	44.2	3.5	5.3	20.3	0.4
Georgia	100.0	55.4	17.8	20.4	7.8	9.3	44.6	1.5
Hawaii	100.0	84.6	40.0	24.4	6.7	13.5	15.4	*
Idaho	100.0	53.4	13.0	3.4	21.2	15.8	46.6	3.0
Illinois	100.0	87.7	49.7	28.2	5.0	4.8	12.3	1.0
Indiana	100.0	67.9	32.4	16.7	10.8	7.8	32.1	4.1
Iowa	100.0	68.3	30.0	10.2	13.4	14.7	31.7	6.3
Kansas	100.0	74.5	25.2	15.4	23.8	10.2	25.5	3.3
Kentucky	100.0	42.0	13.4	12.8	6.7	9.1	58.0	5.1
Louisiana	100.0	62.9	25.7	19.0	7.4	10.8	37.1	1.1
Maine	100.0	50.6	19.6	5.7	10.8	14.5	49.4	0.7
Maryland	100.0	78.2	34.8	37.7	2.7	3.0	21.8	1.2
Massachusetts	100.0	87.9	47.1	34.2	3.0	3.5	12.1	0.1
Michigan	100.0	73.1	33.1	32.0	2.9	5.2	26.9	1.0
Minnesota	100.0	69.8	26.8	27.4	7.8	7.8	30.2	4.8
Mississippi	100.0	43.1	11.4	7.9	13.5	10.3	56.9	2.0
Missouri	100.0	66.4	29.7	21.0	6.4	9.4	33.6	3.2
Montana	100.0	51.1	19.2	8.3	12.7	10.9	48.9	4.1
Nebraska	100.0	72.4	39.6	8.8	14.6	9.4	27.6	3.9
Nevada	100.0	88.1	34.6	43.7	4.5	5.3	11.9	*
New Hampshire	100.0	59.0	31.1	6.1	13.7	8.1	41.0	0.5
New Jersey	100.0	90.0	22.9	63.2	1.8	2.2	10.0	0.2
New Mexico	100.0	63.8	22.9	7.1	19.9	13.9	36.2	0.8
New York	100.0	85.5	62.2	17.8	2.9	2.5	14.5	0.7
North Carolina	100.0	41.5	16.4	11.5	7.4	6.2	54.6	2.1
North Dakota	100.0	51.1	28.0	1.3	12.9	8.8	48.9	9.5
Ohio	100.0	74.7	40.1	20.9	8.2	5.5	25.3	2.7
Oklahoma	100.0	68.5	29.2	10.9	14.2	14.3	31.5	1.3
Oregon	100.0	69.6	22.5	25.0	10.8	11.4	30.4	1.6
Pennsylvania	100.0	65.6	35.0	22.1	3.1	5.4	34.4	3.8
Rhode Island	100.0	90.3	43.8	43.8	1.1	1.6	9.7	*
South Carolina	100.0	51.1	10.9	25.5	4.1	10.7	48.9	1.0
South Dakota	100.0	41.6	17.7	3.3	12.2	8.5	58.4	10.6
Tennessee	100.0	51.6	29.7	5.2	8.3	8.3	48.4	2.9
Texas	100.0	80.9	48.6	14.7	9.5	8.0	19.1	0.8
Utah	100.0	86.9	26.2	50.7	3.9	6.1	13.1	0.8
Vermont	100.0	38.2	9.5	4.5	5.5	18.7	61.8	3.2
Virginia	100.0	56.0	24.4	22.6	3.6	5.4	44.0	1.9
Washington	100.0	73.4	26.0	35.0	4.3	8.1	26.6	1.4
West Virginia	100.0	26.8	9.1	5.9	4.0	7.9	73.1	0.5
Wisconsin	100.0	67.1	40.9	13.5	5.0	7.7	32.9	4.9
Wyoming	100.0	63.7	18.2	4.8	22.4	18.3	36.3	1.6

Source: Derived from Bureau of the Census, *1980 Census of Population, General Social and Economic Characteristics, Part 1, United States Summary,* p. 71; and *Parts 2-52, the States and the District of Columbia,* table 66, various pages.

NA = not applicable.

*Less than an estimated 0.1 of a percent.

cities ranged from less than one in ten in West Virginia to more than three out of five in New York. The proportions of undereducated youth, aged 16 to 19, living in suburbs ranged from fewer than 4 percent in Idaho and South Dakota to 63.2 percent in New Jersey. There were seven states in which the majority of these youth lived in rural areas in 1980: Arkansas, Kentucky, Mississippi, North Carolina, South Dakota, Vermont, and West Virginia.[7]

WHO ARE THE UNDEREDUCATED YOUTH?

Undereducation in the United States is not only a minority problem or a problem of the poor. The majority of undereducated youth were born in this country, have monolingual English-speaking backgrounds, and live in families with incomes above the poverty level. Nevertheless, there are substantial numbers of minority youth who have not completed the minimum number of years of schooling considered essential for success as productive citizens. Minority youth are at greater risk of undereducation, as discussed in the next chapter. They complete fewer years of schooling than white majority youth, and as suggested by the High School and Beyond Study, young people who complete fewer years of schooling are less likely to obtain a high school diploma or its equivalent at a later time.[8]

The identification of at-risk students and programs designed to meet their needs must begin early in the school years. In 1980 there were more than a million native-born young people who had left school before the ninth grade. Almost half of those with only five to eight years of schooling and 37.5 percent of those with fewer than five years were white majority youth. The disproportionate numbers of minority youth, however, especially native-born as well as foreign-born language minority youth, among young people who never reach high school, suggest the need for more attention to linguistic and cultural differences in the elementary and intermediate grades.

Undereducated minority youth constitute larger proportions of the undereducated population in certain states and in certain types of environments within states than in others. Accordingly, dropout prevention programs that reflect the diversity of at-risk populations are more critical in certain states and in certain school districts than in others.

NOTES

1. Bureau of the Census, U.S. Department of Commerce, *1980 Census of Population, General Social and Economic Characteristics, Part 1, United States Summary* (Washington, D.C.: U.S. Government Printing Office, 1983), p. 71.

2. Bureau of the Census, U.S. Department of Commerce, *1980 Census of Population, Detailed Population Characteristics, Part 1, United States Summary* (Washington, D.C.: U.S. Government Printing Office, 1984), p. 7.

3. Bureau of the Census, U.S. Department of Commerce, *Race of the Population by States: 1980* (Washington, D.C.: U.S. Government Printing Office, 1981), p. 8.

4. Bureau of the Census, *General Social and Economic Characteristics,* pp. 79 and 200.

5. Ibid., p. 71.

6. Ibid., pp. 13, 97–98, and 118.

7. Bureau of the Census, *General Social and Economic Characteristics, Parts 2-52, the States and the District of Columbia,* table 66, various pages.

8. Andrew J. Kolstad and Jeffery A. Owings, "High School Dropouts Who Change Their Minds about School" (Paper presented at the annual meeting of the American Educational Research Association, San Francisco, April 16, 1986), pp. 12–13.

3

The Risk of Undereducation

If white majority youth from more economically advantaged families constitute the largest portion of the undereducated population in the United States, they are neither the most nor the least at risk of undereducation. Hispanics, American Indians, Eskimos, and Aleuts, and African Americans are considerably more likely to be undereducated than majority youth. The disadvantage of these groups is apparent even when the comparison is with the least at risk among them, and it is a measure of the extent to which they must still struggle to reach educational equity. In contrast, Asians and Pacific Islanders as a group and non-Hispanic white minority youth—whites with non-English language backgrounds—are less at risk of undereducation than majority youth. Youth from poor families, among whom minorities are overrepresented, are more at risk than youth from families with incomes above the poverty level.

In 1980, 15 percent of all youth, aged 16 to 24, and 13 percent of white majority youth—native-born non-Hispanic youth from monolingual English-speaking backgrounds—were undereducated. The overall undereducation rates ranged from 10 percent of Asians and Pacific Islanders to 32 percent of Hispanics. Hispanic and American Indian and Alaska Native youth were more than twice as likely to be undereducated as white majority youth; African Americans were 1.6 times as likely. Asians and Pacific Islanders and non-Hispanic white minority youth, on the other hand, were 1.3 and 1.1 times less likely to be undereducated, respectively, than white majority youth.

American Indians, Eskimos, and Aleuts, overwhelmingly native born, are more likely than all other native-born groups and foreign-born groups, except foreign-born Hispanics, to be out of school without high school diplomas. Their 1980 rate was 29.2 percent.

Foreign-born youth, except African Americans, are more likely to be undereducated than their counterparts who were born in this country. In 1980, the undereducation rate of young people born outside the United States, excluding blacks, was twice that of young people born in this country. In contrast, native-born African Americans were 1.4 times more likely to be out of school without having completed at least 12 years of schooling than foreign-born blacks.

The high overall undereducation rate of Hispanics in comparison with other minority youth is associated with nativity and language background. Native-born Hispanics from monolingual English-speaking households are about as likely to be undereducated as non-Hispanic blacks. In 1980, one out of five native-born English language-background Hispanics—and one out of five blacks—was out of school and had not completed 12 years of schooling. In contrast, nearly three out of ten native-born Spanish language-background Hispanics and 45 percent of foreign-born Hispanics were undereducated.

Having a non-English language background is a positive factor for Asians and Pacific Islanders, African Americans, and non-Hispanic whites. In 1980 native-born members of these groups from households in which non-English languages are spoken were 1.2 to 1.4 times less likely to be undereducated than their counterparts from monolingual English-speaking households.

Youth from families with incomes below the poverty level are much more likely to be undereducated than youth from more economically advantaged families. Because minority youth are more likely to be from poor families than majority youth, more minority than majority youth are, proportionally, at risk. However, the risk associated with poverty is greater for the groups with the lowest overall undereducation rates—native-born non-Hispanic whites and Asians and Pacific Islanders—than for groups whose overall rates are high—African Americans, Hispanics, and Native Americans. In 1980 poor white majority youth, Asians and Pacific Islanders, and native-born white minority youth were at least twice as likely to be undereducated as members of their groups in more economically advantaged circumstances. The risk factor associated with poverty for blacks, Hispanics, and American Indians, Eskimos, and Aleuts ranged from 1.6 to 1.8.

Even the most advantaged native-born African Americans, Hispanics, and American Indians, Eskimos, and Aleuts are more likely to be undereducated than white majority youth. Native-born blacks from homes with family incomes above the poverty level had an undereducation rate of 16.7 percent in 1980; economically advantaged native-born English language-background Hispanics and Native Americans had rates of 17.9 percent and 24.3 percent, respectively. In contrast, white majority youth had an undereducation rate of 13.0 percent.

Youth in certain regions of the country and in certain states are more at risk than youth in other regions and states. In 1980 those living in the Northeast and the Midwest were the least likely to be undereducated, and those living in the South, the most likely. Among the states, the undereducation rates ranged from 8 percent of youth in Minnesota to a quarter of those in Kentucky.

Young people living in certain kinds of environments within regions and states are more at risk of undereducation than young people living in other kinds of environments in those same regions and states. The disturbingly high dropout rates of youth in urban high schools are widely acknowledged.[1] The high rates of youth in the rural areas of some states are less well known. The risks associated with urbanicity generally parallel the risks associated with poverty, and just as poverty is more prevalent among urban populations in some states and among rural populations in others, the comparative undereducation risk of urban and rural young people in different states varies. The variation in the undereducation rates of all youth according to the type of environment in which they live within a state reflects qualitative differences among school districts and raises serious questions of educational equity for the minority and poor youth who disproportionately live in high risk environments as noted in the previous chapter.

In the nation as a whole, youth who live in the central cities of metropolitan areas are the most likely to be undereducated. The second most likely are rural youth as a whole—those living in places with fewer than 2,500 inhabitants. Those few youth living on productive rural farms, however—mostly white—are the least likely to be undereducated. Their risk of undereducation is even less than that of youth living in the suburbs of metropolitan areas, although suburban populations are economically the most advantaged of all. In 1980 civilian young people, aged 16 to 19, living on rural farms were 1.9 times less likely to be undereducated than those living in central cities and 1.3 times less likely than those living in suburban areas.[2]

The following sections of this chapter contain an examination of these and other factors related to the risk of undereducation. They contain a comparison of the undereducation rates of the racial/ethnic groups associated with nativity, language background, gender, age, and poverty status and a discussion of the possible contribution of educational delay—being older than one's classmates—to the undereducation of certain groups. The chapter ends with an examination of the regional and state undereducation rates, the rates of the racial/ethnic groups related to urban or rural residence within states, and the different proportions of poor, foreign born, or language minority members of each racial/ethnic group in the individual states. The information for the examination of the association of undereducation with school delay and urbanicity comes from the published volumes of the 1980 census.

RACE AND ETHNICITY AND UNDEREDUCATION

The risk of undereducation is much greater for most minority youth than for the majority, and it is greater even when the most advantaged youth are compared as will be apparent in the succeeding sections of this chapter. In 1980 one in six young people—5.9 million out of 38.1 million youth, aged 16 to 24, in the United States—was not enrolled in school and had not completed the twelfth grade, as shown in table 3.1. Among white majority youth, the number was one in eight, and among Asians and Pacific Islanders, one in ten. In contrast, a third of Hispanics, aged 16 to 24; nearly three in ten American Indians, Eskimos, and Aleuts; and one in five African Americans was undereducated.

NATIVITY AND UNDEREDUCATION

Foreign-born youth, except African Americans, are more likely to be undereducated than youth born in the United States, Puerto Rico, or another outlying area, as shown in figure 3.1, which contrasts the undereducation rates of foreign-born groups with non-English language backgrounds with those of native-born English language-background and non-English language-background groups. In 1980, among all foreign-born youth, 28.3 percent were undereducated; among all native-born youth, 14.8 percent were. Excluding blacks, these proportions were 29.5 percent and 13.9 percent, respectively. Foreign-born Asians and Pacific Islanders were twice as likely to be undereducated as their native-born counterparts—12.4 percent in comparison with 6.3 percent. Among Hispanics the difference was 1.7 times—45.4 percent and 26.6 percent—and among white minority youth, 1.6 times—17.6 percent and 11.2 percent. In contrast, foreign-born African Americans were 1.4 times less likely to be undereducated than native-born African Americans. Their rate was 14.6 percent in comparison with 20.6 percent for the native-born group.

Many adults born in Caribbean and African countries and many adults born in some of the Asian countries are high school and even college graduates. In contrast, many foreign-born Hispanics and Southeast Asian refugees have limited schooling. The differences in the extent of education of foreign-born adults, as evidenced by the 1980 census, parallel the differences in the undereducation rates of foreign-born youth in the various racial/ethnic groups. The differences among African American, Hispanic, Asian/Pacific, and white minority adults born in various foreign countries are discussed in the individual chapters on these groups.

Table 3.1
Estimated Numbers of Undereducated Youth and Undereducation Rates, by Nativity and Selected Characteristic: United States, 1980

Characteristic	Total		Native born		Foreign born	
	Number	Rate	Number	Rate	Number	Rate
Total	5,883,000	15.4	5,340,000	14.8	543,000	28.3
Racial/ethnic group						
African Americans	1,023,000	20.4	1,000,000	20.6	22,000	14.6
American Indians, Eskimos, and Aleuts	82,000	29.2	81,000	29.2	1,000	31.2
Asians and Pacific Islanders	55,000	9.8	15,000	6.3	40,000	12.4
Hispanics	923,000	32.2	535,000	26.6	387,000	45.4
Non-Hispanic white minority	337,000	12.0	277,000	11.2	60,000	17.6
White majority	3,426,000	13.0	3,426,000	13.0	NA	
Other non-Hispanics	38,000	13.6	5,000	17.2	33,000	13.2
Language background						
English only	4,576,000	14.3	4,523,000	14.3	53,000	13.9
Non-English	1,307,000	21.3	817,000	17.8	490,000	31.9
Gender						
Males	3,163,000	16.6	2,870,000	15.9	293,000	29.4
Females	2,720,000	14.3	2,470,000	13.6	250,000	27.2
Age						
16 to 19	2,327,000	13.7	2,161,000	13.3	166,000	22.7
20 to 24	3,556,000	16.9	3,179,000	16.0	377,000	31.9
Poverty status in 1979[1]						
Above poverty level	4,097,000	13.7	3,718,000	13.0	379,000	27.7
Below poverty level	1,498,000	28.1	1,345,000	27.5	153,000	35.5

Note: Percentages calculated on unrounded numbers. Detail may not add to total number or to 100.0 percent because of rounding. NA = not applicable.

[1]Not determined for people living in group quarters.

Some of the variation in undereducation among foreign-born youth reflects the levels of schooling that immigrants from certain countries bring with them. In some cases it reflects visa preference or eligibility: applicants from certain countries or in certain categories must be high school graduates to be admitted legally to the United States. In other cases it reflects decisions or experiences after arrival. Some young people who have completed fewer than 12 years of schooling before immigrating never enroll here either because they arrive at age 16 or later and need to begin

Figure 3.1

Undereducation Rates of Native-Born English Language Background and Language Minority Youth and Foreign-Born Language Minority Youth, 1980

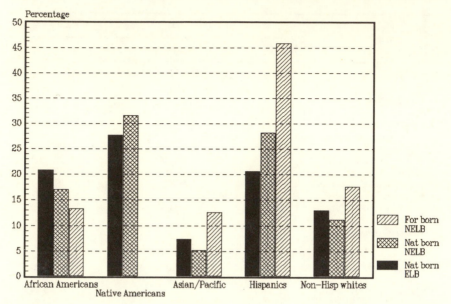

earning to support themselves and their families or because school programs do not meet their needs. Some enroll only to be held back or otherwise discouraged. As indicated in the previous chapter, data are not available to determine whether foreign-born youth were enrolled in school and failed to complete 12 years in this country or whether their educational level reflects only schooling completed abroad. Nevertheless, for whatever reasons, foreign-born youth, especially Hispanics and some Asians, are very likely to be undereducated. They represent a large and growing group of teenagers and young adults in the United States who need help to achieve their full potential in American society.

LANGUAGE BACKGROUND AND UNDEREDUCATION

As measured by their undereducation rates, having a non-English language background is an advantage for Asians and Pacific Islanders, African Americans, and non-Hispanic whites; it is a disadvantage for Hispanics. In 1980 native-born Asian/Pacific youth living in households in which one or more people speak a language other than English were 1.4 times less likely to be undereducated than native-born Asian/Pacific youth in monolingual English-speaking households, as shown in table 3.2. Native-born African Americans and whites in households in which non-English

Table 3.2
Undereducation Rates of Youth, by Language Background, Nativity, and Racial/Ethnic Group: United States, 1980

Nativity and racial/ethnic group	Total	English only	Non-English
Total	15.4	14.3	21.3
African Americans	20.4	20.7	16.5
American Indians, Eskimos, and Aleuts	29.2	27.8	31.5
Asians and Pacific Islanders	9.8	7.8	10.5
Hispanics	32.2	20.8	34.3
Non-Hispanic whites	12.9	13.0	12.0
Native born	14.8	14.3	17.8
African Americans	20.6	20.8	17.0
American Indians, Eskimos, and Aleuts	29.2	27.7	31.6
Asians and Pacific Islanders	6.3	7.4	5.2
Hispanics	26.6	20.6	28.2
Non-Hispanic whites	12.9	13.0	11.2
Foreign born	28.3	13.9	31.9
African Americans	14.6	15.2	13.3
American Indians, Eskimos, and Aleuts	31.2	33.6	27.3
Asians and Pacific Islanders	12.4	10.0	12.6
Hispanics	45.4	24.9	45.9
Non-Hispanic whites	15.5	12.5	17.6

languages are spoken were 1.2 times less likely to be undereducated than their counterparts in all English households. In contrast, native-born Spanish language-background Hispanics were 1.4 times more likely to be undereducated than their native-born counterparts with English language backgrounds.

American Indians, Eskimos, and Aleuts with backgrounds in which American Indian and Alaska Native languages are spoken were 1.1 times more likely to be undereducated than those with monolingual English-speaking backgrounds in 1980. This difference is probably more closely related to poverty and other conditions that affect Native Americans who live on reservations or in rural areas where many people speak their tribal languages than to the effect of language background per se, as discussed in chapter 8.

The high risk of undereducation associated with foreign birth and a Spanish language background explains the high undereducation rate of Hispanics as a group in comparison with other minorities. Native-born Hispanics are less at risk than American Indians, Eskimos, and Aleuts who, regardless of language background, are the most likely of native-born groups to be out of school and not high school graduates. Native-born Hispanics from monolingual English-speaking homes are no more likely to be undereducated than native-born African Americans. In 1980 the rate of all native-born Hispanics was 26.6 percent in comparison with that of American Indians and Alaska Natives, 29.2 percent. The undereducation rate of native-born English language-background Hispanics and that of native-born African Americans was about 21 percent.

Language background is an ambiguous risk factor because language minority youth have other characteristics that are more closely related to success or failure in U.S. schools. Youth from households in which one or more people speak a language other than English may or may not be proficient in English and able to profit from school programs designed for students whose native language is English. They may or may not be proficient in their home languages and ready to learn a second language—English—or to progress in the mastery of English. They may or may not have the self-esteem necessary to succeed despite being members of a minority in a majority classroom. Conversely, minority youth with English language backgrounds may have lost an essential sense of self that comes from participating in the language community of their ethnic affiliation.

The 1980 census contains information on one of the components of English proficiency—English-speaking ability. This information—from self-rating—suggests that people in the United States who speak French, German, and Italian at home—the languages of the backgrounds of the largest groups of non-Hispanic white minority youth—speak English better on the average than people who speak Spanish at home and that speakers of Filipino languages and Japanese—the second and third largest groups of speakers of Asian languages—also tend to speak English better than Spanish speakers. The census data also suggest that home speakers of Chinese languages—the largest group of speakers of Asian languages—speak English less well than Spanish speakers. They suggest, not surprisingly, that recent immigrants have less English-speaking ability than those who have been in the country at least ten years and much less than native-born home speakers of languages other than English.[3] The correspondence between the undereducation rates of certain groups and the English-speaking ability of some of their members reinforces what should be obvious: the possession by language minority students of sufficient English proficiency to profit from school programs offered in English or, alternately, the availability of programs designed to meet their special linguistic needs are important factors in the school success of this group.

The census provides no information on proficiency or speaking ability in another language, much less on self-esteem. Thus there is no way to determine whether or not the groups for whom having a non-English language background is an advantage might be better prepared to succeed because they have solid foundations in their home languages or because they derive increased self-esteem from being a part of their language communities.

GENDER AND UNDEREDUCATION

Young men are more at risk of undereducation than young women, as illustrated in figure 3.2. Young African American men are the most at risk comparatively. The gender ratio varies among the other racial/ethnic groups according to whether the youth are native born or foreign born. In particular, foreign-born Asian/Pacific and non-Hispanic white minority women are more likely to be undereducated than their male counterparts. In 1980 young men as a whole and white majority men were 1.2 times more likely than their female counterparts to be out of school and not high school graduates, as shown in table 3.3. Native-born African American men were 1.3 times more likely than native-born African American women, and foreign-born African American men, 1.2 times more likely than foreign-born African American women, to be undereducated. Native-born non-Hispanic white minority men, American Indian, Eskimo, and Aleut men, and Hispanic men, both native-born and foreign-born, were no more than 1.1 times more likely to be undereducated than their female counterparts.[4] Among foreign-born Asians and Pacific Islanders, women were 1.3 times more likely to be undereducated, and among non-Hispanic white minority youth, 1.2 times more likely, than their male counterparts in 1980. Many recently arrived Asian women have low levels of education, as discussed in chapter 9. In 1980 more than

Figure 3.2
Undereducation Rates of Men and Women, 1980

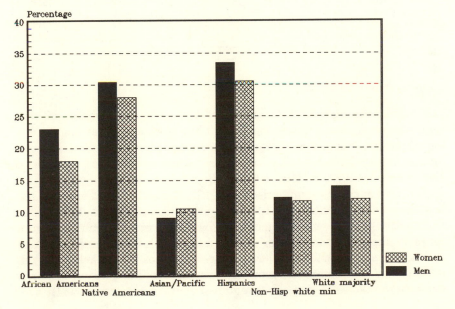

half of all Asian and Pacific Islander youth with fewer than five years of schooling were foreign-born women.

Table 3.3
Undereducation Rates of Youth, by Gender, Nativity, and Racial/Ethnic Group: United States, 1980

Nativity and racial/ethnic group	Total	Men	Women
Total	15.4	16.6	14.3
African Americans	20.4	23.0	18.0
American Indians, Eskimos, and Aleuts	29.2	30.4	28.0
Asians and Pacific Islanders	9.8	9.1	10.5
Hispanics	32.2	33.5	30.9
Non-Hispanic white minority	12.0	12.3	11.7
White majority	13.0	14.0	12.0
Native born	14.8	15.9	13.6
African Americans	20.6	23.2	18.1
American Indians, Eskimos, and Aleuts	29.2	30.4	27.9
Asians and Pacific Islanders	6.3	6.7	6.0
Hispanics	26.6	27.1	26.1
Non-Hispanic white minority	11.2	11.8	10.7
White majority	13.0	14.0	12.0
Foreign born	28.3	29.4	27.2
African Americans	14.6	16.2	13.2
American Indians, Eskimos, and Aleuts	31.2	28.4	33.9
Asians and Pacific Islanders	12.4	11.0	13.9
Hispanics	45.4	47.4	43.1
Non-Hispanic white minority	17.6	16.0	19.4

AGE AND UNDEREDUCATION

Young adults, aged 20 to 24, are more likely to be out of school without high school diplomas than teenagers. This is especially so among foreign-born youth in general, among Hispanics and African Americans, and among foreign-born but not native-born Asians and Pacific Islanders, as shown in table 3.4. In 1980, 16.9 percent of young adults, aged 20 to 24, were undereducated in comparison with 13.7 percent of the teenagers. Native-born young adults were 1.2 times more likely to be undereducated than native-born teenagers; among foreign-born young people, the factor representing additional risk for young adults was 1.4. Hispanics and African Americans, aged 20 to 24, were 1.4 to 1.5 times more likely to be undereducated than than their younger counterparts. The greatest disparity between the rates of young adults and teenagers of any group was that for

Table 3.4
Undereducation Rates of Youth, by Age Group, Nativity, and Racial/Ethnic Group: United States, 1980

Nativity and racial/ethnic group	Total	Aged 16 to 19	Aged 20 to 24
Total	15.4	13.7	16.9
African Americans	20.4	16.0	24.3
American Indians, Eskimos, and Aleuts	29.2	27.2	31.0
Asians and Pacific Islanders	9.8	7.5	11.5
Hispanics	32.2	25.5	37.8
Non-Hispanic white minority	12.0	10.9	13.0
White majority	13.0	12.1	13.7
Native born	14.8	13.3	16.0
African Americans	20.6	16.2	24.6
American Indians, Eskimos, and Aleuts	29.2	27.1	31.0
Asians and Pacific Islanders	6.3	6.1	6.5
Hispanics	26.6	22.2	30.8
Non-Hispanic white minority	11.2	10.5	11.9
White majority	13.0	12.1	13.7
Foreign born	28.3	22.7	31.9
African Americans	14.6	11.6	16.8
American Indians, Eskimos, and Aleuts	31.2	30.5	31.7
Asians and Pacific Islanders	12.4	8.8	14.9
Hispanics	45.4	35.5	51.7
Non-Hispanic white minority	17.6	14.8	19.3

foreign-born Asians and Pacific Islanders; older foreign-born Asian/Pacific youth were 1.7 times more likely to be undereducated than younger foreign-born Asian/Pacific youth in 1980. There was little or no difference between the rates for younger and older native-born Asian/Pacific youth.

As indicated in the previous chapter in the discussion of the numbers of undereducated youth by age group, at any given time many teenagers are behind in school. In 1980, 48.3 percent of all 16-year-olds and 3.7 percent of all 17-to-19-year-olds were enrolled in school but were still no further than the tenth grade.[5] Many 16-year-olds who are still in school, even if only in grade 10, may go on to graduate at age 18 or 19. Fewer of those who are still in the tenth or earlier grades at age 17 or older are likely to stay to complete the twelfth grade, although some teenagers who do not stay to graduate with their classmates—and some older youth now counted as undereducated—will complete high school at a later time by alternate methods such as the General Educational Development (GED) credential.

EDUCATIONAL DELAY AND UNDEREDUCATION

The students in U.S. schools who are older than most of their class-mates are disproportionately members of minority groups. They enter late, they are held back, and they leave and return to a greater extent than majority students. Moving through the grades, as depicted in figure 3.3, they fall further and further behind. Finally, as shown in this study, they disproportionately abandon their schooling without completing 12 years. Educational delay—being older than one's classmates—and the un-dereducation of youth are related measures of the extent to which schools fail some students more than others. Moreover, educational delay is fre-quently considered to be a factor that causes youth to drop out.

Figure 3.3
Proportions of Students Two or More Years Older Than the Modal Age for Their Grades, 1980

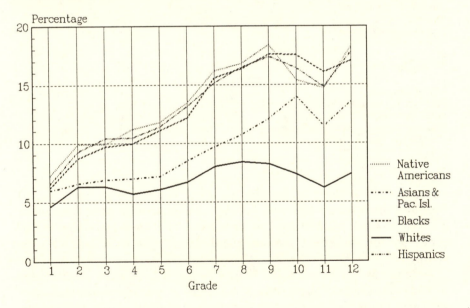

In 1980, about 97 percent of white and Asian/Pacific 6-year-old chil-dren and 95 to 96 percent of Hispanic, African American, and American Indian, Eskimo, and Aleut 6-year-olds were enrolled in nursery school, kindergarten, or elementary school.[6] Among children enrolled in grade 1, 4.6 percent of whites and 6 to 7 percent of minority students were eight or more years old, as shown in table 3.5. Already by the fourth grade, 7.0 percent of Asians and Pacific Islanders, 10.0 percent of blacks, 10.5 per-cent of Hispanics, and 11.2 percent of American Indians, Eskimos, and Aleuts, in comparison with 5.7 percent of white students, were at least 11

Table 3.5
Estimated Numbers of Students, Aged 3 to 24, Enrolled in Kindergarten through Grade 12, and Estimated Numbers and Percentages Who Are Two or More Years Older Than the Modal Age for Their Grades, by Race, Hispanic Ethnicity, and Grade Level: United States, 1980 (Numbers in thousands)

Grade level	Total	Amer. Indians, Eskimos, & Aleuts	Asians & Pacific Islanders	Blacks	Whites	Hispanics[1]
Total enrolled	46,833	409	799	6,972	37,139	3,872
2+ yrs older than modal age	3,585	52	69	869	2,188	470
Percentage	7.7	12.7	8.7	12.5	5.9	11.5
Enrolled in kindergarten	3,210	30	66	498	2,487	319
7+ years old	50	1	1	9	36	6
Percentage	1.5	2.5	1.6	1.7	1.5	1.8
Enrolled in grade one	3,349	33	68	512	2,605	327
8+ years old	167	2	4	31	120	21
Percentage	5.0	7.2	6.0	6.2	4.6	6.5
Enrolled in grade two	3,400	32	67	516	2,657	321
9+ years old	232	3	4	45	166	30
Percentage	6.8	9.9	6.6	8.7	6.3	9.3
Enrolled in grade three	3,681	34	67	556	2,893	329
10+ years old	260	3	5	54	183	34
Percentage	7.1	9.9	6.9	9.7	6.3	10.4
Enrolled in grade four	3,689	33	65	539	2,929	315
11+ years old	245	4	5	54	168	33
Percentage	6.6	11.2	7.0	10.0	5.7	10.5
Enrolled in grade five	3,608	32	63	520	2,874	302
12+ years old	256	4	5	58	175	34
Percentage	7.1	11.8	7.2	11.1	6.1	11.4
Enrolled in grade six	3,570	32	58	527	2,837	297
13+ years old	280	4	5	65	189	39
Percentage	7.8	13.5	8.5	12.2	6.7	13.2
Enrolled in grade seven	3,639	33	57	549	2,885	297
14+ years old	346	5	6	86	230	45
Percentage	9.5	16.2	9.7	15.6	8.0	15.2
Enrolled in grade eight	3,752	34	57	576	2,969	302
15+ years old	378	6	6	95	250	50
Percentage	10.1	16.8	10.7	16.4	8.4	16.5

Source: Derived from Bureau of the Census, *1980 Census of Population, Detailed Population Characteristics, Part 1, United States Summary*, pp. 26–37.

Note: Percentages calculated on unrounded numbers.

[1]May be of any race.

Table 3.5—Continued

Grade level	Total	Amer. Indians, Eskimos, & Aleuts	Asians & Pacific Islanders	Blacks	Whites	Hispanics[1]
Enrolled in grade nine	3,931	35	61	602	3,110	312
16+ years old	397	6	7	106	254	54
Percentage	10.1	18.4	12.1	17.6	8.2	17.4
Enrolled in grade ten	3,994	32	61	598	3,190	292
17+ years old	373	5	9	105	234	48
Percentage	9.3	15.4	14.0	17.5	7.3	16.4
Enrolled in grade eleven	3,646	26	55	522	2,951	244
18+ years old	292	4	6	84	183	36
Percentage	8.0	14.7	11.4	16.1	6.2	14.8
Enrolled in grade twelve	3,363	22	52	458	2,752	215
19+ years old	309	4	7	78	204	38
Percentage	9.2	18.3	13.6	17.1	7.4	17.8

years old. By the eighth grade, black, Hispanic, and American Indian, Eskimo, and Aleut students were twice as likely as white students, and Asian and Pacific Islander students, 1.3 times as likely, to be at least 15 years old. Among the blacks, Hispanics, and Native Americans who had survived into the high school years in 1980, about 17 percent were at least two years older than the age of the largest number of their classmates; 12.8 percent of Asians and Pacific Islanders were also at least two years older than the modal age. In comparison, only 7.3 percent of whites enrolled in grades 9 to 12 were as much as two years older than the modal age.[7]

Youth interviewed as high school sophomores in 1980 in the Department of Education's High School and Beyond study who had been held back or repeated a grade were more than twice as likely not to be high school graduates or still enrolled in 1982 as those who had never been held back or repeated a grade. The correlation was much stronger for whites than for either blacks or Hispanics, and it was stronger for blacks than for Hispanics. Whites were 2.4 to 2.6 times as likely; blacks, 1.8 to 1.9 times as likely; and Hispanics, 1.5 times as likely.[8] There was also a correlation in the High School and Beyond study between being older than the expected age at the start of the ninth grade and dropping out—a correlation, again, less strong for Hispanics than for the other groups. The 1980 sophomores who had entered the ninth grade at age 15½ were 1.8 times more likely not to be graduates or still enrolled in 1982 than those who had entered at age 15, and the latter were twice as likely as those who had entered at age 14½. For Hispanics, the factors were 1.3 to 1.7 for those who had entered ninth grade at age 15½ in comparison with those who had entered at age 15, and 1.4 for those who had entered at age 15 in comparison with those who had entered at age 14½.[9] Fernández and Shu, analyzing the same data, found that, "regardless of age, Hispanic students' chances of dropping out of school are generally greater . . . than those of students in the national sample."[10] Neither of these analyses of the HS&B data considered differences related to nativity and language background within groups.

In a national survey conducted by the Bureau of the Census in 1976, failure to complete high school and educational delay were both found to be related to language background, and the correlations were stronger for Hispanics on both measures than for non-Hispanics. Hispanics with non-English language backgrounds enrolled in grades 5 to 8 were four times more likely to be older than the expected ages for their grades than Hispanics with English language backgrounds, in comparison with a difference of 1.4 times between non-Hispanics with non-English language backgrounds and those with English language backgrounds in grades 5 to 8. In grades 9 to 12, the differences were 1.6 times for Hispanics and 1.3 times for non-Hispanics. Hispanic youth, aged 14 to 25, with non-English language backgrounds were 1.6 times more likely not to be enrolled in school and not to have completed the twelfth grade than Hispanics with English language backgrounds. For non-Hispanics, the factor related to language background was 1.2. On both measures, Hispanics were disadvantaged in comparison with non-Hispanic youth with similar language backgrounds.[11]

This study does not provide any information on the extent to which educational delay among youth in general or among white majority youth may be correlated with the failure to complete high school. The 1980 census did not identify out-of-school youth who were older than their classmates at the time they were enrolled or even determine, as noted in connection with foreign-born youth, if they had been enrolled in U.S. schools at all. However, the study findings on undereducation, especially the comparative rates of undereducation by age group and the years of schooling completed by undereducated minority youth in relation to nativity and language background, have implications with regard to the relationship of educational delay and the likelihood of minority youth not to complete high school. First, just as nativity and language background are underlying factors in the extent of undereducation, they are probably underlying factors in school delay. Second, regardless of nativity and language background, the relationship between educational delay and undereducation, at least for minority youth, is not simple.

If information were available on the educational delay of the various racial/ethnic groups by nativity and language background in 1980, it would probably show that the students who are most likely to be behind in school are those who were born outside the United States, and it would reconfirm the 1976 finding that Hispanics with Spanish language backgrounds are more likely to be held back than their counterparts from monolingual English-speaking backgrounds. If so, a lower delay rate for native-born Hispanics would be consistent with the finding in this study that native-born Hispanics are less likely to be undereducated than native-born American Indians, Eskimos, and Aleuts whose delay rate is approximately the same as that of Hispanics in general. A still lower rate for native-born English language-background Hispanics, in comparison with African Americans, whose delay rate is also about the same as that of Hispanics as a group, would indicate, however, that these Hispanic students are less likely to be older than their classmates when they are in school but just as likely not to graduate. A possible confirmation of this hypothesis is that African Americans complete more years of schooling than other youth who fail to graduate;[12] Hispanics drop out when they reach the school-leaving age, while blacks continue on into the eleventh or even the twelfth grade.

With regard to other racial/ethnic groups, the available data seem to indicate that even though Asian/Pacific students lag behind white students in their progress through school, native-born Asian and Pacific Islander youth are less likely, and foreign-born Asian and Pacific Islander youth are no more likely, to be undereducated than whites; that blacks are more likely to be both undereducated and behind but that those who leave school without high school diplomas are just as likely to complete at least 9 years of schooling and more likely to complete 11 years than whites who leave without high school diplomas;[13] and that, although American Indians, Eskimos, and Aleuts are no more likely to be delayed than African Americans, they are less likely to reach the ninth grade before discontinuing their education, and they are the most likely of all native-born groups to be undereducated.

The declines in educational delay rates in the tenth and eleventh grades, depicted in figure 3.3, and in enrollment in those grades, as shown in table 3.5, reflect the grade levels at which many youth leave school. As older youth leave school, those who remain are closer to the modal ages for their grades. The declines reinforce the findings of this study that Hispanics tend to complete fewer years of schooling than African American or white students. However, in the twelfth grade, larger proportions of students in all groups are likely to be older than the modal age in comparison with their proportions in the eleventh grade. Many youth, close to graduation, stay in school, regardless of age or racial/ethnic group.

POVERTY AND UNDEREDUCATION

Young people whose families have incomes below the poverty level are more likely to be undereducated than those in more economically advantaged circumstances. This is especially so for native-born non-Hispanic whites and Asians and Pacific Islanders, as illustrated in figure 3.4, which contrasts the undereducation rates of poor and more advantaged native-born youth. It is less so for native-born African Americans, Hispanics, and American Indians, Eskimos, and Aleuts and for foreign-born youth. In 1980, as shown in table 3.6, poor youth in general, and native-born non-Hispanic whites, were twice as likely to be out of school without high school diplomas as their counterparts from families with incomes above the poverty level. Native-born Asians and Pacific Islanders from poor families were 2.3 times more likely to be undereducated than their better-off counterparts. In contrast, poor native-born blacks and Hispanics were 1.8 times more likely to be undereducated, American Indians and Alaska Natives, 1.6 times more likely, and foreign-born youth, 1.3 times more likely, than their counterparts from families with incomes above the poverty level.

Figure 3.4
Undereducation Rates of Native-Born Youth from Families with Incomes Above and Below the Poverty Level, 1980

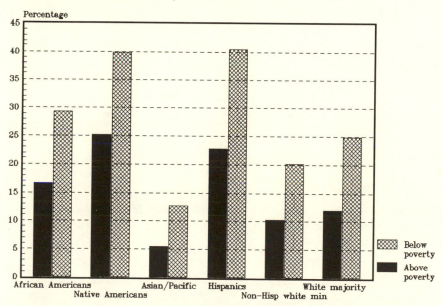

Although poverty is not as great an undereducation risk factor for some of the minorities as it is for native-born whites and Asian/Pacific youth, all minority youth are more likely than white majority youth to come from poor families, as shown in table 3.7. This factor increases the risk of undereducation among native-born minorities disproportionately. In 1980, among those for whom poverty status is determined, African Americans

Table 3.6
Undereducation Rates of Youth, by Poverty Status, Nativity, and Racial/ Ethnic Group: United States, 1980

Nativity and racial/ethnic group	Total	Above poverty	Below poverty
Total	15.4	13.7	28.1
African Americans	20.4	16.6	29.1
American Indians, Eskimos, and Aleuts	29.2	25.2	40.0
Asians and Pacific Islanders	9.8	8.6	17.2
Hispanics	32.2	28.9	44.8
Non-Hispanic white minority	12.0	11.3	19.1
White majority	13.0	12.0	24.9
Native born	14.8	13.0	27.5
African Americans	20.6	16.7	29.3
American Indians, Eskimos, and Aleuts	29.2	25.2	39.9
Asians and Pacific Islanders	6.3	5.5	12.7
Hispanics	26.6	22.8	40.4
Non-Hispanic white minority	11.2	10.3	20.2
White majority	13.0	12.0	24.9
Foreign born	28.3	27.7	35.5
African Americans	14.6	13.3	20.3
American Indians, Eskimos, and Aleuts	31.2	24.2	46.2
Asians and Pacific Islanders	12.4	11.4	18.8
Hispanics	45.4	43.6	54.0
Non-Hispanic white minority	17.6	19.3	14.9

Note: Poverty status not determined for people living in group quarters.

Table 3.7
Estimated Percentages of Youth from Families with Incomes Below the Poverty Level, by Nativity and Racial/Ethnic Group: United States, 1980 (Non-institutional population)

Racial/ethnic group	Total	Native born	Foreign born
Total	15.1	14.6	24.0
African Americans	31.1	31.3	26.9
American Indians, Eskimos, and Aleuts	30.1	30.0	39.2
Asians and Pacific Islanders	20.1	12.3	25.8
Hispanics	23.7	22.9	25.4
Non-Hispanic white minority	12.5	11.3	21.3
White majority	11.1	11.1	NA

NA = not applicable.

and American Indians, Eskimos, and Aleuts were more than 2.7 times as likely, and Hispanics, more than twice as likely, as white majority youth to be from families with incomes below the poverty level.[14] The even higher poverty rates of foreign-born youth in general are not only an undereducation risk factor for those who are young enough at the time they immigrate to enroll in U.S. schools but also an additional indicator of the extent of social and economic disadvantage of many newcomers in this country.

African American, Hispanic, and Native American youth from families with incomes above the poverty level and with other advantages in terms of the risk factors described in the previous sections of this chapter are nevertheless more likely to be out of school without high school diplomas than white majority youth. As shown in table 3.8, among more economically advantaged youth, native-born English language-background American Indians, Eskimos, and Aleuts were twice as likely, and Hispanics with similar characteristics, 1.5 times as likely, to be undereducated as white majority youth in 1980. Foreign-born African Americans, with the lowest overall rates among blacks, are more likely to be undereducated than white majority youth as group; those from more economically advantaged families are also more likely to be undereducated than similarly advantaged white majority youth but to a much smaller degree—13.3 percent in comparison with 12.0 percent.[15] Native-born African Americans from families with incomes above the poverty level do not fare so well. In 1980, with a rate of 16.7 percent, they were 1.4 times more likely to be undereducated than white majority youth from such families.

Table 3.8
Estimated Numbers of Selected Groups of Youth and Percentages and Undereducation Rates of Those from Families with Incomes Above the Poverty Level, by Racial/Ethnic Group: United States, 1980

Racial/ethnic group	Total, non-institutional population	Percentage above poverty	Under-education rate
Foreign-born African Americans	135,000	73.1	13.3
Native-born African Americans	4,455,000	68.7	16.7
Native-born English-language-background American Indians, Eskimos, and Aleuts	163,000	75.6	24.3
Native-born English-language-background Hispanics	396,000	80.4	17.9
Native-born non-English-language-background Asians and Pacific Islanders	111,000	89.9	4.6
Native-born white minority	2,380,000	88.7	10.3
White majority	24,248,000	88.9	12.0

THE RISK OF UNDEREDUCATION BY REGION

The extent to which young people are likely to be undereducated differs according to where they live. Those who live in the Northeast and the Midwest are the least likely to be out of school without high school diplomas and those living in the South are the most likely. In 1980, as shown in table 3.9, the regional rates ranged from 12.1 percent for youth living in the Northeast to 18.9 percent for those living in the South. Youth living in the East South Central states of Kentucky, Tennessee, Alabama, and Mississippi were nearly twice as likely to be undereducated as those living in New England and those living in the West North Central states of Minnesota, Iowa, Missouri, North and South Dakota, Nebraska, and Kansas. Among white majority youth, the rates ranged from 9.3 percent of those in the Northeast to 17.4 percent of those in the South as a whole and 20.7 percent of those in the East South Central states.

Table 3.9
Undereducation Rates of Youth, by Racial/Ethnic Group and Region: United States, 1980

Region	Total	African Americans	Hispanics	Non-Hispanic white minority	White majority
Total, all regions	15.4	20.4	32.2	13.0	13.0
Northeast	12.1	20.0	31.0	11.1	9.3
New England	11.2	17.5	32.3	12.7	9.7
Mid Atlantic	12.4	20.3	30.9	10.4	9.1
Midwest	13.1	21.4	33.0	11.5	11.1
East North Central	13.9	21.5	35.1	11.8	11.5
West North Central	11.3	20.7	22.6	10.3	10.3
South	18.9	21.1	29.9	14.8	17.4
South Atlantic	17.8	21.2	19.8	12.5	16.9
East South Central	20.8	21.5	25.2	18.2	20.7
West South Central	19.3	20.7	33.8	16.4	15.6
West	16.2	14.5	34.0	10.9	12.2
Mountain	15.4	16.7	28.8	10.8	12.2
Pacific	16.5	14.2	35.6	11.0	12.2

The risk of undereducation of minority youth in the various regions and states varies according to their racial/ethnic affiliation. Hispanic, African American, and non-Hispanic white minority youth are also more or less disadvantaged in comparison with majority youth in certain regions and states than in others. Blacks are least at risk in the West and most at risk in the Midwest and the South. In 1980 the range was from 14.5 percent to 21.1 percent. Blacks living in the Northeast were more than twice as likely, and those living in the Midwest nearly twice as likely, as white majority youth in those regions to be undereducated; in contrast, they were only 1.2 times as likely to be undereducated as whites in the South as a whole and in the West. In the East South Central states, African Americans and whites were nearly equally likely to be out of school without high school diplomas. Blacks in these states share the disadvantage of whites, whereas they do not share their advantage in the northern states where overall—and white—undereducation rates are much lower.

Hispanics living in the South, especially in the South Atlantic states, are the least likely to be undereducated and those living in the West, especially in the Pacific states, the most. The 1980 range was from 19.8 percent in the South Atlantic states to 35.6 percent in the Pacific states. The undereducation gap between Hispanics in general and white majority youth was also least in the South, but everywhere it was greater than that of African Americans except in the South Atlantic states where blacks are more likely than Hispanics as a group to be undereducated. The gap in undereducation between Hispanics and majority youth in 1980 ranged from 1.7 times in the South as a whole and 1.1 times in the South Atlantic states to 3.3 times in the Northeast. Non-Hispanic white minority youth living in the South, like white majority youth there, are the most likely of their group to be undereducated. In the South and in the West they have lower rates than white majority youth; in the Northeast they have higher rates.

THE RISK OF UNDEREDUCATION BY STATE

Among the states, the variation in the risk of undereducation is even greater than the variation among the regions, as depicted in figure 3.5. In 1980 youth living in Kentucky were three times more likely than youth living in Minnesota to be out of school before completing 12 years of schooling. There were 20 states, and the District of Columbia, in which the undereducation rate of youth was above the national average.

The risk associated with state of residence is greater for some youth than for others. Hispanics and non-Hispanic white minority youth living in the state with the highest rate were 3.3 times more likely to be undereducated than those living in the state with the lowest rate in 1980: 42.2 percent of all Hispanics living in Illinois were undereducated in comparison with 12.9 percent of those living in Maryland, and 20.4 percent of all non-Hispanic white minority youth living in Rhode Island were undereducated compared with 6.2 percent of those living in Utah. There was a similar gap for white majority youth: 24.0 percent in Kentucky were undereducated in comparison with 7.4 percent in Minnesota. Asian/Pacific

Figure 3.5
Undereducation Rates of Youth in the United States, 1980

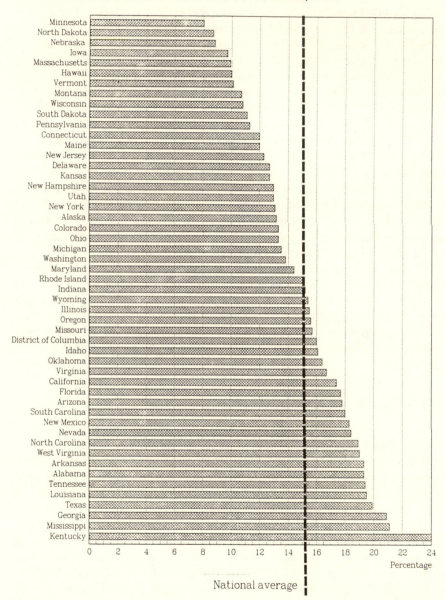

youth living in Texas were 2.4 times more likely to be undereducated than those living in New Jersey: the rates were 17.0 percent and 7.2 percent in 1980. In contrast, the range for African Americans was from 14.1 percent of those living in Iowa to 26.3 percent of those living in neighboring Wisconsin—a difference of 1.9 times—and for American Indians, Eskimos, and Aleuts, from 23.8 percent of those living in California to 34.3 percent of those living in North Carolina—a difference of 1.4 times. The differences in the state undereducation rates of the racial/ethnic groups are explored in relation to the differences in the state populations in the chapters on the various groups.

The state undereducation rates for groups in states in which they numbered at least 1,000 in 1980 are shown in table 3.10. The rates contrasted above and the poverty rates and proportions of foreign-born and language minority youth contrasted in the following sections are those in states in which the total number of a given group was at least 10,000.

POVERTY BY REGION AND STATE

Poverty varies geographically. Residents of some regions and states are poorer than those of other regions and states, and poverty increases the likelihood of youth to be undereducated, as already noted. Not surprisingly, therefore, the regions and states in which youth are the most likely to be poor tend in general to be the regions and states in which they have the highest undereducation rates. This is especially true for non-Hispanic white and Asian/Pacific youth for whom the undereducation risk associated with poverty is the greatest. Poverty and undereducation also generally coincide for American Indians, Eskimos, and Aleuts in the states in which they are concentrated.

In 1980, as shown in table 3.11, youth living in the South were 1.3 times more likely to come from families with incomes below the poverty level than youth living in the Northeast. Those living in the East South Central states were 1.6 times more likely to be poor than those living in New England. As shown in table 3.12, young people living in Mississippi were 2.4 times more likely to be poor than those living in Connecticut; a quarter of the former came from families with incomes below the poverty level in comparison with one in ten of Connecticut youth.

The 1980 poverty rates of non-Hispanic white youth ranged from 9.4 percent in the Middle Atlantic states to 14.3 percent in the East South Central states and from 6.2 percent in New Jersey to 16.9 percent in Kentucky. Among Asian and Pacific Islander youth, poverty ranged from less than 11 percent in New Jersey and Hawaii to 29.6 percent in Texas. The poverty rates of 16-to-24-year-old Native Americans ranged from one in five in California to almost half of those in neighboring Arizona.

Poverty and undereducation do not coincide as closely for African Amer-

Table 3.10
Undereducation Rates of Youth, by Racial/Ethnic Group and State: United States, 1980

State	Total	African Americans	Amer. Indians, Eskimos, & Aleuts	Asians & Pacific Islanders	Hispanics	Non-Hispanic white minority	White majority	Other non-Hispanics
Total	15.4	20.4	29.2	9.8	32.2	12.0	13.0	13.6
Alabama	19.3	20.3	28.6	20.0	21.5	17.5	18.9	11.0
Alaska	13.2	7.2	24.6	22.0	16.1	11.8	10.5	8.7
Arizona	17.8	18.2	33.2	8.2	32.0	12.5	12.9	11.7
Arkansas	19.2	20.3	31.1	17.6	24.3	17.8	18.8	17.6
California	17.4	14.2	23.8	8.1	36.2	10.7	11.7	13.2
Colorado	13.3	14.2	29.1	16.0	29.1	9.0	10.6	13.0
Connecticut	12.0	19.6	20.0	16.0	36.5	10.4	9.7	13.3
Delaware	12.7	21.3	*	5.7	39.3	10.3	10.8	3.3
District of Columbia	16.0	20.8	*	4.2	16.8	1.2	3.0	2.0
Florida	17.7	22.8	35.2	12.5	20.3	13.1	16.5	12.2
Georgia	20.9	23.2	44.9	15.8	23.0	15.7	20.1	17.7
Hawaii	10.0	10.7	24.2	8.9	14.0	8.0	10.7	12.5
Idaho	16.1	14.7	30.9	12.1	48.7	11.2	14.3	12.9
Illinois	15.5	23.5	29.0	8.0	42.4	11.9	11.3	15.2
Indiana	15.2	18.8	23.9	10.0	22.6	15.0	14.7	15.0
Iowa	9.7	14.1	21.9	13.4	20.8	10.4	9.4	19.6
Kansas	12.7	18.9	19.8	18.3	27.0	12.4	11.5	15.1
Kentucky	24.0	23.9	46.0	19.4	37.7	19.9	24.0	21.4
Louisiana	19.5	23.7	43.6	22.8	20.3	18.9	17.0	12.6
Maine	12.0	9.3	19.0	*	32.6	10.1	12.4	14.3
Maryland	14.4	20.0	40.0	8.5	12.9	10.2	12.5	15.7
Massachusetts	9.9	14.3	18.8	7.8	30.9	13.2	8.2	12.8
Michigan	13.5	21.5	27.5	8.7	24.4	11.4	11.9	12.8
Minnesota	8.0	14.3	33.6	17.4	19.8	7.3	7.4	12.2
Mississippi	21.2	24.9	32.7	8.8	20.9	18.9	18.8	17.1
Missouri	15.7	23.1	30.4	10.2	18.6	13.1	14.6	18.7
Montana	10.7	11.5	27.6	*	19.4	14.3	9.2	4.2
Nebraska	8.8	16.5	25.3	12.7	24.1	7.6	8.0	11.9
Nevada	18.4	21.2	30.4	12.1	30.5	16.3	16.9	14.5
New Hampshire	13.0	6.5	*	10.7	25.0	12.8	13.1	15.5
New Jersey	12.3	20.7	30.9	7.2	27.7	10.2	9.0	10.9
New Mexico	18.3	9.7	33.9	20.3	23.1	13.5	11.0	14.3
New York	13.1	20.2	25.9	9.3	31.8	10.2	8.7	12.2
North Carolina	18.9	20.5	34.3	12.2	22.5	12.7	18.3	15.4
North Dakota	8.7	2.4	25.5	*	13.2	10.3	7.7	8.3
Ohio	13.3	18.7	35.4	6.6	21.2	11.7	13.3	9.8
Oklahoma	16.4	15.7	26.4	18.3	31.4	15.6	15.3	13.3
Oregon	15.6	17.3	35.9	8.4	32.2	14.0	15.0	9.3
Pennsylvania	11.3	20.2	29.0	11.9	30.6	10.8	9.9	9.2
Rhode Island	15.1	28.3	*	34.4	35.8	20.4	12.2	23.9
South Carolina	18.0	18.4	36.6	16.3	20.9	13.7	17.9	15.3
South Dakota	11.1	2.4	39.4	*	28.9	14.9	8.4	*
Tennessee	19.4	18.0	31.7	11.4	21.2	16.9	19.9	11.5
Texas	19.9	19.2	23.8	17.0	34.4	15.1	14.7	19.6
Utah	13.0	30.4	28.5	19.4	32.1	6.2	11.9	16.3
Vermont	10.1	*	*	*	17.2	9.4	10.3	2.0
Virginia	16.7	22.0	20.8	10.3	14.4	11.6	15.6	12.5
Washington	13.8	15.5	28.3	9.6	30.8	11.2	13.0	13.0
West Virginia	19.0	14.5	*	†	24.8	14.7	19.4	14.7
Wisconsin	10.8	26.3	25.6	18.3	29.2	10.1	9.5	11.9
Wyoming	15.4	5.6	31.2	*	33.8	12.0	14.2	23.5

*Base number less than an estimated 1,000.

†Less than an estimated 0.1 of a percent.

Table 3.11
**Estimated Percentages of Youth from Families with Incomes Below the
Poverty Level, by Racial/Ethnic Group and Region: United States, 1980
(Non-institutional population)**

Region	Total	African Americans	Hispanics	Non-Hispanic whites
Total, all regions	15.1	31.1	23.7	11.2
Northeast	13.6	30.6	32.9	9.7
New England	12.3	27.3	36.7	10.6
Mid Atlantic	14.0	31.0	32.3	9.4
Midwest	13.0	29.2	20.4	10.6
East North Central	12.8	29.1	20.7	10.0
West North Central	13.4	29.8	18.7	12.0
South	17.4	32.9	24.5	12.0
South Atlantic	16.4	30.6	19.6	11.4
East South Central	20.2	39.5	32.2	14.3
West South Central	17.3	32.6	25.8	11.5
West	15.5	25.7	20.4	12.8
Mountain	16.2	26.9	21.7	13.4
Pacific	15.3	25.5	20.1	12.5

icans and Hispanics. The 1980 poverty rates of blacks ranged from 25.5
percent in the Pacific states to 39.5 percent in the East South Central
states. Their rates were lowest in Nevada—20.8 percent—and highest in
Arkansas and Mississippi—42.7 and 42.5 percent, respectively. Black
youth in Nevada were more likely than blacks nationally to be undereducated;
those in Mississippi had the second highest undereducation rate in
1980, but those in Arkansas were only about as likely as blacks nationally
to be undereducated. The range of poverty for Hispanic youth was from
19.6 percent of those living in the South Atlantic states to 36.7 percent for
those living in New England and from 14.6 percent of those in Virginia to
39.8 percent of those in Massachusetts. Hispanics living in Virginia had the
third lowest undereducation rate of their group in 1980 while those living
in Massachusetts were more likely than Hispanics nationally to be undereducated.
However, Hispanics in Illinois—the most likely to be undereducated—were
less likely than Hispanics nationally to be poor in 1980.

Poverty does not present the same risk for youth in all states. The risk
factor associated with coming from a poor family in comparison with
coming from a family in more advantageous economic circumstances in
1980 ranged from as low as 1.3 to 2.6 for non-Hispanic whites, as shown

Table 3.12
Estimated Percentages of Youth from Families with Incomes Below the Poverty Level, by Racial/Ethnic Group and State: United States, 1980 (Non-institutional population)

State	Total	African Americans	Amer. Indians, Eskimos, & Aleuts	Asians & Pacific Islanders	Hispanics	Non-Hispanic whites
Total	15.1	31.1	30.1	20.1	23.7	11.2
Alabama	21.3	39.4	24.2	23.3	33.3	13.7
Alaska	13.1	11.1	24.8	9.1	16.1	10.1
Arizona	17.8	29.7	47.3	24.3	20.8	13.7
Arkansas	19.7	42.7	18.1	*	36.8	14.0
California	15.5	25.9	21.3	19.1	19.9	12.0
Colorado	14.9	22.6	28.4	29.0	20.9	13.2
Connecticut	10.1	24.6	*	26.7	34.5	7.1
Delaware	14.8	28.6	*	*	39.3	11.4
District of Columbia	25.0	23.6	*	*	34.6	29.6
Florida	16.8	34.8	27.0	18.8	18.4	12.1
Georgia	18.2	34.6	25.6	26.2	22.4	11.0
Hawaii	12.5	11.0	*	10.9	15.8	14.2
Idaho	17.0	*	34.0	30.0	36.0	15.5
Illinois	13.4	31.2	28.0	20.7	21.2	8.6
Indiana	11.5	25.5	16.4	33.8	16.1	10.0
Iowa	13.2	33.8	25.4	41.6	24.8	12.5
Kansas	13.2	30.3	18.3	34.7	13.2	11.8
Kentucky	18.9	39.4	*	33.8	28.4	16.9
Louisiana	19.2	36.5	24.1	38.1	21.9	10.7
Maine	14.5	*	*	*	*	14.2
Maryland	12.2	23.8	29.7	12.4	19.0	7.6
Massachusetts	12.6	29.4	31.2	26.4	39.8	10.8
Michigan	12.6	26.1	22.4	26.8	20.2	10.2
Minnesota	12.2	30.8	29.0	42.6	21.7	11.5
Mississippi	24.6	42.5	36.5	*	35.7	12.5
Missouri	13.8	29.1	16.7	20.8	19.2	11.5
Montana	16.9	*	36.4	*	19.4	15.6
Nebraska	12.5	32.1	30.7	34.0	21.1	11.4
Nevada	11.7	20.8	23.8	15.3	16.7	10.0
New Hampshire	11.9	*	*	*	*	11.8
New Jersey	10.9	27.5	12.0	10.8	25.1	6.2
New Mexico	20.3	32.3	42.3	38.6	22.6	13.0
New York	16.4	31.3	32.8	18.4	34.1	10.4
North Carolina	16.8	31.3	25.7	23.0	27.7	11.4
North Dakota	15.0	*	41.6	*	*	13.9
Ohio	12.9	30.2	23.7	26.3	22.5	10.5
Oklahoma	15.0	27.9	24.9	30.6	25.7	12.6
Oregon	15.7	31.7	23.3	37.0	30.1	14.4
Pennsylvania	12.5	33.2	22.4	27.9	36.0	9.7
Rhode Island	12.8	32.8	*	44.6	32.9	11.3
South Carolina	17.9	32.1	16.2	20.9	28.0	10.3
South Dakota	20.0	*	53.3	*	*	17.2
Tennessee	17.6	36.1	29.1	22.9	31.5	13.1
Texas	16.9	28.1	17.6	29.6	25.9	10.9
Utah	15.3	59.3	44.4	32.0	22.0	13.7
Vermont	16.5	*	*	*	*	16.4
Virginia	14.8	26.4	20.4	19.5	14.6	11.4
Washington	14.4	21.8	28.4	23.3	23.3	13.3
West Virginia	16.7	35.1	*	*	25.8	15.9
Wisconsin	12.6	30.1	29.2	39.6	18.5	11.4
Wyoming	10.8	*	34.6	*	14.5	10.0

*Base number less than an estimated 1,000.

in table 3.13. Poor whites in North Dakota had an undereducation rate of 10.7 percent in comparison with the 8.3 percent of their better-off counterparts;[16] those in Maryland and Ohio had rates of about 29 percent in comparison with 11 percent of more advantaged white youth in those states. The poverty risk factor for African Americans ranged from statistical insignificance to 2.0. In Massachusetts, 17.8 percent of poor blacks (plus or minus 2.4 percent) and 14.1 percent of more economically advantaged blacks (plus or minus 1.4 percent) were undereducated, whereas in Maryland, New Jersey, and Ohio, the comparative rates were 28.4 to 30.9 percent of poor blacks and under 16 percent of their more advantaged counterparts. The Hispanic poverty risk gap ranged from 1.4 for youth in Illinois to 1.9 for those in Florida.

OTHER UNDEREDUCATION RISK FACTORS IN THE STATES: NATIVITY AND LANGUAGE BACKGROUND

States differ widely in the proportions of youth who are foreign born or have non-English language backgrounds. As shown in table 3.14, in 1980, fewer than 1 percent of 16-to-24-year-olds in West Virginia were born abroad in comparison with 15.1 percent of those in California. In all, there were 22 states in which more than 98.0 percent of youth were born in the United States, Puerto Rico, or another outlying area. Among Asians and Pacific Islanders—the most likely to be foreign born nationally—the range was from 18.5 percent of those in Hawaii to 78.4 percent of those in Texas. Only 6.4 percent of Hispanics in New Mexico were foreign born, in comparison with 58.3 percent of those in Florida. The foreign-born proportion among non-Hispanic white minority youth ranged from 1.7 percent of those living in North Dakota to more than one in five of those living in Rhode Island and that among African Americans from 0.4 percent of those in Mississippi to 16.2 percent of those in New York.

The variation in the proportions of language minority youth is even greater than that in the proportions born abroad. In 1980, as shown in table 3.15, the range was from less than 5 percent in the southern states of Arkansas, Kentucky, West Virginia, Mississippi, and Tennessee to more than half in New Mexico, the most multilingual state.[17] Among Hispanics—the group most likely to come from language minority homes— the proportions of non-English language-background youth ranged from 43.6 percent of those living in Hawaii to 94.0 percent of those living in Texas. The range for Asians and Pacific Islanders was from half of those in Hawaii to 86.5 percent of those in Illinois. The widest range of any group was that of American Indians, Eskimos, and Aleuts—from 8.0 percent of those in North Carolina to 90.2 percent of those in New Mexico. The 1980 range for African Americans was from 3.9 percent of those in Mississippi to 11.9 percent of those in New York.

Table 3.13
Undereducation Rates of Youth, by Racial/Ethnic Group, Poverty Status, and State: United States, 1980 (Non-institutional population)

State	Total Above pov	Total Below pov	African Americans Above pov	African Americans Below pov	Hispanics Above pov	Hispanics Below pov	Non-Hispanic whites Above pov	Non-Hispanic whites Below pov
Total	13.7	28.1	16.6	29.1	28.9	44.8	12.0	24.1
Alabama	17.3	29.4	16.6	27.6	19.8	27.4	17.4	31.6
Alaska	11.6	27.6	*	*	*	*	9.5	22.2
Arizona	15.9	30.0	12.9	31.5	28.3	46.8	12.3	19.8
Arkansas	17.3	31.0	17.3	25.4	*	*	17.1	35.0
California	15.5	28.2	11.3	20.7	32.9	50.3	10.4	18.3
Colorado	12.2	22.0	11.7	24.6	25.3	46.0	10.2	14.8
Connecticut	10.7	28.5	14.7	32.7	30.9	49.5	9.5	21.0
Delaware	11.4	24.2	17.5	31.4	*	*	10.2	20.6
District of Columbia	15.4	26.1	17.9	33.2	*	*	*	*
Florida	15.8	28.6	18.4	31.1	17.6	33.3	15.1	26.1
Georgia	18.4	32.8	18.5	32.2	16.6	30.6	18.4	33.6
Hawaii	7.7	21.9	*	*	10.9	*	7.5	21.0
Idaho	14.5	26.4	*	*	41.4	64.2	13.1	21.3
Illinois	13.5	30.8	19.1	32.3	39.5	56.6	10.5	24.2
Indiana	14.0	32.2	15.7	29.4	22.6	31.5	13.8	32.9
Iowa	9.3	17.0	12.2	19.4	19.2	*	9.1	16.5
Kansas	11.9	20.5	14.3	25.4	25.2	49.4	11.2	18.4
Kentucky	19.5	45.2	14.6	36.9	33.1	40.3	19.7	47.0
Louisiana	17.2	30.7	19.7	31.3	19.4	28.1	16.2	30.0
Maine	11.1	23.8	*	*	*	*	11.1	24.1
Maryland	12.3	29.7	15.8	30.9	11.0	*	11.3	29.1
Massachusetts	9.3	20.1	14.1	17.8	28.5	42.5	8.6	17.9
Michigan	12.0	26.3	18.1	30.6	21.7	38.5	11.0	24.2
Minnesota	7.2	14.7	*	27.4	20.1	*	6.9	13.1
Mississippi	19.4	32.0	22.2	31.6	20.1	*	18.2	33.0
Missouri	13.8	28.7	19.0	32.4	14.2	*	13.2	27.5
Montana	9.0	22.2	*	*	*	*	8.3	18.9
Nebraska	7.9	17.2	9.9	29.9	22.1	*	7.5	15.1
Nevada	17.1	29.2	19.8	*	26.6	51.2	15.8	26.7
New Hampshire	13.3	22.5	*	*	*	*	13.4	22.5
New Jersey	10.1	28.8	15.9	32.1	22.9	41.9	8.2	21.1
New Mexico	16.0	30.8	*	*	20.1	35.2	11.3	16.2
New York	10.7	27.5	15.1	29.2	26.3	42.9	8.2	19.0
North Carolina	18.5	28.4	19.1	26.9	20.9	31.2	18.1	29.3
North Dakota	8.7	13.0	*	*	*	*	8.3	10.7
Ohio	11.4	28.7	14.5	28.4	18.3	34.5	11.1	28.7
Oklahoma	14.9	27.4	11.0	22.6	28.9	43.8	14.2	26.1
Oregon	14.3	25.3	12.6	28.0	29.9	41.2	13.7	24.1
Pennsylvania	9.9	25.4	15.6	29.6	26.2	43.0	9.2	22.5
Rhode Island	14.9	29.5	24.1	49.4	40.8	*	14.0	25.7
South Carolina	16.8	26.2	16.2	23.3	16.7	*	16.9	30.8
South Dakota	9.4	21.7	*	*	*	*	8.2	15.4
Tennessee	17.6	33.4	14.3	26.3	23.2	27.4	18.1	38.3
Texas	18.1	31.9	15.6	28.1	31.2	45.2	14.3	22.1
Utah	12.2	18.5	*	41.1	29.7	44.0	11.1	14.1
Vermont	9.9	18.2	*	*	*	*	9.8	18.3
Virginia	15.3	27.9	18.9	32.0	12.0	*	14.6	25.8
Washington	12.0	25.9	11.6	19.1	27.7	47.0	11.4	24.4
West Virginia	16.8	35.0	13.0	19.3	*	*	16.9	36.8
Wisconsin	9.9	19.0	22.5	36.0	27.6	43.6	9.1	15.7
Wyoming	15.0	24.0	*	*	30.8	*	13.9	19.9

*Base number less than an estimated 1,000.

72

Table 3.14
Estimated Percentages of Foreign-Born Youth, by Racial/Ethnic Group and State: United States, 1980

State	Total	African Americans	Amer. Indians, Eskimos, & Aleuts	Asians & Pacific Islanders	His-panics	Non-Hispanic white minority
Total	5.0	3.0	1.7	57.3	29.8	12.1
Alabama	1.1	0.6	1.0	78.6	12.0	7.4
Alaska	3.0	4.6	0.9	54.2	11.4	9.5
Arizona	5.1	1.7	1.3	50.6	15.5	8.6
Arkansas	1.0	0.7	0.8	78.4	11.8	7.0
California	15.1	2.6	1.9	56.3	41.0	19.4
Colorado	3.8	2.9	0.5	58.3	8.2	11.1
Connecticut	5.0	8.7	*	69.8	16.9	15.8
Delaware	1.7	1.2	†	60.0	8.2	7.0
District of Columbia	5.4	3.1	†	47.9	45.1	15.1
Florida	8.9	4.4	3.0	74.7	58.3	11.1
Georgia	1.8	0.8	3.1	75.8	19.1	10.6
Hawaii	11.8	1.2	3.0	18.5	11.4	11.2
Idaho	3.1	23.5	1.0	41.4	29.9	4.5
Illinois	5.5	1.3	5.9	77.8	42.1	14.6
Indiana	1.3	1.2	6.0	69.5	13.7	6.3
Iowa	1.3	4.4	3.1	73.2	22.0	5.2
Kansas	2.2	2.3	1.0	82.3	14.9	6.9
Kentucky	1.1	1.1	6.0	72.0	11.8	6.7
Louisiana	2.1	0.9	2.6	78.4	23.2	2.9
Maine	1.8	4.7	*	†	17.2	4.1
Maryland	3.2	2.1	2.7	71.2	31.5	11.8
Massachusetts	5.5	11.7	5.9	67.3	31.4	18.9
Michigan	2.3	1.2	1.9	71.7	11.5	12.6
Minnesota	1.6	6.7	2.0	77.4	15.2	4.8
Mississippi	1.1	0.4	*	59.6	14.3	7.0
Missouri	1.4	0.9	0.7	70.8	12.7	6.8
Montana	1.2	*	1.9	†	4.7	3.3
Nebraska	1.6	1.9	1.2	73.2	19.0	4.6
Nevada	6.0	1.6	1.5	70.7	31.2	10.9
New Hampshire	2.3	6.5	†	64.3	34.1	6.4
New Jersey	6.5	4.2	7.4	73.3	34.4	16.8
New Mexico	3.9	4.0	0.6	62.5	6.4	5.7
New York	9.3	16.2	5.5	77.3	27.5	16.9
North Carolina	1.6	0.9	1.5	72.8	16.1	7.5
North Dakota	1.5	4.9	*	†	22.7	1.7
Ohio	1.4	0.9	2.1	67.2	11.1	7.9
Oklahoma	2.7	2.2	0.3	74.2	18.7	16.9
Oregon	3.8	3.1	1.1	61.1	22.4	14.1
Pennsylvania	1.6	1.8	0.9	80.0	13.8	6.1
Rhode Island	6.3	8.6	†	62.5	46.7	20.8
South Carolina	0.9	0.9	1.2	64.1	12.6	5.9
South Dakota	1.2	4.9	0.5	†	23.5	4.8
Tennessee	1.2	0.9	3.2	66.7	13.8	7.0
Texas	6.4	1.7	2.6	78.4	19.2	9.2
Utah	3.6	6.5	2.2	59.0	13.1	7.3
Vermont	2.4	†	†	†	21.4	6.7
Virginia	3.1	1.3	6.4	77.7	29.5	12.3
Washington	4.7	4.2	2.7	54.7	24.2	10.6
West Virginia	0.8	1.6	†	56.8	10.1	2.8
Wisconsin	1.5	2.1	1.0	75.4	18.5	5.8
Wyoming	1.7	5.6	1.2	†	12.2	3.3

*Less than an estimated 0.1 of a percent.

†Base number less than an estimated 1,000.

73

Table 3.15
Estimated Percentages of Youth with Non-English Language Backgrounds, by Racial/Ethnic Group and State: United States, 1980

State	Total	African Americans	Amer. Indians, Eskimos & Aleuts	Asians & Pacific Islanders	Hispanics
Total	16.1	7.3	36.4	73.9	84.2
Alabama	5.1	5.4	7.1	77.1	35.6
Alaska	19.1	4.6	59.0	57.6	54.3
Arizona	30.4	10.6	87.6	68.0	87.0
Arkansas	4.4	4.2	11.5	80.4	39.1
California	32.3	8.5	22.3	78.1	83.9
Colorado	18.4	8.8	33.5	65.8	69.6
Connecticut	20.1	9.0	30.0	80.9	89.1
Delaware	8.8	6.3	*	68.6	61.6
District of Columbia	13.1	8.1	*	66.7	75.0
Florida	17.8	8.0	14.4	68.7	89.6
Georgia	6.1	5.1	12.2	77.9	52.4
Hawaii	34.3	9.3	18.2	50.2	43.6
Idaho	11.6	20.6	46.4	48.3	76.3
Illinois	16.0	7.3	24.9	86.5	88.0
Indiana	7.6	5.9	7.5	67.9	69.8
Iowa	6.6	11.6	20.2	76.8	59.2
Kansas	9.6	8.8	24.5	76.8	67.6
Kentucky	4.4	5.3	20.0	76.3	43.3
Louisiana	16.1	10.4	30.8	86.2	54.8
Maine	17.2	7.0	47.6	*	48.3
Maryland	9.9	7.4	10.7	79.4	62.7
Massachusetts	17.9	11.8	23.5	81.9	86.0
Michigan	10.2	6.2	7.7	75.5	65.3
Minnesota	8.7	10.5	21.1	80.0	53.9
Mississippi	4.7	3.9	56.4	75.4	34.4
Missouri	6.4	6.3	9.5	73.6	52.0
Montana	9.3	7.7	37.8	*	41.1
Nebraska	7.7	5.9	32.5	64.8	63.4
Nevada	16.1	6.6	38.5	79.3	69.9
New Hampshire	15.4	10.9	*	67.9	61.0
New Jersey	20.9	7.3	13.8	82.9	90.8
New Mexico	51.8	10.9	90.2	68.7	88.9
New York	25.2	11.9	27.1	86.0	91.9
North Carolina	6.1	5.5	8.0	74.4	50.1
North Dakota	14.0	9.8	44.2	*	56.8
Ohio	8.7	6.6	13.2	75.1	65.3
Oklahoma	8.6	6.3	22.6	74.2	60.8
Oregon	10.6	8.4	18.7	65.3	59.0
Pennsylvania	10.5	6.9	18.7	82.3	75.7
Rhode Island	21.0	15.5	*	79.7	73.3
South Carolina	6.3	5.9	9.8	69.6	39.8
South Dakota	11.2	14.6	47.3	*	49.0
Tennessee	4.9	5.7	19.0	79.8	37.9
Texas	29.0	7.1	19.7	84.0	94.0
Utah	15.5	8.7	59.6	71.4	66.5
Vermont	6.7	*	*	*	61.9
Virginia	8.2	5.7	14.4	80.0	63.3
Washington	12.7	11.4	18.0	74.3	67.6
West Virginia	4.5	4.2	*	56.8	27.5
Wisconsin	9.2	5.0	14.3	76.6	72.6
Wyoming	11.0	2.8	37.5	*	65.8

*Base number less than an estimated 1,000.

Foreign birth and a non-English language background are not risk factors for all youth, as previously noted, and they do not affect the undereducation rates of the racial/ethnic groups in the same way in all states. The relationship between the characteristics of the various state racial/ethnic populations and the undereducation rates of youth in those states is examined in the individual chapters on the racial/ethnic groups.

URBANICITY AND UNDEREDUCATION

Where young people live within regions and states affects the risk of undereducation. The differences between the undereducation rates of those living in central cities, in their suburbs, or in rural areas in individual states suggest qualitative differences between school districts in different environments. They reflect fundamental inequities between districts serving predominantly poor and minority students and districts serving more affluent and more largely majority students. In 1980, 16-to-19-year-old civilians living in the central cities of metropolitan areas were nearly twice as likely to be out of school without high school diplomas as those on rural farms, as shown in table 3.16. The undereducation rate of central city youth was 15.5 percent compared with 8.2 percent for youth living on farms of an acre or more producing at least $1,000 in agricultural income in 1979. Youth living in rural areas in general had a rate of 14.2 percent; those in smaller cities, 13.6 percent; and those in the suburbs of metropolitan areas, 10.5 percent.[18]

Table 3.16
Undereducation Rates of Civilian Youth, Aged 16 to 19, by Urbanicity, Race, and Hispanic Ethnicity: United States, 1980

| Race and Hispanic ethnicity | Total | Urban | | | | Rural | |
		Total	Central cities	Urban fringe	Places of 2,500+	Total	Rural farm
Total	13.4	13.1	15.5	10.5	13.6	14.2	8.2
American Indians, Eskimos, and Aleuts	26.5	26.0	27.9	25.4	24.3	27.0	18.8
Asians and Pacific Islanders	7.7	7.6	8.5	6.5	8.4	8.5	3.6
Blacks	15.8	15.5	16.3	12.6	16.2	17.5	14.3
Hispanics[1]	25.4	25.4	27.4	21.8	26.1	25.4	25.7
Whites	12.2	11.7	14.0	9.9	12.6	13.5	7.8

Source: Derived from Bureau of the Census, 1980 Census of Population, General Social and Economic Characteristics, Part 1, United States Summary, pp. 71, 97–98, and 118.

[1]May be of any race.

White undereducation rates follow those of youth in general. They ranged from 7.8 percent of white youth living on rural farms to 14.0 percent of those living in central cities in 1980. Blacks living in rural areas in general are the most likely to be undereducated and those living in the fringe areas of central cities the least likely—17.5 percent in comparison with 12.6 percent in 1980. Central cities are the most educationally hazardous environments, and fringe areas the least educationally hazardous environments, for both Hispanics and Asians and Pacific Islanders.[19]

The differing undereducation rates of youth living in urban and rural environments in the various states are displayed in table 3.17. In 1980 there were 27 states in which civilian young people, aged 16 to 19, living in central cities were more likely to be undereducated than their counterparts in rural areas and 22 states in which the reverse was true.[20]

For the most part, higher undereducation rates coincide with higher poverty rates in urban or rural areas in the various states, especially for non-Hispanic whites. (See discussion in chapter 4 beginning on page 81 and table 4.2.) The relationship of poverty in urban or rural areas and the undereducation of youth living in urban or rural areas accounts for some of the variation in the comparative undereducation rates of African Americans and white majority youth, as discussed in chapter 5. It accounts for the considerable educational disadvantage of blacks in comparison with whites in certain highly urbanized northern states, where poverty characterizes the inner cities where most blacks, but few whites, live and the similarity of disadvantage of blacks and whites in certain states in the South, where substantial proportions of both groups live in poverty in the rural areas. (See tables 5.4 and 5.5 in chapter 5.)

AT-RISK POPULATIONS

U.S. schools are failing all young people. As discussed in the previous chapter, undereducated youth are overwhelmingly white, native born, and from more economically advantaged homes in which only English is spoken. Nevertheless, minority youth and young people from poor homes are more likely than majority youth and youth from more economically advantaged homes to be out of school without high school diplomas. The disadvantage of African Americans, Hispanics, and American Indians, Eskimos, and Aleuts is apparent even when those least likely to be undereducated are compared with majority youth. Minority students are also those mostly likely to fall behind their majority classmates, and many who discontinue their schooling without graduating from high school leave earlier than undereducated majority students and, thus, further diminish their likelihood of returning to complete graduation requirements. American Indians and Alaska Natives are the most at risk. The risk of Hispanic youth, and that of some other minority youth, is complicated

Table 3.17
Undereducation Rates of Civilian Youth, Aged 16 to 19, by Urbanicity and State: United States, 1980

State	Total	Urban					Rural	
		Total	Central cities	Urban fringe	Places of 10,000+	Places of 2,500–10,000	Total	Rural farm
Total	13.4	13.1	15.5	10.5	12.8	14.3	14.2	8.2
Alabama	16.3	14.4	13.4	14.6	15.7	16.5	19.2	8.2
Alaska	12.9	12.2	12.6	*	*	*	13.9	*
Arizona	18.2	17.3	19.5	14.0	13.2	19.9	22.7	*
Arkansas	16.7	15.7	14.1	19.5	14.1	18.3	17.9	9.7
California	14.7	14.7	16.3	13.3	14.8	18.9	14.6	11.9
Colorado	13.1	13.5	14.0	12.9	13.6	13.2	11.6	*
Connecticut	10.4	11.3	16.3	7.2	7.7	15.3	7.3	*
Delaware	11.5	9.7	19.1	7.9	*	*	16.5	*
District of Columbia	12.7	12.7	12.7	NA	NA	NA	NA	NA
Florida	16.8	16.0	16.3	15.3	20.0	18.4	20.8	*
Georgia	17.8	15.8	15.5	13.9	17.9	20.5	21.1	12.5
Hawaii	7.1	6.9	6.5	6.7	*	9.2	8.6	*
Idaho	14.8	14.2	12.0	*	12.5	20.8	15.7	*
Illinois	12.9	13.6	18.0	10.1	10.2	12.0	9.5	4.4
Indiana	13.7	14.3	15.6	11.2	17.6	14.0	12.6	10.9
Iowa	8.4	9.5	10.8	9.2	8.5	8.3	6.7	3.6
Kansas	11.6	12.9	15.4	10.8	13.0	11.5	8.7	5.2
Kentucky	21.5	17.5	18.7	15.8	14.3	22.4	25.8	15.8
Louisiana	17.2	15.8	14.6	15.7	15.5	20.8	20.3	12.7
Maine	10.6	10.6	15.2	5.9	9.7	10.4	10.6	*
Maryland	12.1	12.0	19.9	8.7	15.1	11.2	12.7	*
Massachusetts	8.8	9.1	14.4	6.1	8.1	8.4	7.2	*
Michigan	11.5	11.9	17.1	9.4	7.7	11.7	10.6	5.2
Minnesota	7.3	7.5	9.7	6.8	6.0	6.7	6.8	3.8
Mississippi	17.5	16.7	14.0	17.0	17.8	19.0	18.1	11.3
Missouri	13.9	13.5	16.4	10.4	12.2	16.6	14.9	7.3
Montana	10.8	10.0	10.2	14.2	7.8	10.9	11.8	*
Nebraska	7.8	8.7	9.2	8.0	9.2	7.2	6.1	*
Nevada	18.6	19.1	19.2	19.7	*	14.9	10.7	*
New Hampshire	11.6	12.1	15.4	6.2	12.9	10.0	11.0	*
New Jersey	10.2	10.3	21.6	8.6	14.9	10.2	9.6	*
New Mexico	16.5	14.8	11.8	12.7	18.5	18.8	20.8	*
New York	10.7	10.9	15.5	5.8	8.1	6.5	9.5	7.9
North Carolina	16.3	14.3	12.7	15.3	15.5	16.0	18.2	11.9
North Dakota	8.0	7.8	7.9	*	8.5	*	8.3	*
Ohio	10.4	10.8	15.1	7.0	10.5	10.5	9.6	9.7
Oklahoma	14.3	14.7	15.5	11.5	13.5	17.7	13.4	*
Oregon	15.4	16.0	16.0	15.8	14.1	18.9	14.3	*
Pennsylvania	9.6	9.1	13.1	6.2	9.1	8.1	10.9	22.3
Rhode Island	13.9	14.2	14.9	13.6	*	*	11.3	*
South Carolina	14.4	13.8	11.9	14.6	11.5	15.2	15.1	*
South Dakota	11.1	9.0	10.0	*	6.3	10.8	13.2	6.9
Tennessee	16.7	14.0	13.4	9.6	17.6	18.4	21.0	13.6
Texas	17.6	17.8	18.2	15.5	17.8	20.4	17.0	7.8
Utah	13.7	13.9	13.7	15.1	7.9	12.3	12.4	*
Vermont	9.0	8.7	*	*	*	11.7	9.1	*
Virginia	13.9	11.9	15.3	9.6	8.5	13.8	17.6	13.1
Washington	12.9	12.8	13.3	12.1	10.2	17.6	13.2	7.4
West Virginia	17.4	12.6	13.8	12.6	9.0	14.0	20.2	*
Wisconsin	9.5	9.8	12.3	7.0	7.7	8.4	9.0	9.6
Wyoming	15.2	15.1	13.3	*	15.2	16.2	15.5	*

Source: Derived from Bureau of the Census, *1980 Census of Population, General Social and Economic Characteristics, Part 1, United States Summary*, p. 71; and *Parts 2–52, the States, and the District of Columbia*, table 66, various pages.

NA = not applicable.

*Base number less than an estimated 1,000.

by the factors of nativity and language background. Foreign-born students present a particular challenge. Some, especially among the most recent arrivals, come with limited schooling. Their educational needs are complicated by the fragile economic existence of many newcomers.

With the exception of American Indians and Alaska Natives, minority youth, as noted in chapter 2, live predominantly in urban areas, most of them in the inner cities of large metropolitan areas. Youth living in inner cities nationally and in many northern states have considerably greater risk of undereducation than youth living elsewhere. However, urban youth are less at risk than rural youth in many states of the South. The differences in the undereducation rates within states according to whether youth live in urban or rural environments reflect differences in the quality of school districts. They raise issues of educational equity, especially for the minority and poor students who disproportionately live in the inner cities of the North and for white majority as well as black youth in rural areas in many states in the South. The following chapters discuss the characteristics of undereducated youth and the undereducation rates of young people in the six racial/ethnic groups identified for this study. They examine the populations of which the youth are a part in the various states in which they are concentrated. Finally, they look at the educational and demographic trends for youth in each group in the final years of this century.

NOTES

1. As many as half of all ninth graders fail to graduate four years later according to a report on urban school districts across the country. Office of Educational Research and Improvement, U.S. Department of Education, *Dealing with Dropouts: The Urban Superintendents' Call to Action* (Washington, D.C.: U.S. Government Printing Office, 1988), p. 1.

2. Bureau of the Census, U.S. Department of Commerce, *1980 Census of Population, General Social and Economic Characteristics, Part 1, United States Summary* (Washington, D.C.: U.S. Government Printing Office, 1983), p. 71.

3. Dorothy Waggoner, "Language Minorities in the United States in the 1980s: The Evidence from the 1980 Census," in *Language Diversity, Problem or Resource?* ed. Sandra Lee McKay and Sau-ling Cynthia Wong (New York: Newbury House Publishers, 1988), pp. 102 and 104.

4. The differences between the rates for American Indian/Alaska Native men and women and between those for Hispanic men and women are significant at the 68 percent confidence level; the difference between the rates for Asian/Pacific men and women is not statistically significant.

5. Bureau of the Census, U.S. Department of Commerce, *1980 Census of Population, Detailed Population Characteristics, Part 1, United States Summary* (Washington, D.C.: U.S. Government Printing Office, 1984), pp. 26–27.

6. Ibid., pp. 28–37.

7. Ibid.

8. Center for Education Statistics, U.S. Department of Education, *Who Drops Out of High School? Findings from High School and Beyond* (Washington, D.C.: U.S. Government Printing Office, 1987), p. 46.

9. Ibid.

10. Ricardo R. Fernández and Gangjian Shu, "School Dropouts: New Approaches to an Enduring Problem," *Education and Urban Society* 20 (August 1988): 378.

11. National Center for Education Statistics, U.S. Department of Health, Education, and Welfare, *The Educational Disadvantage of Language-Minority Persons in the United States, Spring 1976*, NCES Bulletin 78–121, July 26, 1978, pp. 5–6.

12. Bureau of the Census, U.S. Department of Commerce, *School Enrollment—Social and Economic Characteristics of Students: October 1981 and 1980* (Washington, D.C.: U.S. Government Printing Office, 1985), pp. 73–75; see also discussion in chapter 1, pp. 7–10.

13. Ibid.

14. Poverty rates for all groups rose during the early 1980s and then began to fall after 1983. By 1986 the rate of African Americans was about what it had been in 1979, while the rates of whites and Hispanics remained higher than in 1979. Nevertheless, blacks were still the most likely to be poor of the groups for whom data from the current population surveys are available. Bureau of the Census, U.S. Department of Commerce, *Poverty in the United States, 1986* (Washington, D.C.: U.S. Government Printing Office, 1988), pp. 5–6.

15. The difference between 13.3 percent for foreign-born African Americans and 12.0 percent for white majority youth is significant at the 68 percent confidence level.

16. The difference is significant at the 68 percent confidence level.

17. Waggoner, "Language Minorities," pp. 90–91.

18. Bureau of the Census, *General Social and Economic Characteristics*, p. 71.

19. Ibid., pp. 96–98 and 118.

20. Bureau of the Census, *General Social and Economic Characteristics, Parts 2–52, the States and the District of Columbia*, table 66, various pages.

4

White Majority Youth
Who Are Undereducated

Undereducated youth in the United States are predominantly members of the white majority. They are native born and live in monolingual English-speaking homes, the majority with family incomes above the poverty level. There were nearly 3.5 million white majority youth in 1980 who were not enrolled in school and had not completed 12 years of schooling. They constituted one in eight of non-Hispanic native-born whites, aged 16 to 24, with English monolingual backgrounds and three in five of all undereducated youth. At least three-quarters of the undereducated white majority youth were from families with higher-than-poverty-level incomes.

White majority youth are not the least likely of all youth to be undereducated. They are less at risk than African Americans, American Indians and Alaska Natives, and Hispanics, but they are more at risk than Asians and Pacific Islanders and non-Hispanic whites from homes in which non-English languages are spoken who were born in this country. In 1980, 13.0 percent of white majority youth were undereducated in comparison with 9.8 percent of Asian/Pacific youth, 11.2 percent of native-born white minority youth, 20.4 percent of black youth, 20.6 percent of native-born English language-background Hispanics, 28.2 percent of native-born Spanish language-background Hispanics, and 29.2 percent of American Indian/Alaska Native youth.

As members of the majority, white majority youth are the least likely of all youth to come from poor families, and as indicated above, most undereducated white majority youth are not poor. Nevertheless, white majority youth from families with incomes below the poverty level are at much greater risk of undereducation than their counterparts from more economically advantaged families. More than twice as many of the former as of the latter, proportionately, were undereducated in 1980.

Poverty seems to increase the risk of undereducation to a greater extent for white majority youth than for most other youth. In 1980, in contrast with the factor of 2.1 for whites, the factor associated with family economic circumstances for African Americans was 1.8; for Hispanics, American Indians and Alaska Natives, and foreign-born Asians, it was 1.6. The poverty factor for native-born Asians and Pacific Islanders and white minority youth was equal to or greater than that for white majority youth.

White majority youth living in the South are much more likely to be out of school without high school diplomas than those living in other regions of the country. In 1980 the range was from 9.3 percent of those living in the Northeast to 17.4 percent of those living in the South. White majority youth living in Kentucky were more than three times as likely to be undereducated as those living in Minnesota. Non-Hispanic white youth living in the South are the most likely to be poor, and those in the Midwest and the Northwest, the least likely. The undereducation risk associated with poverty for white youth, however, is greatest in some of the northern states where whites in general are the most advantaged.

Like other groups in the United States, the majority of non-Hispanic whites live in urban areas. They differ from other groups in that they are more likely to live in the suburbs of metropolitan areas than in their central cities, and, after the suburbs, the largest group of non-Hispanic whites live in rural areas. In 1980 two-thirds of white civilian undereducated youth, aged 16 to 19, lived in urban areas, and in keeping with their living patterns in general, slightly more undereducated youth lived in the suburbs than in the central cities. However, more lived in rural areas—places with fewer than 2,500 inhabitants—than in either the suburbs or the central cities.[1]

White youth living on rural farms are the least likely of white youth to be out of school without high school diplomas; the most likely are those living in central cities. One in thirteen civilian whites, aged 16 to 19, living on rural farms in 1980 was undereducated, in comparison with one in seven who lived in the central cities of metropolitan areas.[2]

The numbers, characteristics, and distribution of undereducated white majority youth are the subjects of the following sections of this chapter. The undereducation rates of white majority youth in the various states are considered, as well as the differences in state rates in relation to the differences to the proportions of youth in poverty in the various states. The chapter ends with a discussion of the trends in the numbers of non-Hispanic white youth at risk and the undereducation rates of non-Hispanic whites in general in the future.

As native-born non-Hispanic whites from monolingual English-speaking homes, white majority youth are the comparison group for other youth in the study, except when regional and state poverty rates and state poverty risk factors are examined. The comparison group for the latter comprises all non-Hispanic white youth, aged 16 to 24, including non-Hispanic white minority youth and foreign-born non-Hispanic whites from monolingual English-speaking homes. The national undereducation rate for all non-Hispanic white youth from families with incomes above the poverty level was the same as the rate for white majority youth from such families in 1980; the rate for all non-Hispanic white youth from families with incomes below the poverty level was seven-tenths of a percent lower than that for poor white majority youth.

The information from the study discussed in this chapter has been supplemented with information from the published volumes of the 1980 census and other Bureau of the Census sources.

THE NUMBERS AND CHARACTERISTICS OF UNDEREDUCATED WHITE MAJORITY YOUTH

In 1980 there were 3.4 million undereducated white majority youth, as shown in table 4.1. They represented 13.0 percent of all native-born non-Hispanic white youth, aged 16 to 24, from monolingual English-speaking homes.

Undereducated white majority men outnumber undereducated white majority women and are more likely to be undereducated than women. In 1980, 1.9 million white majority men and 1.6 million white majority women were not enrolled in school and had not completed the twelfth grade. One in seven white majority men, but only one in eight white majority women, was undereducated.

Older white majority youth are more likely to be undereducated than teenagers. In 1980 the rate for youth, aged 20 to 24, was 13.7 percent; for 16-to-19-year-olds, it was 12.1 percent. The former outnumbered the latter by a factor of 1.2 per year of age.

White majority youth are the least likely to be poor of all youth. Among those for whom poverty status was determined in 1980, 11.1 percent were from families whose incomes were below the poverty level; in contrast, 12.5 percent of non-Hispanic white minority youth and up to three in ten African Americans and American Indians and Alaska Natives were poor by this standard. (See table 3.7 in chapter 3.)

Youth from poor families are at greater risk of undereducation than those whose families are more economically advantaged, and the differential is greater for white majority youth than for most other youth. White majority youth from poor families had an undereducation rate of 24.9 percent in 1980 in comparison with a rate of 12.0 percent for those whose

Table 4.1
Estimated Numbers and Distribution of Undereducated White Majority
Youth and White Majority Undereducation Rates, by Selected
Characteristic: United States, 1980

Characteristic	Number	Percentage distribution	Undereducation rate
Total	3,426,000	100.0	13.0
Gender			
Males	1,853,000	54.1	14.0
Females	1,573,000	45.9	12.0
Age			
16 to 19	1,404,000	41.0	12.1
20 to 24	2,022,000	59.0	13.7
Poverty status in 1979[1]			
Above poverty level	2,594,000	75.7	12.0
Below poverty level	669,000	19.5	24.9
Years of schooling completed			
Fewer than 5	94,000	2.7	NA
5 to 8	556,000	16.2	NA
9 to 11	2,776,000	81.0	NA

Note: Percentages calculated on unrounded numbers. Detail may not add to 100.0 percent
because of rounding. NA = not applicable.

[1]Not determined for people living in group quarters.

families were better off. Poverty also doubled the risk factor for native-
born Asians and Pacific Islanders and non-Hispanic white minority youth
but the difference was no more than 1.8 times for other youth. Poor foreign-born white minority youth actually seemed less likely to be undereducated in 1980 than their more economically advantaged counterparts. (See table 3.6 in chapter 3.) One in five undereducated white
majority young people was poor in 1980.

Poverty status was not determined for the 2.1 million white majority
youth—7.8 percent of all those aged 16 to 24—who lived in college dormitories, military barracks, institutions, and other group quarters in 1980.
This group included 163,000 undereducated youth, or 4.8 percent of undereducated white majority youth.

Most white majority youth who are undereducated complete at least
nine years of schooling before discontinuing their education, and almost
all the rest stay at least through the fifth grade. In 1980, eight in ten white

majority youth had completed the ninth, tenth, or eleventh grades; fewer than 3 percent were minimally educated. White majority youth made up 46.7 percent of all youth who had failed to reach the ninth grade.

UNDEREDUCATED WHITE MAJORITY YOUTH IN THE STATES

As the state with the largest population, California also has the largest number of undereducated white majority youth of any state. These youth, however, constitute a minority of that state's undereducated youth, as they do in eight other states.

In 1980 there were a quarter of a million white majority youth in California who were not enrolled in school and had not obtained their high school diplomas. There were more than 200,000 such youth in Texas. Ohio, Florida, and Pennsylvania each had at least 150,000 undereducated white majority youth. There were nine other states with at least 100,000 undereducated white majority youth apiece. (See table 2.8 in chapter 2.)

Undereducated white majority youth are the minority of undereducated youth in eight states. In New Mexico they constituted a quarter in 1980; in Hawaii, a third; in California and New York, fewer than two in five. Their proportions in Texas, Arizona, New Jersey, and Louisiana ranged from 41.4 percent to 47.0 percent. On the other hand, at least 85 percent undereducated youth in five states—Iowa, Kentucky, New Hampshire, Vermont, and West Virginia—were members of the white majority. (See table 2.9 in chapter 2.)

THE STATE UNDEREDUCATION RATES OF WHITE MAJORITY YOUTH

The risk of undereducation for white majority youth varies greatly according to the region and state in which they live. Youth in the Northeast are the least at risk and those in the South, especially in Kentucky, Tennessee, Alabama, and Mississippi, are the most at risk. In 1980 the undereducation rates for white majority youth were 9.3 percent for those living in the Northeast, 11.1 percent for those in the Midwest, 12.2 percent for those in the West, and 17.4 percent for those in the South. (See table 3.9 in chapter 3.) Rates in individual states ranged from 7.4 percent of white majority youth living in Minnesota to 24.0 percent for those living in Kentucky, as depicted in figure 4.1. (See table 3.10 in chapter 3.)

UNDEREDUCATION, POVERTY STATUS, AND URBANICITY OF NON-HISPANIC WHITE YOUTH IN THE STATES

Like the risk of undereducation, and related to it, the likelihood of poverty for non-Hispanic whites varies by region and state of residence.

Figure 4.1
Undereducation Rates of White Majority Youth, 1980

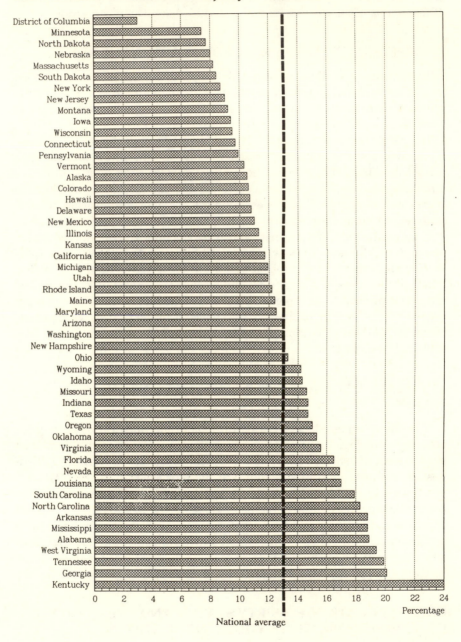

Moreover, the risk of undereducation associated with poverty also varies, and it tends to be greater in some of the states with the lowest white undereducation rates.

White youth in the Northeast, especially in New York, New Jersey, and Pennsylvania—the least likely to be undereducated—are also the least likely to be poor. Those living in the West, as a whole, are more likely to be poor than those living in the South, as a whole, but white youth in Kentucky, Tennessee, Alabama, and Mississippi—the most likely to be undereducated—are the most likely to be poor among white youth in any area of the country. (See table 3.11 in chapter 3.) In the states in 1980, the poverty rates of white youth whose poverty status was determined ranged from 6.2 percent of whites in New Jersey to 16.9 percent of whites in Kentucky. (See table 3.12 in chapter 3.)

The likelihood of undereducation and poverty is greater in certain types of environments than in others. The variation is a reminder of the qualitative differences between school districts serving predominantly poor and minority populations and those serving more economically advantaged populations—differences favoring suburban and rural schools in northern states and urban schools in southern states. In the Middle Atlantic states, as elsewhere in the North, poverty is greatest in the central cities of large metropolitan areas. The minority of whites who lived in the inner cities of Connecticut, Illinois, New Jersey, New York, and Pennsylvania in 1980 were two to three times more likely to have incomes below the poverty level than whites living in the suburbs of those states.[3] (See table 5.5 in chapter 5.) White youth living in the inner cities were more likely to be undereducated, as shown in table 4.2. The undereducation gap between white 16-to-19-year-old civilian inner city and suburban youth in these states, in 1980, ranged from 1.6 in Illinois to 2.6 in New Jersey.[4] Poor white youth in these states were 2.2 to 2.5 times more likely to be undereducated than youth from more advantaged backgrounds. (See table 3.13 in chapter 3.) The undereducation gap between white majority youth and African Americans—who live predominantly in inner cities in these states—was also large. (See table 5.4 in chapter 5.)

In the South, in contrast to the situation in the North, poverty is a rural phenomenon and urban populations, including those living in the central cities of metropolitan areas, are less likely to be poor than populations living in rural areas. White populations in the South are more likely to live in rural areas than in central cities or in suburbs.[5] The 1980 differences in poverty between urban and rural whites in states such as Alabama, Georgia, Kentucky, Mississippi, and North and South Carolina, although not as great as those between inner city whites and others in the northern states, were still significant.[6] White youth living in rural areas in these states in 1980 were decidedly disadvantaged in their likelihood of completing high school in comparison with their counterparts who lived in the

Table 4.2
Undereducation Rates of White Civilian Youth, Aged 16 to 19, by
Urbanicity and Selected State: United States, 1980

State	Total	Central cities	Suburbs	Rural areas
All states	12.2	14.0	9.9	13.4
States in which overall undereducation rates are low				
Connecticut	9.3	14.4	7.2	7.1
Illinois	10.9	14.8	9.3	9.3
New Jersey	8.3	19.6	7.4	9.0
New York	8.6	12.9	5.4	9.0
Pennsylvania	8.8	10.9	6.0	10.8
States in which overall undereducation rates are high				
Alabama	16.8	12.4	15.0	20.2
Georgia	17.6	14.7	13.7	21.3
Kentucky	21.5	18.3	15.9	25.8
Mississippi	16.6	13.3	16.5	17.9
North Carolina	16.4	11.8	15.0	18.8
South Carolina	15.3	9.5	14.9	17.2

Source: Derived from Bureau of the Census, *1980 Census of Population, General Social and Economic Characteristics, Part 1, United States Summary*, p. 97; and selected state parts, table 76, various pages.

urban areas.[7] In these states, except in Kentucky, the undereducation risk factor associated with poverty for whites was less than 2.0 in 1980. There was little or no difference between the undereducation rates of white majority youth and African Americans in most southern states—both were equally disadvantaged. The educational disadvantage of blacks in comparison with whites is discussed in chapter 5.

UNDEREDUCATED WHITE MAJORITY YOUTH IN THE REMAINDER OF THIS CENTURY

In April 1980, when the decennial census was taken, there were 3.4 million white majority youth, aged 16 to 24, who were not enrolled in school and had not completed 12 years of schooling. They comprised 13.0 of all white majority youth. The following fall, in October 1980, there were 4 million undereducated civilian non-institutional white youth, including Hispanics, who comprised 13.3 percent of that population.[8] By October 1988 the number of these youth had fallen to 3.4 million and the undereducation rate to 12.7 percent.[9] (See table 1.1 in chapter 1.)

The non-Hispanic white population is increasing much more slowly than the populations of Hispanics, blacks, and other groups in the United States. Moderate assumptions about non-Hispanic white fertility, mortality, and net immigration produce projected average annual increases in the numbers of non-Hispanic whites of 0.6 percent between 1985 and 1990, 0.4 percent between 1990 and 1995, and 0.3 percent between 1995 and the year 2000. In contrast, moderate assumptions about black fertility, mortality, and net immigration produce projected average annual increases in the black population of 1.5 percent, 1.4 percent, and 1.2 percent during these same periods, whereas moderate assumptions about the fertility, mortality, and net immigration of Hispanics produce projected average annual increases in the Hispanic population of 2.8 percent, 2.5 percent, and 2.5 percent.[10] The projected increases in the numbers of blacks and Hispanics, especially the latter, are probably low; recent legal immigration of these and other minorities has already exceeded the moderate assumptions for net average annual immigration.

By the year 2000, based on moderate assumptions of the growth of all groups, the projected number of school-age children and youth in the United States will be 48.8 million—up by 4.4 million from the projected number in 1985. Only 1.5 million of this growth will be contributed by non-Hispanic whites, whose numbers are projected to grow from 32.3 million in 1985 to 33.8 million in the year 2000.[11] (See table 1.3 in chapter 1.) By the year 2000, with only moderate growth of all groups, the non-Hispanic white proportion of the school-age population would be 69.4 percent, in comparison with 72.8 percent in 1985. The probability is that it will be less and that it will continue to decrease.

White majority students have always been the focus of traditional school programs in the United States. They are the least likely to be adversely affected by efforts to reform schools by raising standards, strengthening the curriculum, and adding time to the school schedule. The fact that so many continue to lack the minimum education deemed necessary for success as productive citizens highlights the extent to which American schools are failing all youth. The additional disadvantage of white youth, especially poor white youth, who live in certain types of environments within states is a reminder of fundamental school district inequities that penalize all students. Nevertheless, as dropout prevention programs become more widespread and successful, at the same time that the growth of the non-Hispanic white population tapers off, white majority youth who are undereducated will be fewer and the proportion who are undereducated will fall.

NOTES

1. Bureau of the Census, U.S. Department of Commerce, *1980 Census of Population, General Social and Economic Characteristics, Part 1, United States Summary* (Washington, D.C.: U.S. Government Printing Office, 1983), pp. 13 and 97.

2. Ibid., p. 97.

3. Bureau of the Census, *General Social and Economic Characteristics, Part 8, Connecticut; Part 15, Illinois; Part 32, New Jersey; Part 34, New York; and Part 40, Pennsylvania,* tables 59 and 82, various pages.

4. Ibid., table 76, various pages.

5. Bureau of the Census, *General Social and Economic Characteristics, Part 2, Alabama; Part 12, Georgia; Part 19, Kentucky; Part 26, Mississippi; Part 35, North Carolina; and Part 42, South Carolina,* table 59, various pages.

6. Ibid., table 82, various pages.

7. Ibid., table 76, various pages.

8. Bureau of the Census, U.S. Department of Commerce, *School Enrollment—Social and Economic Characteristics of Students: October 1981 and 1980* (Washington, D.C.: U.S. Government Printing Office, 1985), p. 60.

9. Bureau of the Census, U.S. Department of Commerce, *School Enrollment—Social and Economic Characteristics of Students: October 1988 and 1987* (Washington, D.C.: U.S. Government Printing Office, 1990), p. 5.

10. Bureau of the Census, U.S. Department of Commerce, *Projections of the Hispanic Population: 1983 to 2080* (Washington, D.C.: U.S. Government Printing Office, 1986), p. 10.

11. Ibid., p. 14.

5

African American Youth Who Are Undereducated

The largest minority group in the United States consists of African Americans, but they are no longer the largest group of undereducated minority youth. During the decade of the eighties, undereducated African Americans have been surpassed in numbers by undereducated Hispanics, and they have almost closed the undereducation gap with white youth. More than a million black young people, aged 16 to 24, were out of school without high school diplomas in 1980. They constituted 17 percent of all undereducated youth and one out of five non-Hispanic black young people in the United States when the 1980 decennial census was taken. By 1988 the number of undereducated African American civilian youth not living in group quarters was just under 700,000—16 percent of the total number of undereducated non-institutional civilian youth—and they constituted one out of seven blacks among civilian youth not living in group quarters.[1]

African Americans are more likely to be undereducated than white majority youth but less likely than American Indians, Eskimos, and Aleuts, and Spanish language-background Hispanics who were born in the United States. In 1980 African Americans were 1.6 times more likely to be undereducated than white majority youth. Their rate was 20.4 percent in comparison with 13.0 percent for whites, 29.2 percent for Native Americans, 28.2 percent for native-born Spanish language-background Hispanics, and 20.6 percent for native-born English language-background Hispanics. By 1988 the rate of African American non-institutional civilians was 14.9 percent in comparison with 12.7 percent of all white civilians, including Hispanics.[2]

African Americans are overwhelmingly native born and from households in which only English is spoken. However, those who are foreign
born and those with non-English language backgrounds are less likely
than native-born English language-background blacks to be undereducated. In fact, foreign-born non-English language-background blacks are
no more likely than white majority youth to be undereducated; undereducated foreign-born blacks from households in which one or more people
speak a language other than English, like undereducated white majority
youth, constituted about one in eight of their group in 1980.

African Americans living in the West are the least likely to be out of
school without having completed the twelfth grade; in the western states
their undereducation rates are close to the moderate rates of white majority youth there. In the remainder of the United States, African Americans
have considerably higher undereducation rates. They share the educational disadvantage of white majority youth in the South, but they do not
participate in the more favorable environment in some of the northern
states with the lowest overall undereducation rates. In 1980 black undereducation rates ranged from 14.5 percent for those living in the West
to more than 20 percent for those elsewhere. The undereducation risk of
blacks was two to three times that of whites in states such as Connecticut,
Illinois, New Jersey, New York, Pennsylvania, and Wisconsin. It was 1.2
times that of white majority youth in California. It was about the same
as that of whites in high undereducation states such as Alabama, Georgia,
Kentucky, North and South Carolina, and Tennessee.

With American Indians, Eskimos, and Aleuts, African Americans are
the poorest of all racial/ethnic groups in the United States, and poverty
increases their risk of undereducation, although not to the extent that it
does for white majority youth. African Americans, aged 16 to 24, were 2.8
times more likely to be poor than white majority youth in 1980. More than
three in ten of them, in comparison with one in nine of whites, were from
families with incomes below the poverty level. Poor blacks were 1.8 times
more likely than blacks from more advantaged families to be out of school
without high school diplomas; in contrast, poor white majority youth were
2.1 times more at risk than more advantaged whites.

African Americans are highly urbanized, and they are the most likely
of all groups to live in the central cities of metropolitan areas where poverty rates are high. In 1980, 57 percent of blacks lived in the central cities
and three in ten of them had incomes below the poverty level. Even
poorer, however, are rural blacks. Of the 26.3 percent of blacks living in
rural areas in 1980—those living in places with fewer than 2,500 inhabitants—more than a third were poor. And, just as rural blacks are poorer
than those in central cities, rural black youth are more likely to be out of
school without high school diplomas than those living in central cities. In
1980, 17.5 percent of rural civilian black youth, aged 16 to 19, were un-

dereducated; the rate for similar youth living in central cities was 16.3 percent.[3]

The national figures on the undereducation of African Americans in different types of environments mask important regional differences. The vast majority of African Americans in northern states live in urban ghettoes where the undereducation and poverty rates differ strikingly from those of youth living in the suburbs, small towns, or rural areas. African Americans are much less urbanized in the South where most rural blacks live. The high undereducation and poverty rates of rural blacks nationally reflect the condition of southern rural populations, who are disadvantaged in comparison with urban populations in their region, including those living in central cities.[4] The intrastate variation in undereducation rates by urbanicity is indicative of qualitative differences between school districts in high poverty areas and other districts in many states. These differences primarily affect African Americans, other minority youth, and the poor.

The following sections of this chapter contain an exploration of the characteristics of undereducated African American youth, aged 16 to 24, and a comparison of the undereducation rates of these youth in the various categories. The rates of African Americans are contrasted with those of white majority and other youth nationally and in the 33 states in which at least an estimated 10,000 African American youth, aged 16 to 24, lived in 1980. Information about people born in Jamaica, Haiti, and other countries of the Caribbean; in Central and South American countries; and in countries of East and Sub-Saharan Africa; who made up part of the black population in the United States in 1980 and who have continued to immigrate to this country since 1980, is also provided. The chapter ends with a consideration of trends in the undereducation of African American youth since 1980 and the possible numbers of those who may be at risk in the future.

The information on foreign-born populations in 1980 is from the published volumes of the 1980 census. Other Bureau of the Census publications provided the information for the discussion of undereducation trends and the projections of the potential growth of the black population in the United States. The information on immigration since 1980 is from the Immigration and Naturalization Service.

THE NUMBERS AND CHARACTERISTICS OF UNDEREDUCATED AFRICAN AMERICAN YOUTH

There were 1,023,000 Africans Americans, aged 16 to 24, in the United States in 1980 who were not enrolled in school and had not completed the twelfth grade, as shown in table 5.1. They constituted a fifth of all African Americans in their age group. Twenty-two thousand of them, or 2.1 per-

Table 5.1
Estimated Numbers and Distribution of Undereducated African American
Youth, by Nativity and Selected Characteristic: United States, 1980

Characteristic	Total		Native born		Foreign born	
	Number	Percent	Number	Percent	Number	Percent
Total	1,023,000	100.0	1,001,000	100.0	22,000	100.0
Gender						
Males	556.000	54.4	545,000	54.4	11,000	52.5
Females	467,000	45.6	456,000	45.6	10,000	47.5
Age						
16 to 19	379,000	37.1	372,000	37.1	7,000	33.4
20 to 24	644,000	62.9	629,000	62.9	15,000	66.6
Language background						
English only	962,000	94.1	947,000	94.6	16,000	71.2
Non-English	60,000	5.9	54,000	5.4	6,000	28.8
Poverty status in 1979[1]						
Above poverty level	524,000	51.2	510,000	51.0	13,000	60.2
Below poverty level	416,000	40.7	409,000	40.8	7,000	33.8
Years of schooling completed						
Fewer than 5	34,000	3.3	32,000	3.2	2,000	7.6
5 to 8	160,000	15.6	156,000	15.6	4,000	17.2
9 to 11	829,000	81.1	813,000	81.2	16,000	75.2

Note: Percentages calculated on unrounded numbers. Detail may not add to total because
of rounding.

[1]Not determined for people living in group quarters.

cent, were foreign born. Sixty thousand, or 5.9 percent, lived in households in which one or more people speak a language other than English
at home. Nearly nine out of ten of the young blacks with non-English language backgrounds were native born.

Foreign-born blacks and blacks with non-English language backgrounds
are less likely to be undereducated than native-born African Americans living in monolingual English-speaking households, as shown in table 5.2.
Among the least likely to be undereducated are foreign-born blacks with
non-English language backgrounds. Their rate is similar to that of white
majority youth. In 1980, 13.0 percent of white majority youth and 13.3 percent of foreign-born non-English language-background blacks were out of
school without high school diplomas. In contrast, 20.8 percent of native-

Table 5.2
Estimated Numbers of Undereducated African American Youth and African American Undereducation Rates, by Nativity and Selected Characteristic: United States, 1980

Characteristic	Total		Native born		Foreign born	
	Number	Rate	Number	Rate	Number	Rate
Total	1,023,000	20.4	1,001,000	20.6	22,000	14.6
Gender						
Males	556.000	23.0	545,000	23.2	11,000	16.2
Females	467,000	18.0	456,000	18.1	10,000	13.2
Age						
16 to 19	379,000	16.0	372,000	16.2	7,000	11.6
20 to 24	644,000	24.3	629,000	24.6	15,000	16.8
Language background						
English only	962,000	20.7	947,000	20.8	16,000	15.2
Non-English	60,000	16.5	54,000	17.0	6,000	13.3
Poverty status in 1979[1]						
Above poverty level	524,000	16.6	510,000	16.7	13,000	13.3
Below poverty level	416,000	29.1	409,000	29.3	7,000	20.3

Note: Detail may not add to total because of rounding.

[1]Not determined for people living in group quarters.

born English language-background blacks, 17.0 percent of native-born non-English language-background blacks, and 15.2 percent of foreign-born English language-background blacks were undereducated.[5]

Among undereducated African Americans, as among undereducated white majority youth, men predominate. In 1980, 54 percent of undereducated black and white majority youth were men and 46 percent were women. Among blacks, as among whites, men are more likely to be undereducated than women. African American men, however, are even more likely to be undereducated in comparison with African American women than white majority men are in comparison with white majority women. The 1980 rates of the former were 23.0 and 18.0; those of the latter, 14.0 and 12.0.

Undereducated African American youth are more likely to be aged 20 to 24 than other native-born youth, and the difference between the undereducation rate of young black adults and that of black teenagers is the greatest of any among native-born and predominantly native-born groups. There were 1.4 times more undereducated young black adults than undereducated black teenagers per year of age in 1980. (See table 2.4 in chapter 2.) Young black adults were 1.5 times more likely than black teenagers to be out of school before completing the twelfth grade. The comparative rates were 24.3 percent for the older group and 16.0 percent for the younger group. In contrast, older white majority youth and native-born Hispanics were 1.1 times more likely than white and Hispanic teenagers to be undereducated—13.7 in comparison with 12.1 for whites and 30.8 in comparison with 22.2 for Hispanics. (See table 3.4 in chapter 3.)

Many African American students are behind in school, as discussed in chapter 3 and illustrated in figure 3.3. They have entered late, have been retained in grade, or have left school and returned. In 1980 nearly one in five of 16- and 17-year-old black students were enrolled two or more grades below the expected grades for their ages. A third of the 18- and 19-year-olds who were still in school had not reached the twelfth grade.[6] African American youth who eventually discontinue their education tend to stay in school at least into the tenth and eleventh grades to a greater extent than most other youth.[7] (See table 1.2 in chapter 1.) Thus more than other youth, 16-to-19-year-old African Americans—still enrolled in school at any given time—may fail to graduate from high school later and become undereducated 20-to-24-year-olds.

Although African Americans tend to stay in school longer than most other youth including whites, black and white majority youth are about equally likely to complete at least eight years of schooling before they discontinue their education, and they are more likely to do so than native-born Hispanics. African Americans are more likely than white majority youth, but less likely than Hispanics and members of other groups, to have very low levels of schooling. Eight in ten undereducated blacks and majority whites in 1980, in comparison with seven in ten undereducated native-born Hispanics, had reached at least the high school years before discontinuing their education. At the same time, 2.7 percent of white majority youth, 3.3 percent of black youth, 4.2 percent of native-born Hispanics, and 7.7 percent of native-born Asians and Pacific Islanders had completed fewer than five years of schooling. (See table 2.6 in chapter 2.)

As is the case with other groups, African Americans from families with incomes below the poverty level are more likely to be out of school without high school diplomas than those whose families are more economically advantaged. However, poverty increases the risk for blacks less than it does for white majority youth. In 1980 poor African American youth were 1.8 times more likely to be undereducated than their counterparts from more advantaged families, whereas poor white majority youth were 2.1 times more at risk than the more well-off members of their group. (See table 3.6 in chapter 3.)

Two out of five undereducated African American Youth were from families with incomes below the poverty level in 1980. There were 83,000 undereducated African American youth in a total 420,000, or 8.4 percent of all African American youth, aged 16 to 24, whose poverty status was not determined because they lived in group quarters, such as college dormitories, military barracks, or institutions of various kinds, in 1980.

UNDEREDUCATED AFRICAN AMERICAN YOUTH IN THE STATES

The largest groups of undereducated African American youth live in New York and Illinois, as depicted in figure 5.1. In 1980 there were 82,000 undereducated African Americans in New York and 74,000 in Illinois. There were six other states with at least 50,000 and 10 states with between 25,000 and 49,000 such youth. Eleven of these states are in the South. Eighty-six percent of all African Americans and about the same percentage of undereducated African American youth lived in these 18 states in 1980.[8] Undereducated blacks, however, are found in all areas of the country. In all, 40 states had at least 1,000 such youth in 1980. In addition, there were 17,000 undereducated blacks in the District of Columbia, where blacks are the majority population. (See table 2.8 in chapter 2.)

The southern states have the highest proportions of African Americans among their undereducated youth. In 1980, 45.6 percent of undereducated youth in Mississippi were black, and there were five other states— Louisiana, Maryland, South Carolina, Georgia, and Alabama—in which at least 30 percent of undereducated youth in 1980 were black. (See table 2.9 in chapter 2.)

THE STATE UNDEREDUCATION RATES OF AFRICAN AMERICAN YOUTH

The likelihood of African Americans to be out of school without high school diplomas varies according to the region of the country and state in which they live. Blacks living in the western states are the least likely to be undereducated, and those in the north central and southern states, the most likely: the 1980 range was from 14.5 percent for those in the West to more than 21 percent for those in the Midwest and the South. (See table 3.9 in chapter 3.) Even within regions, however, the risk of undereducation varies widely for African Americans. In the 33 states with at least 10,000 16-to-24-year-old members of this group in 1980, depicted in figure 5.2, the highest and lowest rates of African Americans, respectively, were 26.3 percent in Wisconsin and 14.1 percent in Iowa, although these are neighboring states in the Midwest. Blacks in Kentucky had the third highest undereducation rate—23.9 percent—while those in the adjoining states of West Virginia had the fifth lowest—14.5 percent. (See table 3.10 in chapter 3.)

Figure 5.1
Undereducated African American Youth in the United States, 1980

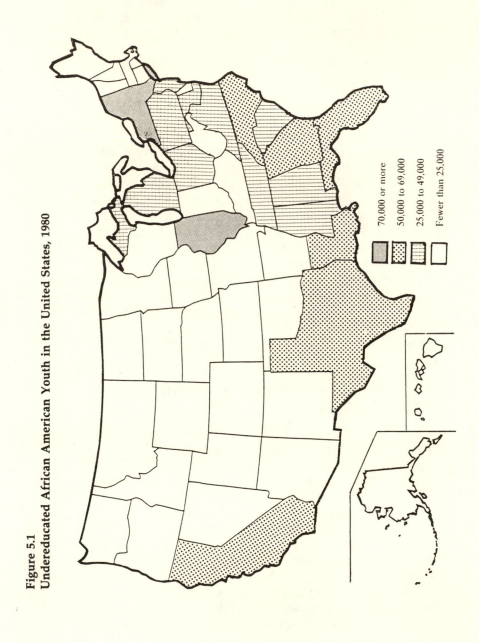

70,000 or more

50,000 to 69,000

25,000 to 49,000

Fewer than 25,000

Figure 5.2
Undereducation Rates of African American Youth, 1980

THE CHARACTERISTICS OF AFRICAN AMERICAN YOUTH IN THE STATES

African American youth differ considerably in the various states. As shown in table 5.3, they are more likely to be poor, to be foreign born, or to live in households in which one or more people speak a non-English language in certain states than in others.

Table 5.3
**Estimated Numbers of African American Youth and Percentages with
Selected Characteristics, by Selected State: United States, 1980**

State	Number	Percentage		
		In poverty[1]	Foreign born	With NELB[2]
Total, all states	5,011,000	31.1	3.0	7.3
Alabama	194,000	39.4	0.6	5.4
Arizona	16,000	29.7	1.7	10.6
Arkansas	68,000	42.7	0.7	4.2
California	353,000	25.9	2.6	8.5
Colorado	22,000	22.6	2.9	8.8
Connecticut	39,000	24.6	8.7	9.0
District of Columbia	82,000	23.6	3.1	8.1
Florida	252,000	34.8	4.4	8.0
Georgia	276,000	34.6	0.8	5.1
Illinois	313,000	31.2	1.3	7.3
Indiana	79,000	25.5	1.2	5.9
Iowa	10,000	33.8	4.4	11.6
Kansas	28,000	30.3	2.3	8.8
Kentucky	56,000	39.4	1.1	5.3
Louisiana	238,000	36.5	0.9	10.4
Maryland	187,000	23.8	2.1	7.4
Massachusetts	42,000	29.4	11.7	11.8
Michigan	212,000	26.1	1.2	6.2
Mississippi	172,000	42.5	0.4	3.9
Missouri	100,000	29.1	0.9	6.3
Nevada	10,000	20.8	1.6	6.6
New Jersey	165,000	27.5	4.2	7.3
New York	405,000	31.3	16.2	11.9
North Carolina	261,000	31.3	0.9	5.5
Ohio	197,000	30.2	0.9	6.6
Oklahoma	43,000	27.9	2.2	6.3
Pennsylvania	187,000	33.2	1.8	6.9
South Carolina	187,000	32.1	0.9	5.9
Tennessee	144,000	36.1	0.9	5.7
Texas	334,000	28.1	1.7	7.1
Virginia	195,000	26.4	1.3	5.7
Washington	24,000	21.8	4.2	11.4
West Virginia	12,000	35.1	1.6	4.2
Wisconsin	36,000	30.1	2.1	5.0

Note: Selected states are those with at least an estimated 10,000 African Americans, aged
16 to 24.

[1]Poverty status not determined for people living in group quarters.

[2]Non-English language background.

African Americans living in the southern states are the most likely to be poor, and those living in the western states, the least likely: in 1980 a third of blacks, aged 16 to 24, in the South came from families with incomes below the poverty level, in comparison with only a little more than a quarter of those in the West. (See table 3.11 in chapter 3.) The individual state poverty rates of this group ranged from 20.8 percent of those in Nevada to nearly 43 percent of those living in Arkansas and Mississippi. In every state, black youth are more likely to be poor, and in some states very much more likely, than non-Hispanic white youth. (See table 3.12 in chapter 3.)

Minorities of African American youth in every state are foreign born or have non-English language backgrounds, and in most states these groups constitute very small minorities. New York and Massachusetts lead in the proportions of foreign-born and language minority blacks. In 1980 one in six young blacks in New York was foreign born, and one in eight had a non-English language background. In Massachusetts, the proportion of both groups was one in eight. One in eleven blacks in Connecticut was foreign born and/or had a non-English language background. At least one in ten blacks in Arizona, Iowa, Louisiana, and Washington had a non-English language background, but the proportion born abroad was less than one in twenty.

Blacks in the southern states are the least likely to be foreign born. In 1980 those born abroad constituted fewer than 1 percent of black youth living in Alabama, Arkansas, Georgia, Louisiana, Mississippi, North and South Carolina, and Tennessee. The proportion of foreign-born blacks in Missouri and Ohio was also less than 1 percent in 1980.

THE EDUCATIONAL DISADVANTAGE OF AFRICAN AMERICAN YOUTH IN THE STATES

There is a striking variation in the comparative undereducation rates of African American and white majority youth in various states. In 1980 the differences ranged from zero in states such as Kentucky and South Carolina to nearly triple in Wisconsin, as shown in table 5.4. This does not indicate that blacks are less disadvantaged in the states where whites are equally likely to be undereducated. Rather, both whites and blacks are disadvantaged in states where many youth are ill-served by their schools. Blacks in Kentucky and other states in the South where the undereducation rates of all groups are high are almost as likely to be undereducated as those in Wisconsin and just as likely as those in other states of the North where whites—and youth in general—have low undereducation rates. Blacks in northern states live overwhelmingly in inner cities where poverty and other social ills are rife. In the South, many live in rural poverty, which is also the plight of many whites in that region.

Table 5.4

Undereducation Rates and Poverty Rates of African American and White Majority Youth, by Selected State: United States, 1980

State	Undereducation rate		Poverty rate[1]	
	African Americans	White majority	African Americans	White majority
Total, all states	20.4	13.0	31.1	11.2
States in which African American and majority undereducation rates are similar				
Alabama	20.3	18.9	39.4	13.7
Georgia	23.2	20.1	34.6	11.0
Kentucky	23.9	24.0	39.4	16.9
Louisiana	23.7	17.0	36.5	10.7
Mississippi	24.9	18.8	42.5	12.5
North Carolina	20.5	18.3	31.3	11.4
South Carolina	18.4	17.9	32.1	10.3
Tennessee	18.0	19.9	36.1	12.9
States in which African American undereducation rates are much higher than majority rates				
Connecticut	19.6	9.7	24.6	7.1
Illinois	23.5	11.3	31.2	8.6
New Jersey	20.7	9.0	27.5	6.2
New York	20.2	8.7	31.3	10.4
Pennsylvania	20.2	9.9	33.2	9.7
Wisconsin	26.3	9.5	30.1	11.4

[1]Poverty status not determined for people living in group quarters.

In 1980 African Americans living in Alabama, Georgia, Kentucky, North and South Carolina, and Tennessee, while much more likely to be poor, were equally or nearly equally as likely to be undereducated as white majority youth. In all of these states, and in Louisiana and Mississippi where blacks were clearly more at risk of undereducation, whites had considerably more likelihood than whites nationally to be undereducated. In these states, many blacks and whites live in rural areas where they are more likely to be poor than people living in central cities or other urban areas and where youth have higher undereducation rates than youth in central cities. Except in Mississippi, proportionally fewer blacks than whites lived in the rural areas in 1980, as shown in table 5.5, and the undereducation risk associated with living in a rural area in comparison with living in a city is less for black youth than for white youth.[9] In a number of the states, as it is nationally, the risk of undereducation associated with poverty is also less for blacks than for whites. (See table 3.13 in chapter 3.)

The differences between African American and white majority undereducation rates in a number of northern states in 1980 were great, in

Table 5.5

Distribution of African American and Non-Hispanic White Populations and Black and White Poverty Rates, by Urbanicity and Selected State: United States, 1980

State	Total		Central cities		Suburbs		Rural areas	
	Black	White	Black	White	Black	White	Black	White
Total, all states	100.0	100.0	57.1	23.8	18.7	33.8	14.7	29.5
Poverty rate	29.9	9.4	30.1	11.1	20.2	6.1	36.4	11.2
States in which African American and majority undereducation rates are similar								
Alabama	100.0	100.0	41.9	24.6	13.1	17.3	30.2	43.4
Poverty rate	38.5	12.1	35.1	10.0	33.9	8.3	43.7	14.6
Georgia	100.0	100.0	37.6	13.2	16.5	31.7	26.5	42.0
Poverty rate	34.1	10.2	35.7	11.1	19.4	6.3	37.0	12.3
Kentucky	100.0	100.0	44.3	13.5	14.3	18.2	14.8	52.0
Poverty rate	33.0	16.4	34.1	12.1	21.7	7.8	33.6	20.7
Louisiana	100.0	100.0	47.2	23.1	10.9	26.1	24.2	34.9
Poverty rate	38.0	10.4	35.9	9.8	28.3	6.6	42.6	12.7
Mississippi	100.0	100.0	16.4	14.2	2.7	11.2	52.8	52.8
Poverty rate	44.4	12.6	31.5	9.4	37.8	8.9	47.8	14.7
North Carolina	100.0	100.0	30.8	18.5	8.6	14.0	43.0	54.6
Poverty rate	30.4	10.0	27.9	8.2	23.5	8.2	31.4	10.9
South Carolina	100.0	100.0	15.6	10.0	16.8	30.4	48.9	44.8
Poverty rate	33.2	9.2	34.9	9.4	25.0	7.7	34.6	10.2
Tennessee	100.0	100.0	72.6	28.6	1.6	11.4	14.0	44.5
Poverty rate	34.2	13.1	34.3	10.0	15.9	7.4	35.6	16.0
States in which African American undereducation rates are much higher than majority rates								
Connecticut	100.0	100.0	78.8	26.5	17.5	45.3	3.0	23.4
Poverty rate	25.4	6.0	29.3	9.8	10.6	4.5	7.0	4.2
Illinois	100.0	100.0	79.7	24.4	16.9	41.7	1.2	20.9
Poverty rate	30.2	7.2	31.5	9.9	23.3	4.2	36.1	8.4
New Jersey	100.0	100.0	33.9	5.3	57.8	78.1	4.1	12.8
Poverty rate	26.0	6.4	34.7	15.2	21.2	5.8	19.1	6.0
New York	100.0	100.0	83.9	35.5	13.3	37.0	1.4	19.8
Poverty rate	28.3	9.4	30.0	13.1	17.4	4.9	19.8	9.4
Pennsylvania	100.0	100.0	77.6	19.4	18.0	37.1	2.6	33.9
Poverty rate	29.8	8.3	32.2	12.0	21.0	5.6	18.4	8.4
Wisconsin	100.0	100.0	94.2	27.9	3.4	19.3	1.4	37.6
Poverty rate	28.8	7.6	29.5	8.8	*	3.8	*	8.8

Source: Derived from the Bureau of the Census, *1980 Census of Population, General Social and Economic Characteristics, Part 1, United States Summary,* pp. 13 and 113; and selected state parts, tables 59 and 82, various pages.

Note: Poverty status not determined for people living in group quarters and unrelated individuals under age 15; population base includes Hispanics.

*Base number less than an estimated 1,000.

contrast to those in the South. Blacks were 2.8 times more likely than white majority youth in Wisconsin, 2.3 times more likely in New Jersey and New York, and twice as likely as whites in Connecticut, Illinois, and Pennsylvania to be undereducated. In these states, as shown in table 5.5, large proportions of blacks live in urban areas, most in central cities, except in New Jersey where the majority live in the New Jersey suburbs of New York City or other metropolitan fringe areas in New Jersey. Whites, in contrast, are more likely to live outside the central cities.[10] Poverty in these states is greatest among people living in the central cities and least among those living in suburbs and rural areas, and young people in the central cities are much more likely to be undereducated than those living outside them.[11]

African American youth living in California (together with those living in Iowa) are the least likely of blacks in any state to be out of school without having completed 12 years of education. Although faring substantially worse educationally than whites in the states with the lowest overall rates, blacks in California have almost closed the undereducation gap with whites in that state. In 1980, 14.2 percent of blacks were undereducated, in comparison with 11.7 percent of white majority youth, or 11.5 percent of all non-Hispanic whites in California, as shown in table 5.6. The majority of blacks in California live in central cities, but a much larger proportion than in the northern states, where their disadvantage is great, live in the suburbs of metropolitan areas, and in the suburbs, they are less likely to be poor.[12] The undereducation risk associated with poverty for African American youth in California was the same as that for white majority youth in 1980. Nevertheless, as in other states, black youth were still more than twice as likely to come from poor families as whites. This differential characterizes the poverty rates of black and white populations living in California, regardless of whether they live in central cities, suburbs, or in rural areas.[13]

FOREIGN-BORN BLACKS IN THE UNITED STATES

There were 150,000 foreign-born non-Hispanic blacks, aged 16 to 24, in the United States in 1980. They were part of a total population of 816,000 foreign-born blacks, including blacks who are Hispanic. The majority—55 percent—were 1970–80 immigrants.[14] Most non-Hispanic foreign-born blacks in the United States are natives of Caribbean countries such as Jamaica, Haiti, Trinidad and Tobago, Barbados, or the Bahamas; the Western Hemisphere mainland countries of Guyana, Belize, or Suriname; or various African countries. There were 506,000 people in the United States in 1980 who were born in predominantly black non-Spanish-speaking Western Hemisphere countries and 116,000 people born in East and Sub-Saharan African countries, as shown in table 5.7. The largest Western

Table 5.6
Undereducation of Youth and Other Characteristics of African Americans and Non-Hispanic Whites: California, 1980

Characteristic	African Americans	Non-Hispanic whites
Youth, aged 16 to 24		
Undereducation rate	14.2	11.5
Poverty rate[1]	25.9	12.0
Undereducation risk factor	1.8	1.8
Proportion foreign born	2.6	4.0
Undereducation rate	11.3	12.3
Proportion with non-English language backgrounds	8.5	12.8
Undereducation rate	10.4	10.7
Total population		
Distribution by urbanicity		
People living in central cities	58.3	30.1
People living in suburbs	37.2	51.2
People living in rural areas	2.1	10.4
Poverty rates by urbanicity[1,2]		
Total	22.5	8.9
People living in central cities	25.3	10.1
People living in suburbs	18.2	7.7
People living in rural areas	21.1	9.8

Source: Data on total population derived from Bureau of the Census, *1980 Census of Population, General Social and Economic Characteristics, Part 6, California,* pp. 57 and 86.

[1]Poverty status not determined for people living in group quarters and unrelated individuals under age 15.

[2]Population base includes Hispanics.

Hemisphere groups consisted of 197,000 people born in Jamaica, 92,000 people born in Haiti, 66,000 people born in Trinidad and Tobago, and 49,000 people born in Guyana. Among those born in African countries, the largest group consisted of 26,000 people born in Nigeria.[15]

Counts of people by country of birth, like counts of people by race, differ from the counts by the mutually exclusive racial/ethnic categories established for this study. The counts by country of birth include people of all races. Nevertheless, the geographical distribution of people born in predominantly black non-Spanish-speaking Western Hemisphere countries and in East and Sub-Saharan Africa parallels the distribution of for-

Table 5.7
Estimated Numbers of People Born in Selected Western Hemisphere and
African Countries, by Country of Birth: United States, 1980

Country of birth	Number	Country of birth	Number
Total	623,000	Trinidad and Tobago	66,000
		Other countries[1]	7,000
Total, Western Hemisphere	506,000		
		Total, Africa	116,000
Antigua-Barbuda	4,000		
Bahamas	14,000	Cape Verde	10,000
Barbados	27,000	Ethiopia	8,000
Belize	14,000	Ghana	8,000
Bermuda	9,000	Kenya	6,000
British Virgin Islands	2,000	Liberia	4,000
Dominica	3,000	Niger	2,000
Grenada	7,000	Nigeria	26,000
Guyana	49,000	Sierra Leone	2,000
Haiti	92,000	South Africa	16,000
Jamaica	197,000	Tanzania	3,000
Netherlands Antilles	8,000	Uganda	4,000
St. Christopher-Nevis	2,000	Zimbabwe	3,000
St. Lucia	2,000	Other countries[2]	25,000
St. Vincent-Grenadines	4,000		

Source: Derived from Bureau of the Census, "Socioeconomic Characteristics of U.S. Foreign-born Population Detailed in Census Bureau Tabulations," pp. 1–3.

Note: Detail may not add to total because of rounding.

[1]Anguilla, Cayman, Guadaloupe, Martinique, Montserrat, and Suriname.

[2]Angola, Botswana, Burundi, Cameroon, Guinea, Ivory Coast, Madagascar, Malawi, Mauritania, Mauritius, Mozambique, Senegal, Somalia, Swaziland, Togo, Zaire, Zambia, and unidentified East and Sub-Saharan African countries.

eign-born non-Hispanic blacks, aged 16 to 24, identified in the study, suggesting that these countries are indeed the birthplaces of most of the foreign-born non-Hispanic black youth.

New York has the largest proportion of 16-to-24-year-old non-Hispanic foreign-born blacks, and it has the largest population of people born in non-Spanish-speaking Western Hemisphere and East and Sub-Saharan African countries. As shown in table 5.8, 303,000 of the 623,000 people born in these countries who lived in the United States in 1980 lived in New York. It was home to nearly three out of five of the people born in the Western Hemisphere countries. Foreign-born New Yorkers included 107,000 people from Jamaica, 55,000 people from Haiti, 42,000 people from Trinidad and Tobago, and 83,000 people from other non-Hispanic Western Hemisphere countries. Sixty-eight thousand people born in these countries, including 25,000 from Jamaica and 17,000 from Haiti, lived in Florida. California matched New York in the size of its population

Table 5.8
Estimated Numbers of People Born in Selected Western Hemisphere and African Countries, by Country of Birth or Group of Countries of Birth and Selected State: United States, 1980

State	Total	Western Hemisphere countries				East and sub-Saharan African countries
		Haiti	Jamaica	Trinidad and Tobago	Other[1]	
Total, all states	623,000	92,000	197,000	66,000	151,000	116,000
California	37,000	1,000	7,000	2,000	11,000	16,000
Florida	68,000	17,000	25,000	3,000	17,000	5,000
Illinois	17,000	3,000	5,000	1,000	3,000	6,000
Massachusetts	27,000	5,000	6,000	3,000	5,000	9,000
New Jersey	32,000	5,000	11,000	3,000	8,000	4,000
New York	303,000	55,000	107,000	42,000	83,000	16,000

Source: Derived from Bureau of the Census, "Socioeconomic Characteristics of U.S. Foreign-born Population Detailed in Census Bureau Tabulations," pp. 1–3 and 9–12.

Note: Detail may not add to total because of rounding. Selected states are those with at least an estimated 10,000 people born in the selected countries.

[1]Belize, Bermuda, Guyana, Suriname, and Caribbean countries, except Cuba, the Dominican Republic, Haiti, Jamaica, and Trinidad and Tobago.

of people born in East and Sub-Saharan African countries: about 16,000 people from these countries lived in each state in 1980.[16]

People born in non-Spanish-speaking Western Hemisphere and African countries living in the United States have educational levels generally comparable to those of whites, and some, especially those from some of the African countries, are much better educated than the average white adult, aged 25 and older, as shown in table 5.9. Their educational levels are reflected in the relatively low undereducation rates of foreign-born black youth. In 1980, 96.7 percent of adults, aged 25 and older, born in Nigeria were high school graduates, and nearly half had completed at least 4 years of higher education; 92.3 percent of Kenyans were high school graduates, and more than half were college graduates; the educational level of people born in Ghana and Ethiopia was almost as high. In contrast to these well-educated immigrants, people born in Cape Verde are considerably less likely to be high school graduates, much less college graduates: in 1980 only a third had received 12 years of schooling, and 5.8 percent were college graduates.[17]

Among adults from Caribbean and other Western Hemisphere countries, Guyanans and Trinidadians had the highest rates of high school completion—71.5 percent and 70.3 percent, respectively—and 15.0 percent of Guyanans and 12.4 percent of Trinidadians were college gradu-

Table 5.9
High School Graduation Rates of People, Aged 25 and Older, Born in
Selected Western Hemisphere and African Countries, by Country of Birth:
United States, 1980

Western Hemisphere countries

Bahamas	52.8
Barbados	62.0
Belize	66.3
Bermuda	71.0
Grenada	66.5
Guyana	71.5
Haiti	64.4
Jamaica	63.5
Netherlands Antilles	67.7
Trinidad and Tobago	70.3

African countries

Cape Verde	34.6
Ethiopia	85.1
Ghana	93.1
Kenya	92.3
Nigeria	96.7
South Africa	89.1

Source: Derived from Bureau of the Census, "Socioeconomic Characteristics of U.S. Foreign-born Population Detailed in Census Bureau Tabulations," pp. 5–7.

ates. Two-thirds of people born in Jamaica had finished high school, and
11.0 percent, at least 4 years of college. Among Haitians, about the same
proportion were high school graduates, and 13.4 percent had finished at
least 4 years of college.[18] In comparison, 68.8 percent of whites and 51.2
percent of African Americans, aged 25 and older, in the total population
in the United States in 1980 had completed 12 years of schooling, and 17.1
percent and 8.4 percent, respectively, were college graduates.[19]

IMMIGRATION FROM CARIBBEAN AND AFRICAN
COUNTRIES SINCE 1980

Since 1980 more than half a million people have legally immigrated to
the United States from non-Spanish-speaking Caribbean and mainland
Western Hemisphere countries and from East and Sub-Saharan African
countries, as shown in table 5.10. They have been averaging 68,000 per
year during the decade. Primarily as a result of the large increase in people
admitted from Haiti, however, legal immigrants from these countries
numbered 92,415 in fiscal year 1988. Despite the harsh reception given to
would-be refugees from Haiti in recent years, the numbers of legally ad-

Table 5.10
Estimated Numbers and Yearly Average Numbers of Immigrants Born in Selected Western Hemisphere and African Countries Admitted to the United States between April 1, 1980, and September 30, 1988, and Numbers Admitted in Fiscal Year 1988, by Country of Birth

Country of birth	Total	Average per year, 1980—88	Admitted, FY 1988
Total	581,000	68,000	92,415
Total, Western Hemisphere	478,000	56,000	77,980
Antiga-Barbuda	11,000	1,000	837
Bahamas	5,000	1,000	1,283
Barbados	15,000	2,000	1,455
Belize	13,000	1,000	1,497
British Virgin Islands	2,000	*	395
Dominica	5,000	1,000	611
Grenada	9,000	1,000	842
Guyana	77,000	9,000	8,747
Haiti	109,000	13,000	34,806
Jamaica	174,000	20,000	20,966
St. Christopher-Nevis	9,000	1,000	660
St. Lucia	5,000	1,000	606
St. Vincent-Grenadines	6,000	1,000	634
Trinidad and Tobago	30,000	4,000	3,947
Other countries[1]	7,000	1,000	694
Total, Africa	103,000	12,000	14,435
Cape Verde	6,000	1,000	921
Ethiopia	20,000	2,000	2,571
Ghana	9,000	1,000	1,239
Kenya	6,000	1,000	773
Liberia	5,000	1,000	769
Nigeria	22,000	3,000	3,343
Sierra Leone	3,000	*	571
South Africa	13,000	2,000	1,832
Tanzania	3,000	*	388
Uganda	3,000	*	216
Zimbabwe	2,000	*	216
Other countries[2]	10,000	1,000	1,469

Source: Derived from Immigration and Naturalization Service, unpublished tabulations. The numbers of immigrants admitted between April 1 and September 30, 1980, are estimated to be half the totals for fiscal year 1980.

Note: Detail may not add to total because of rounding.

*Fewer than an estimated 1,000 per year.

[1]Anguilla, Aruba, Bermuda, Cayman Islands, Guadaloupe, Martinique, Monserrat, Netherlands Antilles, Suriname, and Turks and Caicos Islands.

[2]Other East and Sub-Saharan African countries.

mitted immigrants have been steadily increasing. They rose from 6,540 in FY 1980 to 14,819 in FY 1987, and in FY 1988 the number from Haiti more than doubled to 34,806. In all, 109,000 people have been admitted from Haiti since April 1980. The largest number of immigrants from any of these countries—152,000—came from Jamaica. In addition, 69,000 people were admitted from Guyana and 30,000 from Trinidad and Tobago. The largest numbers from Africa came from Nigeria, 22,000, and Ethiopia, 20,000.[20] Three-quarters of the immigrants from Guyana and more than half of those from Jamaica who were admitted in fiscal year 1987 intended to join the Guyanan and Jamaican communities in New York. Among 1987 immigrants from Haiti, 46.4 percent were headed for New York and a third for Florida.[21]

To the extent that the new immigrants have attained the same level of education as earlier immigrants from their countries, they add to the populations of largely well-educated foreign-born blacks in New York, Florida, California, and the other states where their compatriots are already established. The children of well-educated blacks are likely to complete high school, many to follow their parents to institutions of higher education. Their numbers will not increase the numbers of undereducated African American youth.

UNDEREDUCATED AFRICAN AMERICAN YOUTH IN THE REMAINDER OF THIS CENTURY

In April 1980 when the decennial census was taken, there were a million African American young people, aged 16 to 24, who were out of school and had not completed 12 years of schooling. They constituted one in five of their age group. The October 1980 current population survey counted 912,000 undereducated civilian blacks, aged 16 to 24, not living in group quarters. They constituted 19.4 percent of all civilian noninstitutional blacks, including black Hispanics.[22] By October 1988 the number of undereducated civilian noninstitutional blacks had fallen to 698,000 and the black undereducation rate to 14.9 percent.[23] (See table 1.1 in chapter 1.) Meanwhile, undereducated blacks are staying in school into the upper grades in increasing proportions. In October 1980, 31.7 percent of undereducated 14-to-24-year-old blacks had completed the eleventh grade before discontinuing their education; in October 1986, 33.8 percent had done so.[24] (See table 1.2 in chapter 1.)

The number of African Americans in the United States is increasing faster than the number of whites. Black and other minority youth will constitute a larger proportion of U.S. youth in the future. Using moderate assumptions about fertility, mortality, and net immigration, it is projected that the black population will increase annually by 1.5 percent between 1985 and 1990, by 1.4 percent between 1990 and 1995, and by 1.2 percent between 1995 and the year 2000. In contrast, the non-Hispanic white population is projected to increase annually by 0.6 percent, 0.4 percent, and 0.3 percent in those periods. By the year 2000, if these assumptions prove accurate, the African American school-age population—6.6 million in 1985—will have increased to 8.3 million. (See table 1.3 in chapter 1.) From 14.9 percent of the total school-age population in 1985, its proportion will grow to 17.1 percent. The Hispanic population, increasing even faster, will also constitute a larger proportion of the school-age population in the year 2000. The non-Hispanic white proportion, on the other hand, will fall from 72.8 percent of the school-age population in 1985 to 69.4 percent in the year 2000.[25] Because the numbers of legal immigrants during the eighties have outpaced the Census Bureau's moderate assumptions, the numbers and proportions of black and other minority school-age children and youth in the year 2000 will probably be even greater than these projections.

When the Department of Education issued its 1989 "wall chart," 18 states and the District of Columbia had instituted minimum competency tests for high school graduation.[26] Some states are also using minimum competency testing for grade promotion. Minimum competency testing is only one of the proposals being widely advocated by school reformers. Other proposals concern curricular changes and changes in the amount of time spent in school on academic studies. All of these proposals have negative as well as positive effects, especially for minority youth who are already at risk of being left behind. When the results of the 1990 census are available, it will be possible to determine whether the trend in the undereducation rate of African Americans has continued downward, as the changes being advocated by the school reform movement take effect. In the meantime, however, it is clear that blacks and other minorities will constitute an increasing proportion of the school-age population in the future. Without substantial changes in the way schools educate these youth and without attention to the fundamental inequities among school districts, more and more of the population that is at risk of leaving school without an education adequate to the needs of the twenty-first century will consist of African Americans and other minorities.

NOTES

1. Bureau of the Census, U.S. Department of Commerce, *School Enrollment—Social and Economic Characteristics of Students: October 1988 and 1987* (Washington, D.C.: U.S. Government Printing Office, 1990), pp. 5–6.

2. Ibid.

3. Bureau of the Census, U.S. Department of Commerce, *1980 Census of Population, General Social and Economic Characteristics, Part 1, United States Summary* (Washington, D.C.: U.S. Government Printing Office, 1983), pp. 13, 97, and 113.

4. Bureau of the Census, *General Social and Economic Characteristics, Part 2, Alabama; Part 8, Connecticut; Part 12, Georgia; Part 15, Illinois; Part 19, Kentucky; Part 20, Louisiana; Part 26, Mississippi; Part 32, New Jersey; Part 34, New York; Part 35, North Carolina; Part 40, Pennsylvania; Part 42, South Carolina; Part 44, Tennessee; and Part 51, Wisconsin,* tables 59 and 82, various pages.

5. The differences between 13.3 percent for foreign-born non-English language-background blacks and 15.2 percent for foreign-born English language-background blacks, and between the latter and 17.0 percent for native-born non-English language-background blacks, are significant at the 68 percent confidence level.

6. Bureau of the Census, U.S. Department of Commerce, *1980 Census of Population, Detailed Population Characteristics, Part 1, United States Summary* (Washington, D.C.: U.S. Government Printing Office, 1984), pp. 30–31.

7. Bureau of the Census, U.S. Department of Commerce, *School Enrollment—Social and Economic Characteristics of Students: October 1981 and 1980* (Washington, D.C.: U.S. Government Printing Office, 1985), pp. 73–75.

8. Bureau of the Census, U.S. Department of Commerce, *Race of the Population by States: 1980* (Washington, D.C.: U.S. Government Printing Office, 1981), p. 12.

9. Bureau of the Census, *General Social and Economic Characteristics, Part 2, Alabama; Part 12, Georgia; Part 19, Kentucky; Part 20, Louisiana; Part 26, Mississippi; Part 35, North Carolina; Part 42, South Carolina; and Part 44, Tennessee,* tables 59, 76, and 82, various pages.

10. Bureau of the Census, *General Social and Economic Characteristics, Part 15, Illinois; Part 32, New Jersey; Part 34, New York; Part 40, Pennsylvania; and Part 51, Wisconsin,* table 59, various pages.

11. Ibid., tables 76 and 82, various pages.

12. Bureau of the Census, *General Social and Economic Characteristics, Part 6, California,* pp. 57 and 86.

13. Ibid., p. 86.

14. Bureau of the Census, *Detailed Population Characteristics,* pp. 10–11.

15. Bureau of the Census, U.S. Department of Commerce, "Socioeconomic Characteristics of U.S. Foreign-born Population Detailed in Census Bureau Tabulations," press release, October 17, 1984, pp. 1–3.

16. Ibid., pp. 9–12.

17. Ibid., p. 5.

18. Ibid., pp. 6–7.

19. Bureau of the Census, *Detailed Population Characteristics,* pp. 42–45.

20. Immigration and Naturalization Service, U.S. Department of Justice, unpublished tabulations.

21. Immigration and Naturalization Service, U.S. Department of Justice, *Statistical Yearbook of the Immigration and Naturalization Service, 1987* (Washington, D.C.: U.S. Government Printing Office, 1988), p. 33.

22. Bureau of the Census, *School Enrollment: October 1981 and 1980,* p. 61.

23. Bureau of the Census, *School Enrollment: October 1988 and 1987,* p. 6.

24. Bureau of the Census, *School Enrollment: October 1981 and 1980,* p. 74; and idem, *School Enrollment—Social and Economic Characteristics of Students: October 1986* (Washington, D.C.: U.S. Government Printing Office, 1988), p. 25.

25. Bureau of the Census, U.S. Department of Commerce, *Projections of the*

Hispanic Population: 1983 to 2080 (Washington, D.C.: U.S. Government Printing Office, 1986), pp. 10 and 14.

26. U.S. Department of Education, "State Education Performance Chart, 1982 and 1989," reprinted in *Education Week* (Washington, D.C.), May 9, 1990.

6

Hispanic Youth
Who Are Undereducated

Hispanics as a group are the most likely of all youth to be undereducated, and they are the most likely to discontinue their education before reaching the ninth grade. Native-born Hispanics, however, are less at risk than American Indians and Alaska Natives, and native-born Hispanics from monolingual English-speaking homes have an undereducation rate comparable to that of African Americans. The most likely to be undereducated are foreign-born Hispanics, a very large proportion of whom are not enrolled in school and have not completed 12 years of schooling. They constitute the majority of Hispanics who fail to reach at least the ninth grade.

In 1980 Hispanics were the second largest group among minority young people who were out of school without high school diplomas. By 1988 their numbers had exceeded the numbers of undereducated African Americans, both because Hispanics are increasing faster than other groups in the population and because the overall undereducation rate of Hispanics had remained about the same during the eighties, whereas that of blacks had gone down. In 1980 there were 923,000 undereducated young Hispanics in the United States. They were the second largest minority group after African Americans and one in six of all undereducated youth. By 1988 there were more than a million undereducated civilian Hispanics not living in group quarters, in comparison with fewer than 700,000 civilian non-institutional blacks, and they constituted more than a quarter of all undereducated civilian non-institutional youth.[1]

The overall undereducation rate of Hispanics misrepresents the educational status of Hispanic youth and obscures important differences. In 1980 a third of all Hispanics were out of school and had not completed 12 years of schooling. However, among native-born Hispanics from Spanish-speaking homes—the largest group of Hispanics in 1980—the rate was 28.2 percent—under three in ten—and among native-born Hispanics from monolingual English-speaking homes it was 20.6 percent, or one in five—virtually the same as that of African Americans. Foreign-born Hispanics are much more likely to be undereducated; their 1980 rate was 45.4 percent, and they accounted for the high overall rate. These groups were, respectively, 2.2 times, 1.6 times, and 3.5 times more likely to be undereducated than white majority youth in 1980. The higher undereducation rate of native-born Spanish language-background Hispanics in comparison with English language-background Hispanics and the fact that these and other language minority youth are likely to have completed fewer years of schooling than their English language-background counterparts underline the need for more attention to linguistic differences in U.S. school programs.

The majority of Hispanics are native born. In 1980, 70.2 percent of the total age group 16 to 24, and 58 percent of those who were undereducated, were born in one of the states, the District of Columbia, Puerto Rico, or another outlying area. Hispanics are the most likely of all youth to have non-English language backgrounds. In 1980 more than four out of five native-born Hispanics and almost all of the foreign-born Hispanics lived in households in which one or more people speak a language other than English at home, presumably Spanish.

For Hispanics, having a non-English language background and being foreign born are associated with higher undereducation rates, as indicated above. These characteristics are both negative factors for them. In contrast, for African Americans, both characteristics are associated with lower undereducation rates. For Asians and Pacific Islanders and for non-Hispanic whites, foreign birth is associated with higher undereducation rates, but a non-English language background is a positive factor.

Greater than average poverty characterizes Hispanics as it does other minorities in the United States, but Hispanics are not quite as likely to be poor as African Americans or as American Indians, Eskimos, and Aleuts, even after allowances are made for the differential effects of the greater poverty experienced by all groups in 1982 and 1983.[2] In 1980 nearly a quarter of all Hispanics had incomes below the poverty level;[3] Hispanic youth, aged 16 to 24, were more than twice as likely as white majority youth to come from poor families. They were 1.3 times less likely to be poor than blacks or Native Americans.

Poverty represents a smaller undereducation risk for Hispanics than for some other youth, and it is mediated by language background and nativity. In 1980 poor native-born Hispanic youth from monolingual English-speaking homes were 1.9 times more likely to be undereducated than their counterparts from more economically advantaged families. Native-born Hispanics from Spanish-speaking homes were 1.7 times more likely, and foreign-born Hispanics were 1.2 times more likely, to be undereducated than their more advantaged counterparts. The comparable poverty risk factor for white majority youth was 2.1; that for Asians and Pacific Islanders, 2.0.

A large majority of Hispanics in the United States live in urban areas. They are more urbanized than African Americans but not as urbanized as the Asian and Pacific Islander population. After African Americans, Hispanics are the most likely to live in the central cities of metropolitan areas, but more, proportionally, than blacks live in the suburbs or in smaller cities. Nine out of ten Hispanics lived in urban areas in 1980. Among Asians and Pacific Islanders, 93.2 percent lived in urban areas; the proportions of African Americans and non-Hispanic whites were 85.3 percent and 70.5 percent, respectively. Just under half of the Hispanics, in comparison with 57.1 percent of the blacks, lived in central cities.[4] (See table 2.10 in chapter 2.)

Hispanics living in the suburbs and other urban areas outside the central cities are the least likely to be poor; those in central cities and rural areas, the most likely.[5] Youth living in central cities have the highest undereducation rates. In 1980, 27.4 percent of civilian Hispanics, aged 16 to 19, living in central cities were undereducated, in comparison with 25.4 percent of those living in rural areas and 21.8 percent of those living in the suburbs of central cities.[6] (See table 3.16 in chapter 3.)

Like Asians and Pacific Islanders, Native Americans, and non-Hispanic white minority youth, Hispanics are not homogeneous, and differences among the subgroups are related to the likelihood of Hispanic youth to be undereducated, as shown by the differences in undereducation rates of Hispanic young people in the various states where the different subgroups are concentrated. In 1980 three out of five Hispanics in the United States were Mexican American, one in seven was Puerto Rican, and 5.5 percent were Cuban American. In addition, about a fifth of Hispanics did not identify with any of these groups in 1980.[7] These "other" Hispanics are people of mixed Hispanic heritage, immigrants or children of immigrants from Spanish-speaking Western Hemisphere countries other than Mexico or Cuba, immigrants or children of immigrants from Spain, or, especially in New Mexico and Colorado, descendants of the early Spanish settlers in the Southwest.

The following sections of this chapter contain discussions of the characteristics of undereducated Hispanic youth and comparisons of the undereducation rates of Hispanics in the various categories. The discussions highlight the differences in undereducation among native-born English language-background Hispanics, native-born non-English language background Hispanics, and foreign-born Hispanics. They contrast Hispanic undereducation rates with those of white majority youth and other minority youth. The undereducation rates of Hispanics in the 29 states with at least an estimated 10,000 Hispanics in the age group that is the focus of this study and the undereducation rates of native-born and foreign-born Hispanics in states with at least an estimated 10,000 Hispanic in those base populations are examined. State undereducation rates are considered in relation to the composition of the state Hispanic populations as a whole and to the composition of state foreign-born Hispanic populations. The chapter ends with an examination of the immigration from Spanish-speaking countries that has contributed to the growing population of Hispanic young people with special educational needs since 1980 and a consideration of what the projected growth of the Hispanic population in the last years of this century may mean for the size of the population at risk by the year 2000.

The study data do not separate Hispanics who live in households in which Spanish is spoken from those who live in households in which other non-English languages are spoken; the discussion treats non-English language-background Hispanics as though all had Spanish language backgrounds, although a few, undoubtedly, have other language backgrounds.[8] In the sections describing the national findings, the foreign-born category includes the 5,000 Hispanics living in monolingual English-speaking households. Some of them are Hispanic immigrants from English-speaking countries; all speak English in households in this country in which only English is spoken. In the discussion of state rates, the foreign-born category includes only non-English language-background Hispanics.

The information on Mexican Americans, Puerto Ricans, Cuban Americans, and "other" Hispanics and on immigrants born in Spanish-speaking countries in the total population in 1980 is from the published volumes of the 1980 census; that on 1980–88 immigrants is from the Immigration and Naturalization Service. Other publications of the Bureau of the Census provided the information on trends in the size of the undereducated Hispanic population and on the potential size of the school-age Hispanic population in the future.

THE NUMBERS AND CHARACTERISTICS OF UNDEREDUCATED HISPANIC YOUTH

There were 535,000 undereducated native-born Hispanic youth and 387,000 undereducated foreign-born Hispanic youth in the United States in 1980, as shown in table 6.1. Of the native-born Hispanics, 446,000, or 83.3 percent, lived in households in which one or more people speak Spanish or another non-English language; the remainder, 90,000, lived in monolingual English-speaking households. Among the foreign-born, 383,000, or 98.8 percent, lived in Spanish-speaking households.

Table 6.1
Estimated Numbers and Distribution of Undereducated Hispanic Youth, by Nativity, Language Background, and Selected Characteristic: United States, 1980 (Numbers in thousands)

| | | | Native born | | | | | |
| | Total | | English only | | Non-English | | Foreign born[1] | |
Characteristic	#	%	#	%	#	%	#	%
Total	923	100.0	90	100.0	446	100.0	387	100.0
Gender								
Males	489	53.0	47	52.3	225	50.5	217	56.0
Females	434	47.0	43	47.7	221	49.5	170	44.0
Age								
16 to 19	332	36.0	35	39.4	181	40.5	116	30.1
20 to 24	590	64.0	54	60.6	265	59.5	271	69.9
Poverty status in 1979[2]								
Above poverty level	605	65.6	57	63.6	279	62.7	269	69.4
Below poverty level	291	31.5	26	28.9	151	34.0	114	29.3
Years of schooling completed								
Fewer than 5	97	10.5	3	3.9	19	4.3	74	19.1
5 to 8	313	34.0	12	13.9	117	26.2	184	47.5
9 to 11	513	55.6	74	81.2	310	69.5	129	33.4

Note: Percentages calculated on unrounded numbers. Detail may not add to total number or to 100.0 percent because of rounding.
[1]Includes an estimated 5,000 people living in monolingual English-speaking households.
[2]Not determined for people living in group quarters.

Foreign-born Hispanics are considerably more likely than native-born Hispanics to be undereducated, and native-born Hispanics from Spanish-speaking homes are more likely to be undereducated than native-born English language-background Hispanics. The latter are about as likely to be undereducated as African Americans. In 1980 Hispanic undereducation rates were 45.4 percent for foreign-born youth as a group, 28.2 percent for native-born youth living in homes in which Spanish is spoken, and 20.6 for native-born youth living in monolingual English-speaking homes, as shown in table 6.2. These rates contrast with those of non-Hispanic whites and Asians and Pacific Islanders, for whom foreign birth is a risk factor but having a non-English language background is not, and with those of African Americans for whom neither foreign birth nor having a

Table 6.2
Estimated Numbers of Undereducated Hispanic Youth and Hispanic Undereducation Rates, by Nativity, Language Background, and Selected Characteristic: United States, 1980 (Numbers in thousands)

			Native born					
	Total		English only		Non-English		Foreign born[1]	
Characteristic	#	Rate	#	Rate	#	Rate	#	Rate
Total	923	32.2	90	20.6	446	28.2	387	45.4
Gender								
Males	489	33.5	47	21.5	225	28.7	217	47.4
Females	434	30.9	43	19.7	221	27.8	170	43.1
Age								
16 to 19	332	25.5	35	19.3	181	22.8	116	35.5
20 to 24	590	37.8	54	21.6	265	33.7	271	51.7
Poverty status in 1979[2]								
Above poverty level	605	28.9	57	17.9	279	24.2	269	43.6
Below poverty level	291	44.8	26	33.4	151	41.9	114	54.0

Note: Detail may not add to total because of rounding.

[1]Includes an estimated 5,000 people living in monolingual English-speaking households.

[2]Not determined for people living in group quarters.

non-English language background are risk factors. (See table 3.2 in chapter 3.)

Undereducated native-born English language-background, native-born Spanish language-background, and foreign-born Hispanics differ in several ways. The native-born groups are about evenly divided between women and men with, perhaps, slightly more men than women in the English language-background group. In contrast, undereducated foreign-born men outnumber foreign-born women. There were 1.3 times as many foreign-born men in 1980 as foreign-born women. Men in all groups, but especially foreign-born men, are more likely to be undereducated than women. In 1980, among native-born English language-background Hispanics, 19.7 percent of women and 21.5 percent of men, and among native-born Spanish language-background Hispanics, 27.8 percent of women and 28.7 percent of men, were undereducated—differences of less than 2 percentage points.[9] At the same time, 43.1 percent of foreign-born Hispanic women and 47.4 percent of foreign-born Hispanic men were undereducated—a difference of more than 4 percentage points.

Undereducated Hispanic youth in all groups are likely to be older, but foreign-born youth are especially likely to be older. There were 1.2 times as many native-born 20-to-24-year-olds per year of age as native-born teenagers and nearly twice as many foreign-born 20-to-24-year-olds per year of age as foreign-born teenagers in 1980.

Hispanic youth, aged 16 to 24, are much more likely to come from poor families than white majority youth in their age group. However, they are less likely to be poor than American Indians, Eskimos, and Aleuts and African Americans. In 1980, 23.7 percent of Hispanic youth whose poverty status was determined were from families with incomes below the poverty level. In comparison, 11.1 percent of white majority youth and 12.5 percent of non-Hispanic white minority youth were from poor families. Among American Indians, Eskimos, and Aleuts, 30.1 percent, and among black youth, 31.1 percent, were poor. (See table 3.7 in chapter 3.) Poverty status is not determined for people who live in group quarters—institutions, college dormitories, military barracks, and the like. This group included 124,000 Hispanic youth, or about 4.3 percent of the age group, in 1980.

Native-born Spanish language-background Hispanics and foreign-born Hispanics are more likely to be from families with incomes below the poverty level than native-born English language-background Hispanics. In 1980, 23.8 percent of the first group and 25.4 percent of the foreign-born group were from poor families. In contrast, 19.6 percent of native-born English language-background Hispanics were from poor families.

Poverty is less closely associated with undereducation for Hispanics than it is for non-Hispanic whites and Asians and Pacific Islanders who have much lower undereducation rates. Whereas white majority, native-born white minority, and Asian/Pacific youth from families with incomes below the poverty level were at least twice as likely to be undereducated as their counterparts who were not from the poorest families in 1980, native-born Hispanics from poor families were 1.8 times more likely to be undereducated than those from more advantaged families. In 1980 a third of native-born English language-background Hispanics from poor families were undereducated in comparison with 17.9 percent of their counterparts from more advantaged families. Among native-born Spanish language-background Hispanics from poor families, two out of five were undereducated in comparison with a quarter of native-born Spanish language-background Hispanics from more advantaged families. (See table 3.6 in chapter 3.)

The difference related to poverty is much less among foreign-born Hispanics because so many in this group are undereducated regardless of family income. In 1980 foreign-born Hispanics from poor families were 1.2 times more likely to be undereducated than those from more advantaged families; their rates were 54.0 and 43.6 percent, respectively.

Undereducated Hispanic youth as a group are the least likely of all youth to have reached high school before discontinuing their education. In 1980, 44.4 percent of those who were not enrolled and had not completed 12 years of schooling had discontinued their education with 8 years or fewer. They constituted 14.3 percent of all Hispanic youth, aged 16 to 24, in 1980.

Low levels of schooling are characteristic of Spanish language-background Hispanics and, especially, of foreign-born Hispanics. Native-born undereducated Hispanics living in monolingual English-speaking homes are just as likely as undereducated white majority and African American youth to continue at least into the high school grades. In 1980 only a third of foreign-born Hispanics had completed at least nine years of schooling and one in five had completed fewer than five years. They constituted over three-quarters of all Hispanics with very low levels of schooling and nearly three out of five of those who had completed between five and eight years of schooling. In contrast, 69.5 percent of native-born undereducated Spanish language-background and 81.2 percent of native-born undereducated English language-background Hispanics had completed at least nine years of schooling, and only 4.3 and 3.9 percent, respectively, had completed fewer than five years. In the proportions completing at least nine years, foreign-born undereducated Hispanics ranked well behind foreign-born undereducated Asians and Pacific Islanders and white minority youth. In the proportions with less than a fifth grade education, they ranked with Asian/Pacific youth and behind white minority youth.[10] Native-born undereducated Hispanics living in Spanish-speaking homes ranked behind native-born undereducated Asian/Pacific and white minority youth in the proportions completing at least the ninth grade but well above Asians in the proportions completing fewer than five years of schooling. (See table 2.6 in chapter 2.)

UNDEREDUCATED HISPANIC YOUTH IN THE STATES

Not surprisingly, undereducated Hispanic youth are found in the states and regions where the Hispanic population as a whole is concentrated. The largest center of Hispanic population is the Southwest where four out of five Hispanics lived in 1980.[11] Two-thirds of all undereducated Hispanic youth in the United States were located in the five southwestern states. A third—336,000—lived in California and one in ten—197,000—in Texas. There were groups of 20,000 to 30,000 undereducated Hispanics in Arizona, New Mexico, and Colorado. The second largest concentration of Hispanics is in the Mid Atlantic states: 14 percent, or 128,000 undereducated Hispanic youth, lived there in 1980. Ninety-five thousand lived in New York, 24,000 in New Jersey, and 10,000 in Pennsylvania. In addition, 55,000 undereducated Hispanic youth lived in Illinois and

29,000 in Florida. There were 33 other states, ranging from Massachusetts to Hawaii, with at least 1,000 undereducated Hispanics in 1980. (See table 2.8 in chapter 2.) The geographical distribution of undereducated Hispanic youth in the United States is depicted in figure 6.1.

Hispanics dominate the undereducated population in certain states. They are the largest minority group among the undereducated in others. In 1980 more than half of all undereducated youth in New Mexico were Hispanic. They constituted 47.7 percent of this population in California. They were the largest minority in Texas where they constituted two out of five undereducated youth, in Arizona where they were a third, and in Colorado and New York where they constituted more than a quarter of the undereducated population. They were also the largest groups of undereducated minority youth in Connecticut and in the western states of Idaho, Nevada, Utah, Washington, and Wyoming. (See table 2.9 in chapter 2.)

THE STATE UNDEREDUCATION RATES OF HISPANIC YOUTH

The likelihood of Hispanics to be undereducated does not vary widely by region but there is considerable range in the state rates, as illustrated in figure 6.2. The range reflects the differences among the Hispanic populations in the various states. It reflects not only the differences in the proportions of youth in the at-risk groups, that is, those who are poor, foreign born, or come from Spanish-speaking homes, but also the underlying differences in the characteristics of the Hispanic subgroups, that is, the Mexican Americans, Puerto Ricans, Cuban Americans, and "other" Hispanics, and the differences among Hispanics born in different countries. These groups are not evenly distributed among the states, as will be seen later in this chapter.

In 1980 three out of ten Hispanics, aged 16 to 24, in the South and the Northeast and a third of those in the Midwest and the West were out of school without having completed 12 years of schooling. (See table 3.9 in chapter 3.) In the 29 states with at least 10,000 Hispanics, aged 16 to 24, in 1980, the undereducation rates ranged from as low as one in eight—in Maryland—to as high as two out of five—in Illinois. Of these 29 states, there were only 7 with rates as high or higher than the national Hispanic undereducation rate. Hispanics in 22 states were less likely than Hispanics nationally to be undereducated. Five of the states in which Hispanics were most at risk were in the West, including the two with the largest numbers of undereducated Hispanic youth—California and Texas. In Texas's neighbor New Mexico, on the other hand, fewer than a quarter of Hispanic youth were undereducated, and in Florida, another state with a substantial number of Hispanic youth, only one in five was undereducated in 1980. (See table 3.10 in chapter 3 for the rates in all the states.)

Figure 6.1
Undereducated Hispanic Youth in the United States, 1980

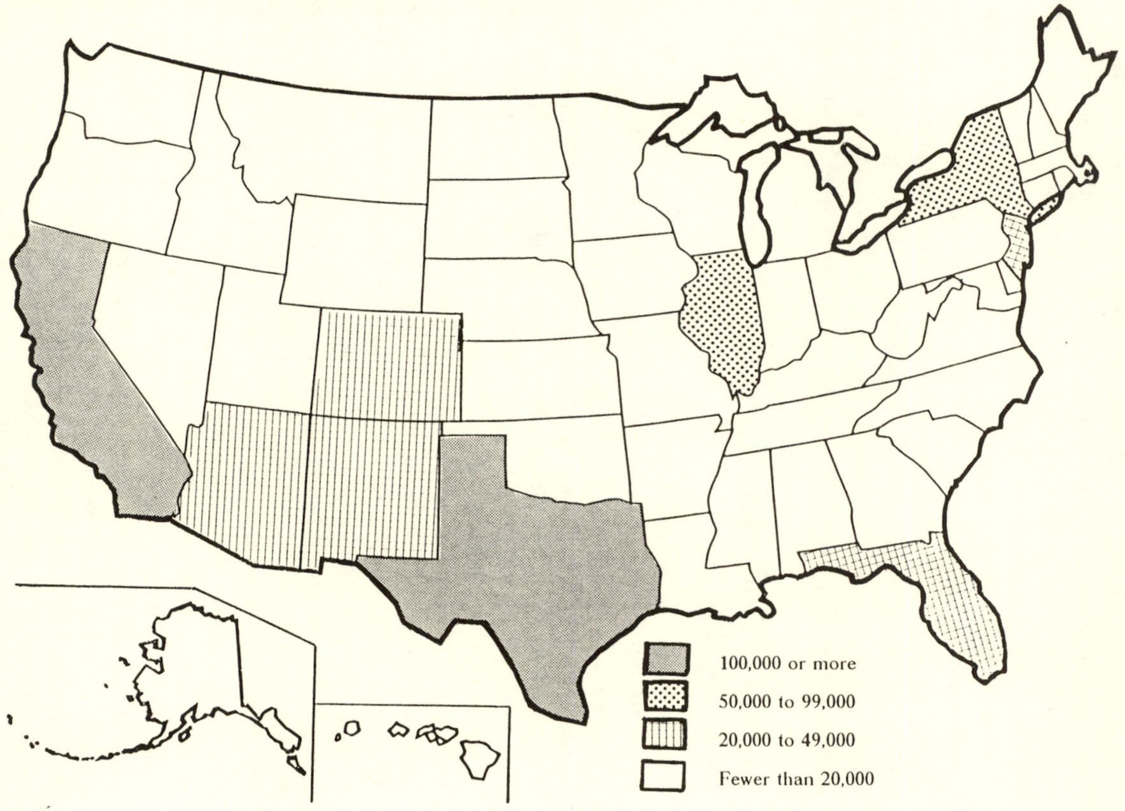

100,000 or more

50,000 to 99,000

20,000 to 49,000

Fewer than 20,000

Figure 6.2
Undereducation Rates of Hispanic Youth, 1980

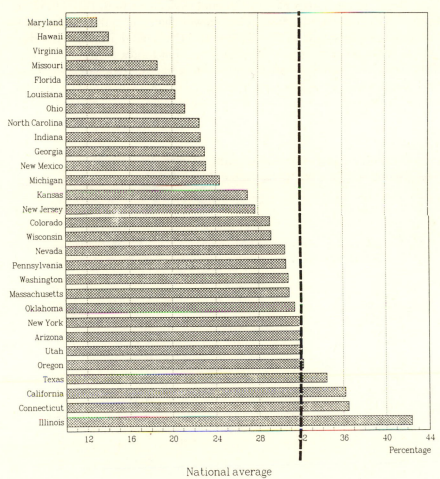

National average

The range in the state undereducation rates of native-born Hispanic youth is not as great as the range of state undereducation rates for Hispanic youth in the aggregate, but it is still considerable. Native-born Hispanics living in monolingual English-speaking homes in Illinois in 1980 were twice as likely to be undereducated as similar Hispanics in New Mexico, as shown in table 6.3; their comparative rates were 26.9 percent and 13.6 percent, respectively. Native-born Hispanics living in Spanish-speaking homes in Connecticut, with a rate of 42.1 percent, were twice as likely to be undereducated as those in Ohio who had a rate of 20.6 percent.

The range in the state rates of foreign-born youth is almost as great as that for Hispanics as whole. Hispanics living in Florida, New Jersey, and New York are much less likely to be undereducated than those living in Illinois, Texas, and California. In 1980 fewer than one in five in this group in Florida, slightly more in New Jersey, and three in ten in New York were undereducated.[12] In contrast, foreign-born Hispanics in Illinois, Texas, California, and Arizona were more likely to be undereducated than not; their rates were 56.8 percent, 56.5 percent, 55.7 percent, and 50.5 percent, respectively.

Table 6.3
Undereducation Rates of Hispanic Youth, by Nativity, Language Background, and Selected State: United States, 1980

State	Native born		Foreign born, non-English
	English only	Non-English	
Total, all states	20.6	28.2	45.9
Arizona	21.4	30.0	50.5
California	18.9	24.2	55.7
Colorado	28.1	26.9	52.2[a]
Connecticut	18.3[a]	42.1	23.4[a]
Florida	21.0	23.7	18.2
Georgia	20.9[a]	29.0[a]	16.0[a]
Hawaii	12.1[a]	17.8[a]	13.3[a]
Illinois	26.9	33.8	56.8
Indiana	19.6[a]	22.9	27.9[a]
Kansas	23.6[a]	24.6[a]	44.2[a]
Louisiana	21.3[a]	18.2[a]	21.0[a]
Maryland	9.9[a]	15.6[a]	14.8[a]
Massachusetts	10.2[a]	39.4	24.9[a]
Michigan	21.5	26.9	22.2[a]
Missouri	17.8[a]	18.1[a]	22.2[a]
Nevada	19.5[a]	26.7[a]	46.5[a]
New Jersey	16.7[a]	33.3	21.3
New Mexico	13.6	22.2	51.2[a]
New York	19.4	34.1	30.0
North Carolina	24.7[a]	22.6[a]	15.4[a]
Ohio	23.7[a]	20.6	16.7[a]
Oklahoma	26.4[a]	28.8[a]	49.6[a]
Oregon	21.6[a]	27.0[a]	60.6[a]
Pennsylvania	18.4[a]	37.7	19.6[a]
Texas	23.6	29.6	56.5
Utah	26.4[a]	34.2[a]	38.5[a]
Virginia	18.2[a]	12.8[a]	12.1[a]
Washington	17.8[a]	26.0	57.7[a]
Wisconsin	24.0[a]	29.5[a]	37.0[a]

Note: Selected states are those with at least an estimated 10,000 Hispanics, aged 16 to 24.
[a]Base number less than an estimated 10,000.

Although native-born Spanish language-background Hispanics are more at risk nationally than native-born Hispanics from monolingual English-speaking backgrounds, and foreign-born Spanish language-background Hispanics are most at risk, this is not the case in every state (see table 6.3). In Florida, foreign-born Hispanics are less likely to be undereducated than either native-born group.[13] In New York and New Jersey, native-born English language-background Hispanics have the lowest undereducation rates of the three groups, but foreign-born Hispanics are less likely than native-born Spanish language-background Hispanics to be undereducated.[14]

Nationally, and in all the nine states with at least 10,000 native-born Hispanics in monolingual English-speaking households except New Mexico, native-born English language-background Hispanics are more likely than white majority youth to be out of school without having completed the twelfth grade. In 1980, their rates were from seven to as much as seventeen percentage points higher than those of white majority youth, as shown in table 6.4. New Mexico Hispanics who live in monolingual English-speaking households are no more at risk of undereducation than white majority New Mexicans; one in seven to one in nine young people in both groups was undereducated in 1980.[15]

In California, Colorado, Illinois, and Texas, native-born English language-background Hispanics are at higher risk than African American youth.[16] Nationally, however, and in Arizona, Florida, Michigan, and New York, native-born Hispanics who live in households in which only English

Table 6.4
Undereducation Rates of Native-Born English Language-Background Hispanic, White Majority, and African American Youth, by Selected State: United States, 1980

State	Hispanics	White majority youth	African Americans
Total, all states	20.6	13.0	20.4
Arizona	21.4	12.9	18.2
California	18.9	11.7	14.2
Colorado	28.1	10.6	14.2
Florida	21.0	16.5	22.8
Illinois	26.9	11.3	23.5
Michigan	21.5	11.9	21.5
New Mexico	13.6	11.0	*
New York	19.4	8.7	20.2
Texas	23.6	14.7	19.2

Note: Selected states are those with at least an estimated 10,000 youth, aged 16 to 24, in each group except where otherwise noted.

*Base number less than an estimated 10,000.

is spoken have about the same likelihood of being out of school and not high school graduates as African American youth.

THE CHARACTERISTICS OF HISPANIC YOUTH IN THE STATES

Hispanic youth in the various states differ widely in the extent to which they come from families with incomes below the poverty level, are foreign-born, and live in Spanish-speaking households, as shown in table 6.5.

Table 6.5
Estimated Numbers of Hispanic Youth and Percentages with Selected Characteristics, by Selected State: United States, 1980

State	Number	Percentage		
		In poverty[1]	Foreign born	With NELB[2]
Total, all states	2,865,000	23.7	29.8	84.2
Arizona	87,000	20.8	15.5	87.0
California	928,000	19.9	41.0	83.9
Colorado	68,000	20.9	8.2	69.6
Connecticut	24,000	34.5	16.9	89.1
Florida	146,000	18.4	58.3	89.6
Georgia	15,000	22.4	19.1	52.4
Hawaii	15,000	15.8	11.4	43.6
Illinois	129,000	21.1	42.1	88.0
Indiana	17,000	16.1	13.7	69.8
Kansas	13,000	13.2	14.9	67.6
Louisiana	21,000	21.9	23.2	54.8
Maryland	12,000	19.0	31.5	62.7
Massachusetts	29,000	39.8	31.4	86.0
Michigan	30,000	20.2	11.5	65.3
Missouri	11,000	19.2	12.7	52.0
Nevada	10,000	16.7	31.2	69.9
New Jersey	88,000	25.1	34.4	90.8
New Mexico	96,000	22.6	6.4	88.9
New York	297,000	34.1	27.5	91.9
North Carolina	15,000	27.7	16.1	50.1
Ohio	23,000	22.5	11.1	65.3
Oklahoma	13,000	25.7	18.7	60.8
Oregon	13,000	30.1	22.4	59.0
Pennsylvania	31,000	36.0	13.8	75.7
Texas	571,000	25.9	19.2	94.0
Utah	13,000	22.0	13.1	66.5
Virginia	17,000	14.6	29.5	63.3
Washington	27,000	23.3	24.2	67.6
Wisconsin	13,000	18.5	18.5	72.6

Note: Selected states are those with at least an estimated 10,000 Hispanics, aged 16 to 24.

[1]Poverty status not determined for people living in group quarters.

[2]Non-English language background.

These are factors that, nationally, are associated with a higher risk of undereducation for Hispanics. Their proportions in each state are related to the characteristics of the particular ethnic subgroup or national origin of the foreign born in that state, and they have differing effects on the likelihood of undereducation according to the subgroup or national origin group, as already noted.

Hispanic youth in Massachusetts are the poorest, reflecting the higher poverty rates of Puerto Ricans who are the predominant Hispanic population in that state.[17] In 1980 two out of five Hispanic youth in Massachusetts whose poverty status was determined came from families with incomes below the poverty level; other states where large proportions of youth are likely to be poor, such as Connecticut, New York, and Pennsylvania, also have substantial Puerto Rican populations, as will be noted in the next section.

Hispanic youth in Florida—largely Cuban American—are the most likely to be foreign born; those in New Mexico, where the descendants of Spanish settlers in the colonial period form a substantial group of Hispanics, the least. In 1980 the proportions of foreign-born Hispanic youth ranged from 6.4 percent in New Mexico to 58.3 percent in Florida.

Almost all Hispanic youth in Texas live in households in which one or more people speak Spanish; Texas had the largest proportion of such youth in 1980—94.0 percent. In all other states with at least 10,000 Hispanic youth in 1980, except Hawaii, at least half of Hispanic youth lived in Spanish-speaking households. In Hawaii in 1980, only 43.6 percent of Hispanic youth lived in Spanish-speaking households.

HISPANIC SUBGROUPS IN THE UNITED STATES

In 1980 there were 14.6 million Hispanics in the United States, as shown in table 6.6. Of these people, 8.7 million, or 59.8 percent, identified themselves as Mexican American; 2 million, or 13.8 percent, as Puerto Rican; and 803,000, or 5.5 percent, as Cuban American. Three million Hispanics, 20.9 percent, did not consider themselves to belong to any of these groups.[18] They are classified as "other" Hispanics.

Hispanic subgroups are concentrated in certain areas of the country. In 1980, 41.6 percent of the Mexican American population lived in California and 31.5 percent in Texas;[19] 49.0 percent of the Puerto Rican population lived in New York and another 12.1 percent in New Jersey;[20] 58.5 percent of the Cuban American population lived in Florida and 10.1 percent in New Jersey.[21] The Mexican American proportion of the total Hispanic population in states with at least 10,000 Hispanic youth varied from 92.2 percent in Texas to 2.3 percent in New York. The Puerto Rican proportion varied from 71.0 in Connecticut to less than 1 percent in New Mexico, Texas, and Arizona. Similarly, the Cuban American proportion

Table 6.6
Estimated Numbers of Hispanics, by Type of Hispanic Origin and Selected
State: United States, 1980

State	Total	Mexican Americans	Puerto Ricans	Cuban Americans	Other Hispanics
Total, all states	14,609,000	8,740,000	2,014,000	803,000	3,051,000
Arizona	441,000	396,000	4,000	1,000	39,000
California	4,544,000	3,637,000	93,000	61,000	753,000
Colorado	340,000	207,000	4,000	1,000	127,000
Connecticut	124,000	4,000	88,000	6,000	26,000
Florida	858,000	79,000	95,000	470,000	214,000
Georgia	61,000	28,000	8,000	6,000	20,000
Hawaii	71,000	9,000	19,000	*	43,000
Illinois	636,000	408,000	129,000	19,000	79,000
Indiana	87,000	57,000	13,000	2,000	15,000
Kansas	63,000	50,000	3,000	1,000	10,000
Louisiana	99,000	29,000	5,000	8,000	58,000
Maryland	65,000	12,000	9,000	5,000	38,000
Massachusetts	141,000	7,000	76,000	7,000	51,000
Michigan	163,000	112,000	12,000	4,000	34,000
Missouri	52,000	32,000	3,000	2,000	16,000
Nevada	54,000	33,000	2,000	4,000	16,000
New Jersey	492,000	13,000	244,000	81,000	154,000
New Mexico	477,000	234,000	2,000	1,000	241,000
New York	1,659,000	39,000	986,000	77,000	557,000
North Carolina	57,000	28,000	7,000	3,000	18,000
Ohio	120,000	53,000	32,000	3,000	31,000
Oklahoma	57,000	39,000	3,000	1,000	15,000
Oregon	66,000	45,000	2,000	1,000	18,000
Pennsylvania	154,000	19,000	92,000	6,000	37,000
Texas	2,986,000	2,752,000	23,000	14,000	196,000
Utah	60,000	38,000	1,000	*	21,000
Virginia	80,000	24,000	10,000	5,000	41,000
Washington	120,000	81,000	5,000	1,000	33,000
Wisconsin	63,000	41,000	10,000	1,000	10,000

Source: Derived from Bureau of the Census, Persons of Spanish Origin by State: 1980, p. 6.

Note: Detail may not add to total because of rounding. Selected states are those with at least
an estimated 10,000 Hispanics, aged 16 to 24.

*Fewer than an estimated 1,000 people.

of Hispanics varied from 54.8 percent in Florida to a tenth of a percent
in New Mexico. The "other" Hispanic population constituted 60.1 percent of the Hispanic population in Hawaii and almost as large a proportion in Maryland and Louisiana. Half of New Mexico's Hispanics were
"other" Hispanics. In Texas, where the Hispanic population is so largely
Mexican American, only 6.6 percent chose the "other" category to identify themselves.[22]

FOREIGN-BORN HISPANICS IN THE UNITED STATES

There were 4.2 million foreign-born Hispanics in the United States in 1980, and they constituted 28.6 percent of the total number of people who identified themselves as Hispanics in the census.[23] Most of them were among the 3.8 million people who were born in Spanish-speaking countries in the Western Hemisphere or in Spain, as shown in table 6.7. Two million people were born in Mexico; nine other Western Hemisphere countries and Spain were the birthplaces of at least 50,000 people. These 11 countries were the birthplaces of 94.5 percent of the immigrants from Spanish-speaking countries counted in 1980.[24]

By far the largest number of people born in Spanish-speaking countries lived in California in 1980, and they were overwhelmingly from Mexico; in all, one-third of the people born in Spanish-speaking countries who were identified in the 1980 census were born in Mexico and lived in Cali-

Table 6.7
Estimated Numbers of People Born in Spanish-Speaking Countries, by Selected State and Country of Birth: United States, 1980 (Numbers in thousands)

Country of birth	Total, all states	Arizona	California	Florida	Illinois	New Jersey	New York	Texas
Total, all Spanish-speaking countries	3,834	74[a]	1,576	479	213	157	409	538
Argentina	69	*	21	6	2	7	16	2
Colombia	144	*	16	24	5	20	48	4
Cuba	608	1	46	366	15	68	57	10
Dominican Republic	169	*	2	7	1	14	131	1
Ecuador	86	*	13	5	4	10	42	1
El Salvador	94	*	68	2	1	2	9	3
Guatemala	63	*	35	3	6	1	7	2
Mexico	2,199	71	1,278	14	168	3	11	498
Panama	61	NA	9	5	1	2	23	3
Peru	55	*	15	5	2	6	13	2
Spain	74	1	13	13	1	10	14	3

Source: Derived from Bureau of the Census, "Socioeconomic Characteristics of U.S. Foreign-born Population Detailed in Census Bureau Tabulations," pp. 2–4 and 11–13; Bureau of the Census, *1980 Census of Population, Detailed Population Characteristics, Part 4, Arizona*, p. 8.

Note: Selected states are those with at least an estimated 10,000 foreign-born Hispanics, aged 16 to 24. Countries of birth are those with at least 50,000 people.

NA = not available.

*Fewer than an estimated 1,000 people.

[a]Listed countries only.

fornia. More than half a million people born in Spanish-speaking countries lived in Texas in 1980, most of them from Mexico. Florida was home to 366,000 Cuban-born people and 113,000 immigrants from other Spanish-speaking countries. Nearly four out of five of Illinois' 213,000 people born in Spanish-speaking countries were from Mexico.[25]

THE EDUCATIONAL ATTAINMENT OF HISPANIC SUBGROUPS AND THE FOREIGN BORN

Mexican Americans, Puerto Ricans, Cuban Americans, and other Hispanics differ in the extent to which they may be undereducated. As already indicated, the differences are reflected in the differences in the state undereducation rates of Hispanic youth. Among the 1980 Hispanic high school sophomores reinterviewed in 1982 in the High School and Beyond study, Puerto Ricans were the most likely to have dropped out, followed by Mexican Americans and Cuban Americans. The rates of these groups ranged from 19.4 percent to 22.9 percent. In contrast, only 11.4 percent of "other" Hispanics were not in school and had not graduated with their class—a rate actually lower than that of non-Hispanic whites in the HS&B study.[26] As shown in table 6.8, there are similar differences in the high school graduation rates of adult members of these groups. Among Hispanics aged 25 and older, "other" Hispanics and Cuban Americans are the best educated; in 1980, 57.4 percent of the "other" Hispanic population and 55.3 percent of Cuban Americans, in comparison with 40.1 percent of Puerto Ricans and 37.6 percent of Mexican Americans, were high school graduates.[27] Hispanic youth in Florida, where Cuban Americans predominate, are among the least likely to be undereducated, and youth in New Jersey, where there are many Cuban Americans and "other" Hispanics, have lower rates than Hispanic youth in New York, where the Puerto Ricans constitute a larger proportion of the Hispanic population. Hispanic youth in New Mexico, where the "other" population is as large as the Mexican American population, have lower undereducation rates than those in Arizona, Texas, and California, where Mexican Americans predominate.

Foreign-born Hispanics also differ in their educational attainment, as shown in table 6.9. Like the differences in the educational attainment of the Hispanic subgroups, the differences in the educational attainment of Hispanic national origin groups parallel the differences in the undereducation rates of foreign-born Hispanic youth in the states in which the various immigrant groups have settled. People from Peru, Panama, and Argentina are the best educated; their 1980 high school graduation rates were 77.3 percent, 74.0 percent, and 70.9 percent, respectively, in comparison with 54.9 percent for Cuban-born Hispanics, 30.1 percent for

Table 6.8
High School Graduation Rates of Hispanics, Aged 25 and Older, by Type of Hispanic Origin and Selected State: United States, 1980

State	Mexican Americans	Puerto Ricans	Cuban Americans	Other Hispanics
Total, all states	37.6	40.1	55.3	57.4
Arizona	41.7	70.2	74.1	61.1
California	38.1	56.7	61.5	61.3
Colorado	46.6	79.5	84.2	50.0
Connecticut	57.9	30.3	66.5	59.4
Florida	35.2	53.7	53.0	62.6
Georgia	38.0	79.0	81.1	69.6
Hawaii	80.4	53.5	*	65.9
Illinois	31.1	32.6	57.0	60.6
Indiana	42.2	45.3	67.4	66.3
Kansas	49.0	75.3	78.8	66.4
Louisiana	47.9	67.8	66.1	59.8
Maryland	57.4	78.7	80.1	74.2
Massachusetts	64.7	31.0	63.8	52.1
Michigan	43.4	44.1	72.4	64.2
Missouri	51.0	80.8	76.9	67.5
Nevada	48.7	55.1	63.3	68.3
New Jersey	52.6	35.7	47.2	52.9
New Mexico	46.4	*	*	53.9
New York	51.1	36.9	53.5	47.2
North Carolina	36.1	74.6	82.7	61.2
Ohio	40.1	39.9	81.7	65.1
Oklahoma	42.1	88.1	82.4	66.7
Oregon	48.6	73.8	76.8	71.7
Pennsylvania	46.0	30.7	72.0	63.5
Texas	33.4	76.1	75.6	53.1
Utah	48.5	57.0	*	57.3
Virginia	51.2	81.0	91.0	76.4
Washington	43.3	77.8	86.9	73.6
Wisconsin	40.3	35.8	87.8	69.1

Source: Derived from Bureau of the Census, *1980 Census of Population, General Social and Economic Characteristics, Part 1, United States Summary,* p. 163; and selected state parts, table 99, various pages.

Note: Selected states are those with at least an estimated 10,000 Hispanics, aged 16 to 24.
*Base number less than an estimated 1,000.

Hispanics born in the Dominican Republic, and 21.3 percent for those born in Mexico.[28] People born in Cuba, the Dominican Republic, and Mexico who came to the United States in the period between 1970 and 1980 had lower levels of schooling than the total immigrant population from those countries. More than a tenth of the 1970–80 Cuban immigrants, a fifth of the Dominicans, and a third of the Mexican immigrants recorded in the decennial census had completed fewer than five years of

Table 6.9
High School Graduation Rates of People Born in Selected Spanish-Speaking Countries, Aged 25 and Older, and of 1970–80 Immigrants, by Country of Birth: United States, 1980

Country of birth	Total	1970—1980 immigrants
Argentina	70.9	NA
Colombia	62.8	NA
Cuba	54.9	40.2
Dominican Republic	30.1	27.1
Ecuador	56.0	NA
El Salvador	41.4	NA
Guatemala	42.7	NA
Mexico	21.3	17.0
Panama	74.0	NA
Peru	77.3	NA
Spain	46.9	NA

Source: Derived from Bureau of the Census, "Socioeconomic Characteristics of U.S. For-eign-born Population Detailed in Census Bureau Tabulations," pp. 5–8; and idem, *1980 Census of Population, Detailed Population Characteristics, Part 1, United States Summary*, p. 13.

NA = not available.

schooling. In contrast, two-thirds of recent immigrants from South American countries as a whole were high school graduates, and only 4.5 percent had completed fewer than five years of schooling.[29]

Foreign-born Hispanic youth in states in which most immigrants come from Mexico, such as Illinois, Texas, California, and Arizona, are more likely to be undereducated than not, and they are more likely not to be enrolled in school and not to have high school diplomas than Hispanics born in this country and living in Spanish-speaking households. Foreign-born Hispanic youth in states in which Cubans and other non-Mexican national origin groups form the majority of the foreign-born Hispanic population, such as Florida, New Jersey, and New York, on the other hand, are much less likely to be undereducated than foreign-born youth in the states with Mexican-born majorities. Moreover, foreign-born Hispanic youth in Pennsylvania, New Jersey, Connecticut, Massachusetts, and New York are less likely to be undereducated than the native-born, Spanish language-background, largely Puerto Rican youth in those states.

IMMIGRATION FROM SPANISH-SPEAKING COUNTRIES SINCE 1980

Spanish-speaking countries currently contribute the largest numbers of immigrants to the United States after the Asian countries. Moreover,

Mexico is the country of birth of the largest number of people immigrating annually from any single country. Since 1980, nearly 1.4 million people born in Spanish-speaking countries have legally entered the United States, as shown in table 6.10. The largest number—nearly 600,000—were born in Mexico. About 192,000 were born in the Dominican Republic and 146,000, in Cuba. Colombia was the country of birth of the largest number of South American immigrants, 91,000.[30]

People born in Spanish-speaking countries are immigrating to the United States at the rate of about 164,000 per year. In fiscal year 1988, 199,893 immigrants born in 18 Latin American countries and Spain were legally admitted. They included 95,039 born in Mexico, 27,189 born in the Dominican Republic, and 17,558 born in Cuba. There were more than 10,000 each who were born in El Salvador and Colombia.[31]

Table 6.10
Estimated Numbers and Yearly Average Numbers of Immigrants Born in Spanish-Speaking Countries Admitted to the United States between April 1, 1980, and September 30, 1988, and Numbers Admitted in Fiscal Year 1988, by Country of Birth

Country of birth	Total	Average per year, 1980—88	Admitted, FY 1988
Total	1,393,000	164,000	199,893
Argentina	18,000	2,000	2,371
Bolivia	8,000	1,000	1,038
Chile	18,000	2,000	2,137
Colombia	91,000	11,000	10,322
Costa Rica	11,000	1,000	1,351
Cuba	146,000	17,000	17,558
Dominican Republic	192,000	23,000	27,189
Ecuador	39,000	5,000	4,716
El Salvador	80,000	9,000	12,045
Guatemala	38,000	5,000	5,723
Honduras	31,000	4,000	4,302
Mexico	597,000	70,000	95,039
Nicaragua	25,000	3,000	3,311
Panama	24,000	3,000	2,486
Paraguay	2,000	*	483
Peru	40,000	5,000	5,936
Spain	13,000	2,000	1,483
Uruguay	6,000	1,000	612
Venezuela	13,000	2,000	1,791

Source: Derived from Immigration and Naturalization Service, unpublished tabulations.

Note: The numbers of immigrants admitted between April 1 and September 30, 1980, are estimated to be half the totals for fiscal year 1980.

*Fewer than an estimated 1,000 per year.

The numbers recorded by the Immigration and Naturalization Service represent only those admitted for legal permanent residence in the United States. To them must be added an unknown number of refugees from political turmoil and economic hardship in Central America and elsewhere who are coming without legal sanction. Many of them are among the least educated.

Immigrants born in Spanish-speaking countries are continuing to flow into the states in which their compatriots already reside. Thus nearly half of the 1987 Mexican-born legal immigrants intended to reside in California and 28 percent in Texas, as shown in table 6.11. Two out of five Cuban-born immigrants planned to reside in Florida. Nearly two-thirds of the Dominicans were headed toward New York.[32] If these immigrants have the same characteristics as previous immigrants born in these countries, the populations of at-risk Hispanic youth are likely to be growing in a number of states.

Table 6.11
Immigrants Admitted to the United States in Fiscal Year 1987, by Selected State of Intended Residence and Spanish-Speaking Country of Birth

Country of birth	Total, all states	Arizona	California	Florida	Illinois	New Jersey	New York	Texas
Total, all Spanish-speaking countries	169,540	3,545	46,951	30,553	6,709	8,334	30,043	22,220
Colombia	11,700	38	859	2,291	367	1,958	3,706	389
Cuba	28,916	40	685	24,287	255	562	1,830	294
Dominican Republic	24,858	3	90	874	53	2,595	15,860	97
Ecuador	4,641	11	378	242	148	755	2,611	65
El Salvador	10,693	39	5,620	310	133	565	1,609	593
Guatemala	5,729	28	2,344	306	543	230	914	201
Honduras	4,751	26	684	761	91	339	1,474	255
Mexico	72,351	3,314	35,228	772	4,959	168	652	20,166
Peru	5,901	46	1,063	710	160	1,162	1,387	160

Source: Derived from Immigration and Naturalization Service, *Statistical Yearbook of the Immigration and Naturalization Service, 1987*, pp. 32–34.

Note: Selected states are those with at least an estimated 10,000 foreign-born Hispanics, aged 16 to 24, in 1980.

UNDEREDUCATED HISPANIC YOUTH IN THE REMAINDER OF THIS CENTURY

In April 1980 when the decennial census was conducted, there were 923,000 undereducated Hispanic youth, aged 16 to 24. They constituted

32.2 percent of all Hispanic youth, aged 16 to 24, who were identified in the decennial census. The following fall, the Census Bureau's current population survey of school enrollment counted 885,000 undereducated civilian Hispanics not living in group quarters; they were 35.2 percent of civilian non-institutional Hispanics, aged 16 to 24.[33] By fall 1988 the current population survey identified 1,169,000 undereducated civilian non-institutional Hispanics, 35.7 percent of civilian Hispanic youth who were not living in group quarters in the 1988 sample.[34] (See table 1.1 in chapter 1.) Among undereducated civilian non-institutional Hispanic youth, aged 14 to 24, the proportion completing no more than eight years of schooling fell from about half in 1980 to 44.0 percent in 1986.[35] (See table 1.2 in chapter 1.) Even so, Hispanics may be losing ground in terms of the years of schooling completed. Fifty-six percent of the undereducated Hispanics, aged 16 to 24, identified in the 1980 census, had completed at least the ninth grade before discontinuing school, but only half of the undereducated civilian non-institutional Hispanics in this age group identified in the October 1988 current population survey had completed this much education. In contrast, the proportion of undereducated non-Hispanic youth completing at least the ninth grade has remained at about 80 percent during the eighties.[36]

An increasing proportion of undereducated youth are Hispanic. Hispanics constituted 15.7 percent of undereducated youth in April 1980. They were the second largest minority group after African Americans. In October 1980 undereducated Hispanics in the sample constituted 17.4 percent of all civilian noninstitutional youth who were undereducated, and they numbered almost as many as blacks.[37] By October 1988 undereducated Hispanics constituted 27.6 percent of the current population survey total and had surpassed blacks in numbers.[38]

The Hispanic population in the United States is growing faster than the non-Hispanic white population and the African American population. Hispanic school-age children and youth will constitute increasingly larger proportions of the school-age population in the future. Using the Bureau of the Census's moderate assumptions about fertility, mortality, and net immigration, the Hispanic population is projected to grow on the average annually by 2.8 percent between 1985 and 1990, by 2.5 percent between 1990 and 1995, and by 2.2 percent between 1995 and the year 2000. At the same time the non-Hispanic white population is projected to grow by 0.6 percent, 0.4 percent, and 0.3 percent; and the African American population, by 1.5 percent, 1.4 percent, and 1.2 percent.[39] These assumptions underlie the projection of the growth of the population of school-age children and youth in the United States from 44.3 million in 1985 to 48.8 million by the year 2000. (See table 1.3 in chapter 1.) About 1.9 million of the increase, following these assumptions, will consist of Hispanics, and African Americans will contribute 1.7 million

and non-Hispanic whites, 1.5 million. The number of school-age Hispanics will grow from 4.3 million, or 9.6 percent of the total, to 6.2 million, or 12.7 percent of the total. The African American population will
grow from 6.6 million to 8.3 million, and its proportion, from 14.9 percent to 17.1 percent. In comparison, the non-Hispanic white school-age
population will increase from 32.3 million in 1985 to 33.8 million in the
year 2000, but the proportion of whites will decrease from 72.8 percent
to 69.4 percent of the total.[40]

The projected numbers and proportions of minorities based on the
moderate assumptions are minimums. Hispanics and other minorities
will very likely constitute larger proportions, and non-Hispanic whites
smaller proportions, of the school-age population by the year 2000. Legal
immigration has already outpaced the net average annual immigration assumed at the moderate level for all groups. In the case of Hispanics, as
already noted, people born in Spanish-speaking countries were being legally admitted to the United States at the rate of 164,000 per year between
1980 and 1988, and nearly 200,000 were admitted in fiscal year 1988.[41] At
the moderate level, the total net annual Hispanic immigration is assumed
to be 143,200, including 138,200 legal immigrants, 5,000 Puerto Ricans
moving from the island to the mainland, and no undocumented immigration. If the high net annual immigration of Hispanics is assumed—
361,500 including both legal and undocumented entrants[42]—and moderate growth is assumed otherwise, the projected number of school-age Hispanics in the year 2000 will be 7.5 million, and their proportion will be 14.7
percent of this age group.[43]

Native-born and foreign-born Hispanics have special needs that must
be met by the schools. The disparity between the undereducation rates
of native-born Hispanics from monolingual English-speaking homes
and those from Spanish-speaking homes demands programs that address linguistic differences and build upon the strengths of these students. Hispanics as a group have failed to make gains in the eighties, and
the effects on them of the school reform movement, as on other "at-risk"
youth, have still to be felt. Whether Hispanic youth in the year 2000 will
be less likely to be undereducated than Hispanics in the eighties will depend on whether their increasing numbers and proportions call forth
genuine efforts to address their unique linguistic and other needs and
whether U.S. education is restructured to provide a greater measure of
equity for all students and not just excellence for those already prepared
to achieve it.

NOTES

1. Bureau of the Census, U.S. Department of Commerce, *School Enrollment—Social and Economic Characteristics of Students: October 1988 and 1987*
(Washington, D.C.: U.S. Government Printing Office, 1990), pp. 5–6.

2. Poverty among African Americans in 1986 was about the same as it had been in 1979, but it was 1.2 times more prevalent among whites and 1.3 times more prevalent among Hispanics because these groups, unlike blacks, failed to regain some of the loss they had experienced in 1982 and 1983. Bureau of the Census, U.S. Department of Commerce, *Poverty in the United States, 1986* (Washington, D.C.: U.S. Government Printing Office, 1988), pp. 5–6.

3. Bureau of the Census, U.S. Department of Commerce, *1980 Census of Population, General Social and Economic Characteristics, Part 1, United States Summary* (Washington, D.C.: U.S. Government Printing Office, 1983), p. 126.

4. Ibid., p. 13.

5. Ibid., p. 126.

6. Ibid., p. 118.

7. Bureau of the Census, U.S. Department of Commerce, *Persons of Spanish Origin by State: 1980* (Washington, D.C.: U.S. Government Printing Office, 1982), p. 8.

8. In 1976, 1.3 percent of the 11.2 million Hispanics of all ages reported non-Spanish non-English language backgrounds. National Center for Education Statistics, U.S. Department of Health, Education and Welfare, *Place of Birth and Language Characteristics of Persons of Hispanic Origin in the United States, Spring 1976,* NCES Bulletin 78-135, October 20, 1978, p. 5.

9. Significant at the 68 percent confidence level.

10. The difference between 19.1 percent for Hispanics and 18.7 percent for Asian/Pacific youth is not statistically significant.

11. Bureau of the Census, *Persons of Spanish Origin,* p. 12.

12. The difference between 18.2 percent for Florida and 21.3 percent for New Jersey is significant at the 68 percent confidence level.

13. The difference between 21.7 percent for native-born English language-background Hispanics and 23.7 percent for native-born non-English language-background Hispanics in Florida is not statistically significant.

14. The difference between 16.7 percent for native-born English language-background Hispanics and 21.2 percent for foreign-born non-English language-background Hispanics in New Jersey is significant at the 68 percent confidence level.

15. The difference between 21.0 percent for Hispanics and 16.5 percent for whites in Florida is significant at the 68 percent confidence level; the difference between 13.6 percent for Hispanics and 11.0 percent for whites in New Mexico is not statistically significant.

16. The difference between 26.9 percent for Hispanics and 23.5 percent for blacks in Illinois is significant at the 68 percent confidence level.

17. Nationally, Puerto Ricans, aged 15 and older, for whom poverty status was determined were 1.7 times more likely to be poor than other Hispanics in 1980. Bureau of the Census, *General Social and Economic Characteristics,* p. 168.

18. Bureau of the Census, *Persons of Spanish Origin,* pp. 6 and 8. Of 14.6 million Hispanics in the 50 states and the District of Columbia in 1980, 974,000 were born on the island of Puerto Rico. Bureau of the Census, U.S. Department of Commerce, *1980 Census of Population, Detailed Population Characteristics, Part 1, United States Summary* (Washington, D.C.: U.S. Government Printing Office, 1984), p. 8. As native-born citizens, they are not included in the numbers of foreign-born Hispanics.

19. Bureau of the Census, *Persons of Spanish Origin,* p. 12.

20. Ibid., p. 13.

21. Ibid.

22. Ibid., p. 8.

23. Bureau of the Census, *Detailed Population Characteristics,* p. 8.

24. Bureau of the Census, U.S. Department of Commerce, "Socioeconomic Characteristics of U.S. Foreign-born Population Detailed in Census Bureau Tabulations," press release, October 17, 1984, pp. 2–4.

25. Ibid., pp. 11–13.

26. Rafael Valdivieso and Martha Galindo, eds., *"Make Something Happen": Hispanics and Urban High School Reform,* Vol. 2 (Washington, D.C.: Hispanic Policy Development Project, 1984), p. 57.

27. Bureau of the Census, *General Social and Economic Characteristics,* p. 163.

28. Bureau of the Census, "Socioeconomic Characteristics," pp. 5–8.

29. Bureau of the Census, *Detailed Population Characteristics,* p. 13.

30. Immigration and Naturalization Service, U.S. Department of Justice, unpublished tabulations.

31. Ibid.

32. Immigration and Naturalization Service, U.S. Department of Justice, *Statistical Yearbook of the Immigration and Naturalization Service, 1987* (Washington, D.C.: U.S. Government Printing Office, 1988), pp. 32–34.

33. Bureau of the Census, U.S. Department of Commerce, *School Enrollment—Social and Economic Characteristics of Students: October 1981 and 1980* (Washington, D.C.: U.S. Government Printing Office, 1985), pp. 60–61.

34. Bureau of the Census, *School Enrollment: October 1988 and 1987,* p. 6. See also comments in notes 17 and 20 in chapter 1 on CPS sample revisions and the institution of independent control numbers for estimating the numbers of Hispanics; these changes affect the reliability of comparisons of data for Hispanics over time.

35. Bureau of the Census, *School Enrollment: October 1981 and 1980,* p. 75; and October 1986, p. 26.

36. National Center for Education Statistics, U.S. Department of Education, *Dropout Rates in the United States: 1988* (Washington, D.C.: U.S. Government Printing Office, 1989), p. 22.

37. Bureau of the Census, *School Enrollment, October 1981 and 1980,* pp. 60–61.

38. Bureau of the Census, *School Enrollment: October 1988 and 1987,* p. 6.

39. Bureau of the Census, U.S. Department of Commerce, *Projections of the Hispanic Population: 1983 to 2080* (Washington, D.C.: U.S. Government Printing Office, 1986), p. 10.

40. Ibid., p. 14.

41. Immigration and Naturalization Service, unpublished tabulations.

42. Bureau of the Census, *Projections,* pp. 24–25.

43. Ibid., pp. 14 and 53.

7

Non-Hispanic White Minority
Youth Who Are Undereducated

After Asians and Pacific Islanders, non-Hispanic white youth from homes
in which one or more people speak a language other than English are the
least likely to be out of school without high school diplomas. In 1980 one
in eight was undereducated—fewer, proportionally, than among white
majority youth and many fewer than among other minority youth except
Asians and Pacific Islanders. There were 337,000 non-Hispanic white minority young people in the United States who were not enrolled in school
and had not completed the twelfth grade. More than four out of five were
born in this country. Undereducated white minority youth constituted 5.7
percent of all undereducated youth, and foreign-born white minority
youth, 11.0 percent of foreign-born youth, in the United States in 1980.

Non-Hispanic white minority youth are part of a non-Hispanic white
language minority population that included nearly 14 million people with
21 different language backgrounds in 1980. They are part of a total language minority population that numbered 34.6 million people in 1980 and
consisted of all of the people with Spanish, non-Spanish European, Near
Eastern, Asian, Pacific Islander, American Indian, Alaska Native, and African language backgrounds identified in the census.[1] The largest groups
of non-Hispanic white minority people consist of those with French, German, Italian, and Polish language backgrounds. Most of these people were
born in the United States.[2] Some are aging populations with few young
people in the age group that is the focus of this study. Other groups are
younger and the size of some groups is being augmented by new
immigration.

For whites, as for Asians and African Americans, a non-English language background is associated with a reduced likelihood of undereducation. Although their undereducation risk is greater than that of Asians and Pacific Islanders, native-born non-Hispanic white minority youth are less likely to be undereducated than native-born non-Hispanic white youth with monolingual English-speaking backgrounds. The overall undereducation rate of non-Hispanic white minority youth in 1980 was 12.0 percent; that of native-born white minority youth was 11.2 percent. The comparable rate for white majority youth was 13 percent; for native-born Asians and Pacific Islanders with language minority backgrounds it was 6.3 percent.

The following sections of this chapter contain discussions of the characteristics and geographical distribution of undereducated non-Hispanic white minority youth, and the undereducation rates of this group, including those who were born in this country and those who were born abroad. They contain analyses of the differences between the rates of native-born white minority youth and those of white majority youth in the 44 states in which there were at least an estimated 10,000 non-Hispanic white minority youth, aged 16 to 24, and between the rates of native-born and foreign-born white minority youth in the 10 states with at least 10,000 foreign-born youth in 1980.

The final sections deal with the numbers and geographical distribution of European and other language minority groups that make up the non-Hispanic white minority population in the United States and the numbers, distribution, and educational attainment of people born in the countries in which the languages of these groups are spoken who lived in the United States in 1980. The chapter concludes with a discussion of immigration from these countries since 1980 and the probable effect of immigration and other factors on the undereducation risk and possible numbers of undereducated non-Hispanic white minority youth in the future.

The information on language minority groups and foreign-born groups in 1980 is from the published volumes of the 1980 census. The Immigration and Naturalization Service provided the information on legal immigrants since 1980.

THE NUMBERS AND CHARACTERISTICS OF UNDEREDUCATED NON-HISPANIC WHITE MINORITY YOUTH

In 1980 there were 337,000 non-Hispanic white youth from language minority backgrounds who were not enrolled in school and had not completed the twelfth grade, as shown in table 7.1. Two hundred and seventy-seven thousand of them—82.2 percent—were native-born citizens of the United States; 60,000 were born in the countries where the languages of

Table 7.1
Estimated Numbers and Distribution of Undereducated Non-Hispanic White Minority Youth, by Nativity and Selected Characteristic: United States, 1980

Characteristic	Total		Native born		Foreign born	
	Number	Percent	Number	Percent	Number	Percent
Total	337,000	100.0	277,000	100.0	60,000	100.0
Gender						
Males	177,000	52.6	148,000	53.4	29,000	48.5
Females	160,000	47.4	129,000	46.6	31,000	51.5
Age						
16 to 19	144,000	42.7	125,000	45.3	19,000	31.0
20 to 24	193,000	57.3	152,000	54.7	41,000	69.0
Poverty status in 1979[1]						
Above poverty level	267,000	79.1	218,000	78.6	49,000	81.7
Below poverty level	64,000	19.1	54,000	19.6	10,000	17.0
Years of schooling completed						
Fewer than 5	14,000	4.2	8,000	2.8	6,000	10.8
5 to 8	76,000	22.5	57,000	20.4	19,000	32.0
9 to 11	247,000	73.3	213,000	76.8	34,000	57.2

Note: Percentages calculated on unrounded numbers. Detail may not add to total because of rounding.

[1]Not determined for people living in group quarters.

their backgrounds are spoken or elsewhere abroad. Those who were foreign-born were 1.6 times more likely to be undereducated than their native-born counterparts, as shown in table 7.2. Foreign-born white minority youth differ from their native-born counterparts in other ways as well.

Like undereducated white majority youth, undereducated non-Hispanic white minority youth in general are likely to be male and aged 20 to 24. However, among foreign-born white minority youth, women predominate and they have higher undereducation rates than foreign-born men. In 1982, 52.6 percent of native-born undereducated youth and 48.5 percent of those who were foreign born were men. The undereducation rates of native-born women and men were 10.7 percent and 11.8 percent, respectively; those of foreign-born women and men were 19.4 percent and 16.0 percent.

The differences in the comparative numbers of undereducated teenagers and older non-Hispanic white minority youth are largely attribut-

Table 7.2
Estimated Numbers of Undereducated Non-Hispanic White Minority Youth and White Minority Undereducation Rates, by Nativity and Selected Characteristic: United States, 1980

Characteristic	Total		Native born		Foreign born	
	Number	Rate	Number	Rate	Number	Rate
Total	337,000	12.0	277,000	11.2	60,000	17.6
Gender						
Males	177,000	12.3	148,000	11.8	29,000	16.0
Females	160,000	11.7	129,000	10.7	31,000	19.4
Age						
16 to 19	144,000	10.9	125,000	10.5	19,000	14.8
20 to 24	193,000	13.0	152,000	11.9	41,000	19.3
Poverty status in 1979[1]						
Above poverty level	267,000	11.3	218,000	10.3	49,000	19.3
Below poverty level	64,000	19.1	54,000	20.2	10,000	14.9

[1]Not determined for people living in group quarters.

able to the foreign-born group. In 1980 about the same number of native-born young adults per year of age as native-born teenagers were undereducated, while the number of foreign-born young adults per year of age exceeded that of foreign-born teenagers by a factor of 1.8. Both native-born and foreign-born teenagers are less at risk of undereducation than older youth. Among the native-born, 10.5 percent of teenagers and 11.9 percent of young adults were undereducated in 1980; among the foreign-born, the comparative rates were 14.8 percent of teenagers and 19.3 percent of young adults.

Native-born non-Hispanic white minority youth are no more likely to come from families with incomes below the poverty level than white majority youth. Poverty is much more prevalent among the foreign-born in this group, as it is among all foreign-born youth. In 1980, of those for whom poverty status is determined—a group that excludes youth living in college dormitories, military group quarters, and institutions of various kinds—11.3 percent of native-born white minority youth and 11.1 percent of majority youth were from poor families. In comparison, foreign-born white minority youth were twice as likely to be poor: 21.3 percent were from poor families. (See table 3.7 in chapter 3.) Fifty-four thousand undereducated native-born white minority youth and 10,000 undereducated foreign-born white minority youth in 1980 were from families with incomes below the poverty level.

As it is for white majority youth and other native-born youth in general, poverty is associated with a greater risk of undereducation for native-born non-Hispanic white minority youth. (See table 3.6 in chapter 3.) Its role in connection with the undereducation of foreign-born white minority youth is less clear. In 1980 native-born white youth from families with incomes below the poverty level were twice as likely to be undereducated as those from more economically advantaged families: 20.2 percent in comparison with 10.3 percent. Foreign-born white minority youth from poor families, on the other hand, were less likely to be undereducated than more advantaged foreign-born youth; their rate was 14.9 percent in comparison with 19.3 percent for those from families with incomes above the poverty level.

Youth who are working contribute income to their families and, in many cases, their contributions may be enough to raise their family incomes above the poverty level. Working means that a higher proportion of youth are not enrolled in school; if they are not already high school graduates, they are, by definition, undereducated. Whether the financial contributions of these youth raise their family incomes above the poverty level and working interferes with school attendance to a greater extent among foreign-born non-Hispanic white minority youth than among other foreign-born youth, distorting their undereducation rate, cannot be determined from the data available in this study.

Native-born and foreign-born non-Hispanic white minority youth, like other native-born and foreign-born youth, differ considerably in the number of years of schooling they complete before discontinuing their education, especially in the proportions with minimal education. Undereducated native-born white minority youth are somewhat less likely than undereducated white majority youth to stay in school at least through the ninth grade; in 1980, 76.8 percent of white minority youth and 81.0 percent of majority youth had completed at least nine years of schooling. In contrast, only 57.2 percent of undereducated foreign-born white minority youth had achieved this much schooling. Foreign-born white minority youth were nearly four times more likely to have completed fewer than five years of schooling than native-born white youth. One in ten had less than a fifth grade education in comparison with fewer than 3 percent of native-born white youth. (See table 2.6 in chapter 2.)

UNDEREDUCATED NON-HISPANIC WHITE MINORITY YOUTH IN THE STATES

Undereducated non-Hispanic white minority youth are found in all states, but there are many more in certain states than in others. California, New York, and Texas, with 36,000, 35,000, and 22,000, respectively, had the largest numbers in 1980, as shown in figure 7.1. There were be-

Figure 7.1
Undereducated Non-Hispanic White Minority Youth in the United States, 1980

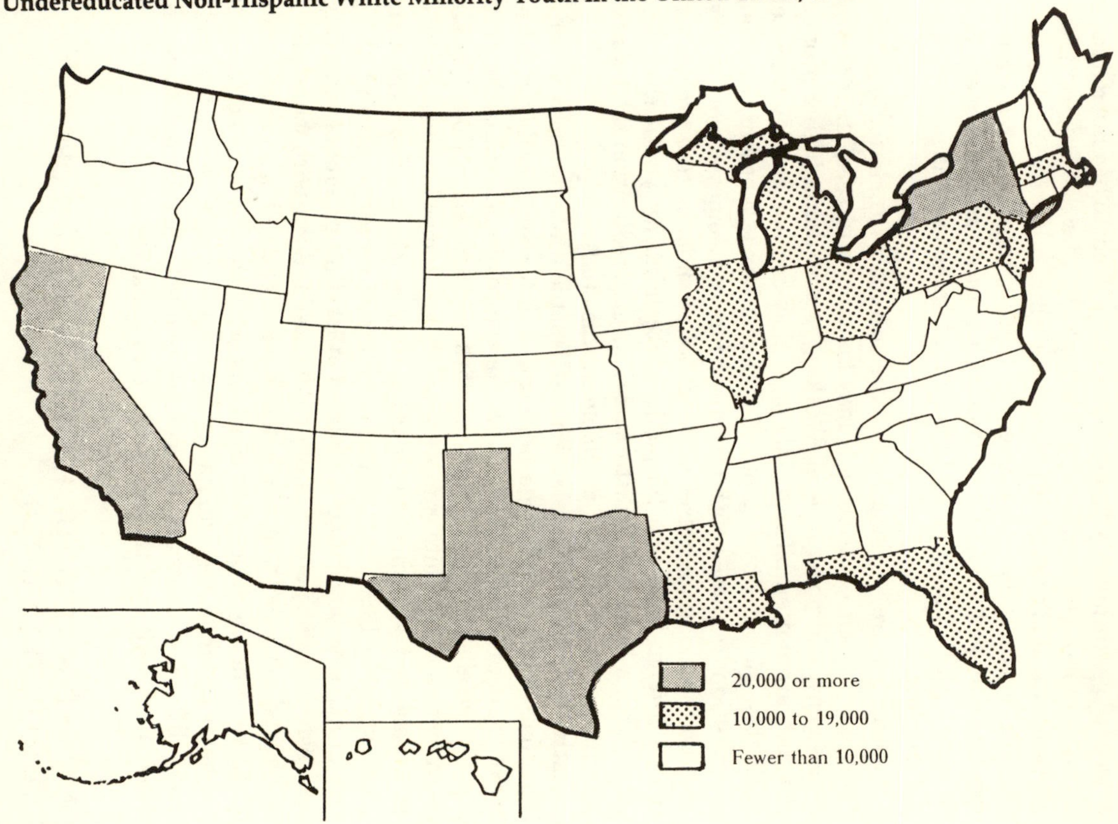

20,000 or more
10,000 to 19,000
Fewer than 10,000

tween 13,000 and 19,000 in eight other states—Massachusetts, Illinois, Pennsylvania, Louisiana, Michigan, New Jersey, Ohio, and Florida. (See table 2.8 in chapter 2.) Undereducated white minority youth constituted substantial proportions of undereducated youth in two states: in Rhode Island they were a quarter; in Massachusetts, 18.4 percent. They comprised at least 10 percent in the other New England states and in North Dakota and Louisiana. (See table 2.9 in chapter 2.) The largest group of undereducated foreign-born white minority youth—11,000—lived in New York; there were groups of 8,000 in California and Massachusetts and 5,000 in Illinois.

THE STATE UNDEREDUCATION RATES OF NON-HISPANIC WHITE MINORITY YOUTH

Non-Hispanic white minority youth living in the South are more likely to be undereducated than those in other regions of the country where the regional undereducation rates are similar. The range of rates by state is much greater, however, reflecting the differences in the non-Hispanic white minority populations in individual states. (See tables 3.9 and 3.10 in chapter 3.) In 1980, in the 44 states with at least 10,000 non-Hispanic white minority youth, the rates ranged from 6.2 percent of those living in Utah to 20.4 percent of those living in Rhode Island: Rhode Island youth were more than three times more likely to be out of school before completing 12 years of schooling than their counterparts in Utah, as illustrated in figure 7.2.

The variation in the rates of native-born non-Hispanic white minority youth parallels that of the rates of white majority youth. In general, native-born white minority youth living in the southeastern states, like white majority youth there, are more likely to be undereducated than youth in the northern tier of states, including New England. The 1980 range for native-born white minority youth was from 5.7 percent in Utah to 20.6 in Kentucky, as shown in table 7.3.

Native-born white minority youth living in Kentucky, Louisiana, Mississippi, South Carolina, Arkansas, Tennessee, and Alabama are the most likely to be undereducated; at least 17 percent of this group in these states were undereducated in 1980. Native-born white minority youth living in Utah, Minnesota, Nebraska, New York, New Jersey, Connecticut, and Massachusetts are the least likely to be undereducated; in 1980 fewer than 9 percent were undereducated.

In almost all of the states, as it is nationally, having a non-English language background is an advantage for native-born non-Hispanic whites. In 1980 native-born non-Hispanic white minority youth were less likely or no more likely to be undereducated than native-born youth from monolingual English-speaking backgrounds in 42 of the 44 states with at least

Figure 7.2
Undereducation Rates of Non-Hispanic White Minority Youth, 1980

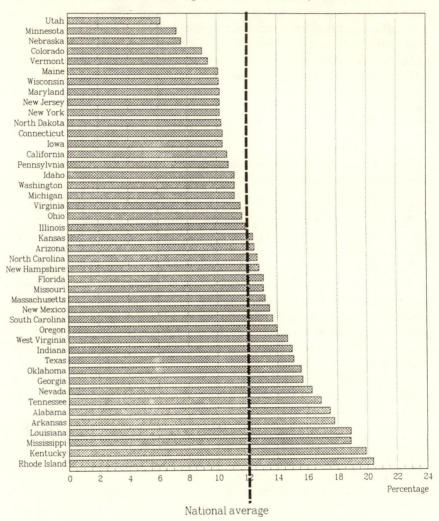

an estimated 10,000 white minority youth, as shown in table 7.3. In two states—Louisiana and North Dakota—they had a marginally higher risk of undereducation than white majority youth.[3]

The rates of foreign-born white minority youth vary even more widely than those of native-born white minority youth, as shown in table 7.4. In the states with at least 10,000 foreign-born non-Hispanic white minority youth, aged 16 to 24, they ranged from 12.9 percent in Texas to 33.0 percent in Massachusetts in 1980.[4]

Table 7.3

Undereducation Rates of Native-Born Non-Hispanic White Minority and White Majority Youth, by Selected State: United States, 1980

State	White minority	White majority	State	White minority	White majority
Total, all states	11.2	13.0	Missouri	13.2	14.6
			Nebraska	8.0	8.0
Alabama	17.3	18.9	Nevada	17.1	16.9
Arizona	12.3	12.9	New Hampshire	12.4	13.1
Arkansas	17.6	18.8	New Jersey	8.3	9.0
California	10.1	11.7	New Mexico	13.6	11.0
Colorado	9.1	10.6	New York	8.2	8.7
Connecticut	8.4	9.7	North Carolina	12.8	18.3
Florida	13.1	16.5	North Dakota	10.2	7.7
Georgia	16.4	20.1	Ohio	11.7	13.3
Idaho	11.3	14.3	Oklahoma	17.0	15.3
Illinois	10.4	11.3	Oregon	14.1	15.0
Indiana	15.2	14.7	Pennsylvania	10.6	9.9
Iowa	10.8	9.4	Rhode Island	14.2	12.2
Kansas	12.5	11.5	South Carolina	17.9	17.9
Kentucky	20.6	24.0	Tennessee	17.4	19.9
Louisiana	19.2	17.0	Texas	15.3	14.7
Maine	10.1	12.4	Utah	5.7	11.9
Maryland	9.9	12.5	Vermont	9.5	10.3
Massachusetts	8.6	8.2	Virginia	11.8	15.6
Michigan	9.7	11.9	Washington	11.4	13.0
Minnesota	7.4	7.4	West Virginia	14.4	19.4
Mississippi	18.7	18.8	Wisconsin	9.9	9.5

Note: Selected states are those with at least an estimated 10,000 non-Hispanic white minority youth, aged 16 to 24.

In addition to being more at risk of undereducation in some states than in others, most foreign-born non-Hispanic white minority youth are at greater risk in comparison with native-born white minority youth in their states as they are nationally. As shown in table 7.4, in Florida and Texas they are no more likely than native-born white minority youth to be undereducated.[5] In all of the other states with at least 10,000 foreign-born white minority youth, however, they are more likely to be undereducated than their native-born counterparts. In Massachusetts, the educational gap was more than 24 percentage points in 1980: foreign-born white minority youth in Massachusetts were 3.8 times more likely to be undereducated than native-born white minority youth.

NATIVE-BORN AND FOREIGN-BORN NON-HISPANIC WHITE MINORITY YOUTH IN THE STATES

Although foreign-born non-Hispanic white minority youth are more likely to be undereducated than native-born white minority youth in al-

Table 7.4
Undereducation Rates of Non-Hispanic White Minority Youth, by Nativity and Selected State: United States, 1980

State	Native born	Foreign born
Total, all states	11.2	17.6
California	10.1	13.4
Connecticut	8.4	21.2
Florida	13.1	13.4
Illinois	10.4	20.8
Massachusetts	8.6	33.0
Michigan	9.7	23.4
New Jersey	8.3	19.7
New York	8.2	20.1
Pennsylvania	10.6	14.9
Texas	15.3	12.9

Note: Selected states are those with at least an estimated 10,000 native-born and 10,000 foreign-born non-Hispanic white minority youth, aged 16 to 24.

most all of the states, as indicated above, the proportions of the higher-risk foreign-born youth in the various states bear little relationship to the differences between the state undereducation rates of these youth with a few exceptions. In 1980 these proportions ranged from 1.7 percent in North Dakota to 20.8 percent in Rhode Island, as shown in table 7.5. White minority youth in Rhode Island, as already noted, are the most likely to be undereducated; the high overall white minority undereducation rate in Rhode Island reflects the rate of foreign-born youth. In 1980 foreign-born non-Hispanic white minority youth in Rhode Island were three times more likely to be undereducated than their native-born counterparts. Their rate was 44 percent (plus or minus 4.1 percent) in comparison with 14.2 percent for native-born non-Hispanic white minority youth who were about as likely to be undereducated as majority youth in that state, as shown in table 7.3.[6] The disparity between the undereducation rates of foreign-born and native-born white minority youth in Massachusetts was even greater as already noted; the high undereducation rate of foreign-born youth pulled the overall rate for white minority youth up. In contrast, in California, the state with the second largest proportion of foreign-born white minority youth in 1980, foreign-born youth are not much more likely to be undereducated than native-born youth, and white minority youth in the state generally are less likely to be undereducated than the average non-Hispanic white minority young person in the nation. In New York, New Jersey, and Connecticut, foreign-born youth are much more at risk than native-born youth, but the low rates of native-born

Table 7.5

Estimated Numbers of Non-Hispanic White Minority Youth and Percentages Who Are Foreign Born, by Selected State: United States, 1980

State	Number	% foreign born	State	Number	% foreign born
Total, all states	2,810,000	12.1	Missouri	36,000	6.8
			Nebraska	15,000	4.6
Alabama	20,000	7.4	Nevada	10,000	10.9
Arizona	35,000	8.6	New Hampshire	22,000	6.4
Arkansas	11,000	7.0	New Jersey	135,000	16.8
California	323,000	19.4	New Mexico	15,000	5.7
Colorado	40,000	11.1	New York	336,000	16.9
Connecticut	72,000	15.8	North Carolina	37,000	7.5
Florida	100,000	11.1	North Dakota	14,000	1.7
Georgia	31,000	10.6	Ohio	124,000	7.9
Idaho	10,000	4.5	Oklahoma	23,000	16.9
Illinois	150,000	14.6	Oregon	30,000	14.1
Indiana	52,000	6.3	Pennsylvania	157,000	6.1
Iowa	27,000	5.2	Rhode Island	29,000	20.8
Kansas	24,000	6.9	South Carolina	20,000	5.9
Kentucky	20,000	6.7	Tennessee	24,000	7.0
Louisiana	82,000	2.9	Texas	143,000	9.2
Maine	30,000	4.1	Utah	26,000	7.3
Maryland	41,000	11.8	Vermont	11,000	6.7
Massachusetts	135,000	18.9	Virginia	45,000	12.3
Michigan	125,000	12.6	Washington	51,000	10.6
Minnesota	51,000	4.8	West Virginia	12,000	2.8
Mississippi	11,000	7.0	Wisconsin	60,000	5.8

Note: Selected states are those with at least an estimated 10,000 non-Hispanic white minority youth, aged 16 to 24.

youth outweigh the rates of the 15.8 to 16.9 percent who were born abroad. In the six states in which white minority youth are most at risk of undereducation after those in Rhode Island—Kentucky, Mississippi, Louisiana, Arkansas, Alabama, and Tennessee—fewer than 8 percent were foreign born.

In the southern states where most non-Hispanic white minority youth are native born, white minority youth share the educational disadvantage of majority youth for the reasons that have been explored in chapter 4.[7] In other states, the differences in state undereducation rates are related to differences in the composition of the language minority populations and the populations of people born in countries in which white minority languages are spoken. These differences will be discussed in the following sections.

EUROPEAN AND NEAR EASTERN LANGUAGE MINORITY GROUPS IN THE UNITED STATES

In 1980 there were an estimated 13.7 million people with 1 of the 21 European or Near Eastern language backgrounds identified in the census that are the principal language backgrounds of the non-Hispanic white minority population in the United States, as shown in table 7.6. The language minority groups consist of people, aged five and older, who speak a non-English language at home or who live in families in which one or more other family members speak a non-English language, and children under five years of age, one or both of whose parents speak a non-English language. The French and German language minority groups are the largest: each had nearly 3 million members in 1980. The Italian language minority group was not far behind with 2.6 million members. There were 1.3 million people with Polish language backgrounds, 548,000 with Greek language backgrounds, 480,000 with Portuguese language backgrounds, 430,000 with Yiddish language backgrounds, and 312,000 with Arabic language backgrounds.[8]

Although these are the principal language backgrounds of non-Hispanic white minority youth, counts of people by language background, like counts of people by country of birth as noted elsewhere, include people of all races. The counts of people with French language backgrounds include French- and Creole-speaking Haitians and other Creole-speaking blacks, and those of people with Portuguese language backgrounds include speakers of Cape Verdean and Crioulo (Portuguese Creole), many of whom have African origins. Other language minority groups are similarly mixed.

Language minority groups vary widely in their age distribution and, accordingly, in the extent to which they are represented among the white minority youth who are the focus of this study, as shown in table 7.6. Among people with Arabic language backgrounds, three in ten were under age 18 in 1980; in contrast, only one in ten members of the Slovak language minority was under age 18. Of the four largest groups, people with French language backgrounds are as young as people living in monolingual English-speaking households: 28.3 percent of both groups were under age 18 in 1980. The proportions of children and youth in the other groups were less: a quarter of the German group, 19.9 percent of the Italian group, and 15.3 percent of the Polish group.[9]

European and Near Eastern language minority groups are widely distributed in the United States, and all states have at least a few members of some of these groups. However, some states have large concentrations, as shown in table 7.7. More than 2 million members of European and Near Eastern language minority groups lived in New York in 1980; 1.3 million lived in California. New Jersey, Pennsylvania, Illinois, and Massachusetts

Table 7.6
Estimated Numbers of People with Selected Non-Hispanic White Minority
Language Backgrounds and Percentages under Age 18, by Language Group:
United States, 1980

Language group	Number	% under age 18
Total	13,745,000	22.7
Arabic	312,000	30.7
Armenian	127,000	20.5
Czech	194,000	15.9
Dutch	252,000	26.1
Finnish	111,000	16.7
French	2,937,000	28.3
German	2,834,000	25.2
Greek	548,000	25.7
Hungarian	266,000	16.7
Italian	2,627,000	19.9
Lithuanian	104,000	13.2
Norwegian	184,000	16.5
Persian	138,000	24.8
Polish	1,285,000	15.3
Portuguese	480,000	28.8
Russian	232,000	19.0
Serbo-Croatian	211,000	21.2
Slovak	141,000	11.7
Swedish	163,000	16.4
Ukrainian	168,000	16.5
Yiddish	430,000	13.4

Source: Derived from Bureau of the Census, 1980 Census of Population, Detailed Population Characteristics, Part 1, United States Summary, pp. 16 and 17.

each had at least 800,000 members of these groups. There were four other states with between 500,000 and 700,000 each in 1980.

Language minority people tend to be concentrated by language group, reflecting their histories in the United States. French language minority people dominate the European and Near Eastern language minority populations in Louisiana, Maine, New Hampshire, and Vermont. In 1980 they constituted 91.3 percent, 88.4 percent, 76.6 percent, and 76.5 percent, respectively, of the total European and Near Eastern language minority populations in those states. Nearly half a million French language minority people lived in Louisiana. The next largest numbers—269,000 and 239,000—lived in New York and Massachusetts, respectively. Five other states—California, Connecticut, Florida, Maine, and New Hampshire—were home to at least 100,000 members of this group in 1980.

German language minority people are the most widely distributed of all the European and Near Eastern language minority groups. They are the largest group in 22 states. In 1980 more than a quarter of a million people

Table 7.7
Estimated Numbers of People with Selected Non-Hispanic White Minority Language Backgrounds, by Language Group and Selected State: United States, 1980 (Numbers in thousands)

State	Total, all groups	Arabic	French	German	Greek	Italian	Persian	Polish	Portu-guese	Yiddish
Total, all states	13,745	312	2,937	2,834	548	2,627	138	1,285	480	430
Alabama	64	1	26	23	2	4	2	1	1	*
Arizona	94	3	18	29	3	14	1	6	2	2
Arkansas	34	1	12	12	1	2	1	2	*	*
California	1,290	55	195	276	50	209	44	35	108	32
Colorado	127	4	22	59	4	13	2	4	1	1
Connecticut	452	3	107	34	14	142	1	62	27	6
Florida	519	10	120	112	22	95	6	31	8	47
Georgia	114	3	45	42	4	6	2	2	1	2
Idaho	26	*	6	12	1	2	*	*	1	*
Illinois	843	21	73	168	59	134	5	201	3	16
Indiana	191	4	33	75	8	10	1	25	1	1
Iowa	98	2	13	49	2	4	1	1	*	1
Kansas	80	1	13	49	1	2	1	1	1	*
Kentucky	60	2	23	24	1	4	1	1	1	*
Louisiana	528	2	482	16	2	15	2	1	1	*
Maine	172	*	152	5	2	4	*	1	1	1
Maryland	214	4	56	47	17	31	4	19	4	9
Massachusetts	821	13	239	35	48	173	3	75	158	15
Michigan	626	45	74	110	21	80	4	147	2	9
Minnesota	265	3	21	105	3	6	1	14	1	2
Mississippi	39	1	22	9	1	3	1	1	1	*
Missouri	139	3	30	60	5	19	2	6	1	3
Nebraska	72	1	7	33	1	4	1	6	*	*
Nevada	37	1	6	11	2	9	1	2	1	1
New Hampshire	137	1	105	7	6	4	*	6	1	*
New Jersey	892	17	63	119	36	320	3	120	44	28
New Mexico	28	1	6	10	1	3	1	1	*	*
New York	2,221	38	269	254	120	816	11	211	29	208
North Carolina	118	4	59	32	6	6	2	2	1	*
North Dakota	101	*	4	65	*	*	*	2	*	*
Ohio	575	15	77	152	26	92	3	61	3	7
Oklahoma	60	4	14	25	1	3	4	1	1	*
Oregon	98	3	18	38	2	6	2	2	1	*
Pennsylvania	861	12	77	155	28	241	2	130	6	27
Rhode Island	193	2	69	5	3	45	*	9	51	2
South Carolina	71	2	38	19	3	3	1	1	1	*
Tennessee	74	2	30	26	2	5	2	2	1	1
Texas	394	13	99	153	9	19	8	18	4	3
Utah	67	1	12	26	4	5	1	1	2	*
Vermont	51	*	39	4	*	3	*	2	*	*
Virginia	166	7	59	46	10	15	5	5	3	1
Washington	184	4	31	71	4	12	3	4	2	1
West Virginia	47	2	12	10	2	10	1	3	*	*
Wisconsin	303	2	24	138	5	18	1	50	1	2

Source: Derived from Bureau of the Census, *1980 Census of Population, Detailed Population Characteristics, Part 1, United States Summary,* pp. 16 and 17; and selected state parts, tables 197 and 198, various pages.

Note: Selected states are those with at least an estimated 10,000 non-Hispanic white minority youth, aged 16 to 24.

*Fewer than an estimated 1,000 people.

with German language backgrounds lived in California and another quarter of a million in New York. There were nine other states with at least 100,000 German language minority people each in 1980.

The largest numbers of Italian language minority people live in the Middle Atlantic states where they constitute the largest European/Near Eastern language minority group. In 1980 there were 816,000 in New York, 320,000 in New Jersey, and 241,000 in Pennsylvania. More than 200,000 Italian language minority people also lived in California; three other states—Connecticut, Illinois, and Massachusetts—were home to at least 100,000 each in 1980. Italian language minority people constituted a third of the European/Near Eastern language minority population in New York and New Jersey, 31.4 percent of this population in Connecticut, and 28.0 percent of this population in Pennsylvania.

The largest groups of people with Polish language backgrounds live in New York and Illinois, which had more than 200,000 each in 1980. Michigan, New Jersey, and Pennsylvania each had at least 100,000 Polish language minority people in 1980. People with Polish language backgrounds constituted the largest European/Near Eastern language minority groups in Illinois and Michigan.

Nearly half of the total number of people with Yiddish language backgrounds lived in New York in 1980; New York was also home to one in five members of the Greek language minority population. A third of the people with Portuguese language backgrounds lived in Massachusetts; the second largest group lived in California. Portuguese language minority people, while not the largest European/Near Eastern language minority group in Rhode Island, constituted a quarter of the total in that state. The largest numbers of people with Arabic language backgrounds were located in California, Michigan, and New York in 1980.[10]

PEOPLE IN THE UNITED STATES WHO WERE BORN IN COUNTRIES IN WHICH NON-HISPANIC WHITE MINORITY LANGUAGES ARE SPOKEN

In 1980 there were 4.9 million people in the United States who were born in one of the countries in which the languages of the backgrounds of non-Hispanic white minority youth are spoken, as shown in table 7.8. They include people born in countries in which the 21 European and Near Eastern languages identified in the census are spoken, other European countries, and Israel and Turkey. Although not all foreign-born people continue to speak their mother tongues in their new homes and some may live in monolingual English-speaking environments, most form part of the language minority populations examined in the last section. Thus part of the German language minority group consists of many of nearly a million U.S. residents born in Germany and Austria who were recorded in the 1980 census, as well as Ger-

Table 7.8
Estimated Numbers of People Born in Countries in Which Non-Hispanic White Minority Languages Are Spoken and Percentages by Year of Immigration, by Country or Group of Countries of Birth: United States, 1980

Country of birth	Number	Percentage, by year of immigration			
		1975—80	1970—74	1960—69	≤1959
Total	4,897,000	12.8	8.1	17.6	61.4
Total, countries speaking European languages[1]	4,421,000	9.0	7.1	17.6	66.2
Austria	146,000	2.7	1.8	7.6	87.9
Belgium	36,000	10.6	4.6	14.6	70.2
Brazil	41,000	32.1	16.0	31.3	20.6
Canada[2]	173,000	9.8	5.4	20.1	64.7
Czechoslovakia	113,000	3.3	4.3	15.0	77.4
Denmark	43,000	8.4	3.9	15.1	72.6
Finland	29,000	10.4	4.7	15.1	69.9
France	120,000	13.9	7.2	23.9	55.0
Germany	849,000	6.2	4.4	20.6	68.8
Greece	211,000	12.9	19.1	27.7	40.3
Hungary	144,000	3.8	4.5	10.8	81.0
Italy	832,000	4.0	8.1	18.2	69.8
Lithuania	48,000	1.5	1.2	4.8	92.6
Netherlands	103,000	8.3	4.4	21.2	66.1
Norway	63,000	6.0	2.3	9.5	82.2
Poland	418,000	6.0	5.0	14.5	74.5
Portugal	212,000	21.7	23.3	34.0	21.0
Romania	67,000	17.0	10.2	16.8	56.0
Soviet Union	406,000	21.1	3.2	5.3	70.4
Sweden	77,000	7.9	2.8	8.8	80.5
Switzerland	43,000	14.3	5.8	17.5	62.4
Yugoslavia	153,000	7.4	16.2	23.9	52.5
Other countries	476,000	48.1	17.0	17.5	17.4
Arabic-speaking countries[3]	236,000	45.5	18.9	18.7	16.9
Iran	122,000	71.9	12.7	9.7	5.7
Israel	67,000	34.1	18.9	25.0	22.0
Turkey	52,000	22.7	15.4	21.1	40.7

Source: Derived from Bureau of the Census, "Socioeconomic Characteristics of U.S. Foreign-born Population Detailed in Census Bureau Tabulations," pp. 2–4.

Note: Detail may not add to total number or to 100.0 percent because of rounding.

[1]Except English- and Spanish-speaking countries, French- and Dutch-speaking Caribbean islands, and Cape Verde.

[2]Number and percentages for the 20.5 percent of people born in Canada who are estimated to speak a non-English language at home. Bureau of the Census, "Socioeconomic Characteristics," p. 7.

[3]Algeria, Bahrain, Egypt, Iraq, Jordan, Kuwait, Lebanon, Libya, Malta, Morocco, People's Democratic Republic of Yemen, Qatar, Saudi Arabia, Sudan, Syria, Tunisia, United Arab Emirates, and Yemen Arab Republic.

man-speaking people born in Switzerland who cannot be separately counted. Similarly, the 832,000 people born in Italy overlap with the Italian language minority group, the 418,000 people born in Poland with the people with Polish language backgrounds, and the 406,000 people born in the Soviet Union with people with backgrounds of Russian, Ukrainian, Lithuanian, and other languages spoken in the Soviet Union. In all, 13 European countries in which the languages of the backgrounds of non-Hispanic white minority people in the United States are spoken were the birthplaces of at least 100,000 U.S. residents in 1980. There were also 236,000 people born in Arabic-speaking countries and 122,000 born in Iran living in the United States in 1980.[11]

Some of the people born in European and other countries in which non-Hispanic white minority languages are spoken are recent immigrants, some of whom are 16-to-24-year-olds. Others have been here for many years and are well beyond the age group of interest in this study. As shown in table 7.8, people born in Iran and in Arabic-speaking countries are among the most recent immigrants. More than seven out of ten of the 1980 Iranian-born population and 45.5 percent of the population born in Arabic-speaking countries immigrated to the United States between 1975 and 1980. A third of Israeli-born people and three in ten Brazilians were recent immigrants. Among immigrants from European countries, those born in Portugal and the Soviet Union are more likely to be recent arrivals: a fifth of each group in the United States in 1980 had come after 1974. In contrast, most people born in Austria, Czechoslovakia, Hungary, Italy, Lithuania, Norway, and Poland are long-time residents: 6 percent or fewer of the these populations were 1975–80 immigrants.[12]

As shown in table 7.9, the geographical distribution of people born in the countries in which major white minority languages are spoken supports the assumption that the foreign-born and language minority populations overlap. Like the European and Near Eastern language minorities in general, the largest related foreign-born groups live in New York, California, and New Jersey, and like German and Italian language background people, the largest groups of immigrants born in Germany and Austria live in New York and California, and the largest groups of immigrants born in Italy live in New York and New Jersey. The distribution of Greek and Portuguese immigrants also parallels the distribution of the Greek and Portuguese language minority groups.[13]

THE EDUCATIONAL ATTAINMENT OF EUROPEAN AND NEAR EASTERN LANGUAGE MINORITY PEOPLE AND PEOPLE BORN IN THE COUNTRIES IN WHICH THE LANGUAGES ARE SPOKEN

The differences in the undereducation rates of non-Hispanic white minority youth in the various states are related to the differences in educa-

Table 7.9
Estimated Numbers of People Born in Countries in Which Non-Hispanic White Minority Languages Are Spoken, by Selected State and Country or Group of Countries of Birth: United States, 1980 (Numbers in thousands)

Country of birth	Total, all states	California	Connecticut	Florida	Illinois	Massachusetts	Michigan	New Jersey	New York	Pennsylvania	Rhode Island	Texas
Total	4,897	700	154	267	356	263	226	380	1,048	243	50	98
Total, countries speaking European languages[1]	4,421	566	150	250	331	248	187	356	974	231	48	78
Austria	146	17	3	12	10	3	5	10	39	12	*	2
Brazil	41	7	1	3	2	2	1	4	8	1	*	1
Canada[2]	173	33	6	14	4	16	16	3	15	3	2	4
Czechoslovakia	113	11	3	7	11	1	4	9	24	10	*	3
Denmark	43	11	1	3	3	1	1	2	4	1	*	1
Finland	29	5	1	3	1	2	2	1	4	*	*	*
France	120	24	3	8	5	4	3	7	21	4	1	5
Germany	849	113	16	53	55	15	31	57	135	38	2	34
Greece	211	18	5	8	25	18	8	15	55	10	1	3
Hungary	144	21	4	11	8	2	7	14	32	9	*	2
Italy	832	67	48	29	49	55	26	100	284	68	10	4
Lithuania	48	4	2	3	11	4	3	2	6	3	*	*
Netherlands	103	27	2	5	4	2	11	7	8	2	*	3
Norway	63	8	1	3	3	2	1	3	11	1	*	1
Poland	418	27	19	27	64	17	27	41	113	21	2	3
Portugal	212	41	15	2	1	75	*	29	14	3	20	1
Romania	67	10	1	4	6	1	4	4	22	3	*	1
Soviet Union	406	59	8	35	26	16	13	25	113	27	2	4
Sweden	77	13	3	6	9	4	2	3	8	1	1	1
Switzerland	43	11	1	2	2	1	1	3	7	1	*	1
Yugoslavia	153	20	2	4	23	1	12	9	29	7	*	1
Other countries	476	133	4	17	25	15	39	24	74	12	2	20
Arabic-speaking countries[3]	236	57	2	8	15	8	31	13	32	7	1	10
Iran	122	49	1	3	4	3	3	2	10	2	*	7
Israel	67	16	1	3	4	2	3	4	20	2	*	2
Turkey	52	12	1	3	2	3	3	4	12	2	1	1

Source: Derived from Bureau of the Census, "Socioeconomic Characteristics of U.S. Foreign-born Population Detailed in Census Bureau Tabulations," pp. 1–4 and 9–14; and idem, *1980 Census of Population, Detailed Population Characteristics, Part 8, Connecticut;* and *Part 41, Rhode Island*, p. 8.

Note: Detail may not add to total because of rounding. Selected states are those with at least an estimated 10,000 foreign-born non-Hispanic white minority youth, aged 16 to 24, and Rhode Island.

*Fewer than an estimated 1,000 people.

[1]Except English- and Spanish-speaking countries, French- and Dutch-speaking Caribbean islands, and Cape Verde.

[2]Numbers for the 20.5 percent of people born in Canada who are estimated to speak a non-English language at home. Bureau of the Census, "Socioeconomic Characteristics," p. 7.

[3]Algeria, Bahrain, Egypt, Iraq, Jordan, Kuwait, Lebanon, Libya, Malta, Morocco, People's Democratic Republic of Yemen, Qatar, Saudi Arabia, Sudan, Syria, Tunisia, United Arab Emirates, and Yemen Arab Republic, except in Connecticut and Rhode Island where the totals consist of numbers for Lebanon and North African countries only.

tional attainment among the language minority and recent immigrant groups that make up the non-Hispanic white minority populations in the states. Members of certain groups are less likely than members of other groups to be high school graduates and their children are more likely to be members of the at-risk groups. In 1980 some of the most recent immigrant groups varied most in educational attainment, as shown in table 7.10. Among people born in Portugal, aged 25 and older, 22.3 percent were high school graduates; in comparison, 87.0 percent of people born in Egypt and Iran were high school graduates.[14] Portuguese immigrants constituted two in five of the immigrants born in countries in which white minority languages are spoken in Rhode Island and nearly three in ten of those in Massachusetts.[15] The low educational attainment of Portuguese-born adults parallels the high undereducation rates of foreign-born white minority youth in those states. In contrast the undereducation rates of foreign-born white minority youth are low in California, perhaps because the numbers of Portuguese immigrants are balanced by those of immigrants from Arabic-speaking countries and Iran who have higher educational attainment.[16]

Adults born in most of the European countries where white minority languages are spoken are less likely to be high school graduates than white adults as a whole, whose 1980 high school graduation rate was 68.8 percent.[17] The lower rates of the longtime resident foreign-born populations reflect the lower educational attainment of older populations in general.[18]

No information is available on the educational attainment of language minority groups by language, except for the Spanish language minority. However, in Louisiana and North Dakota—states in which European and Near Eastern language minorities, excluding the Spanish language minority, comprised 86.6 percent and 93.5 percent, respectively, of all language minorities in 1980—the high school graduation rates of non-Hispanic language minority adults are strikingly lower than those of people from monolingual English-speaking backgrounds. In Louisiana, 44.2 percent of non-Hispanic language minority adults and 60.4 percent of English language background adults were high school graduates; in North Dakota, the rates were 43.9 percent and 73.4 percent.[19] Louisiana and North Dakota are states in which non-Hispanic white minority youth are marginally more likely to be undereducated than white majority youth.

POST-1980 IMMIGRATION FROM COUNTRIES IN WHICH NON-HISPANIC WHITE MINORITY LANGUAGES ARE SPOKEN

Immigrants are continuing to come to the United States from countries in which the non-Hispanic white minority languages are spoken. As

Table 7.10
**High School Graduation Rates of People, Aged 25 and Older, Born in
Selected Countries in Which Non-Hispanic White Minority Languages Are
Spoken, by Country or Group of Countries of Birth: United States, 1980**

Countries speaking European languages	51.4[a]
Austria	50.2
Brazil	69.2
Canada	61.8[b]
Czechoslovakia	47.7
Denmark	60.1
Finland	48.2
France	74.3
Germany	67.3
Greece	40.4
Hungary	53.4
Italy	28.6
Lithuania	48.8
Netherlands	67.7
Norway	48.6
Poland	40.5
Portugal	22.3
Romania	53.2
Soviet Union	47.2
Sweden	48.0
Switzerland	67.8
Yugoslavia	41.1
Arabic-speaking countries	NA
Egypt	87.3
Iraq	60.1
Jordan	66.6
Lebanon	59.8
Syria	53.8
Other countries	NA
Iran	87.1
Israel	78.8
Turkey	49.3

Source: Derived from Bureau of the Census, "Socioeconomic Characteristics of U.S. Foreign-born Population Detailed in Census Bureau Tabulations," pp. 5–8.

NA = not available.

[a]Rate of people born in European countries, including Ireland, Malta, Spain, and the United
Kingdom.

[b]Rate of all people born in Canada.

shown in table 7.11, between April 1, 1980, when the census was taken, and September 30, 1988, an estimated 436,000 people legally immigrated to the United States from countries speaking European languages, except English and Spanish, and 320,000 immigrated from countries in which other languages of the backgrounds of white minority youth are spoken. The largest numbers of 1980–88 immigrants came from Arabic-speaking countries and Iran—139,000 from the former and 114,000 from the latter.[20]

People are being admitted from countries in which white minority languages are spoken at the rate of about 89,000 per year; 91,379 were admitted from these countries in fiscal year 1988. The largest groups of 1988 immigrants consisted of 17,660 people who were born in Arabic-speaking countries and 15,246 people who were born in Iran. The largest group from a European country consisted of 9,507 people born in Poland.[21] Among the immigrants admitted to the United States in 1987, half of those born in Iran intended to live in California, and a quarter of those born in Poland intended to live in Illinois and 18.1 percent in New York.[22]

UNDEREDUCATED NON-HISPANIC WHITE MINORITY YOUTH IN THE REMAINDER OF THIS CENTURY

In April 1980 there were 337,000 undereducated non-Hispanic white minority youth, aged 16 to 24, in the United States. They constituted 12.0 percent of all non-Hispanic white minority youth. At the same time, 3.3 million white majority youth, 13.0 percent of their group, were out of school without having completed 12 years of schooling. The October 1980 current population survey identified 4.1 million white civilians not living in group quarters, including white minority and Hispanic youth, who were undereducated. They constituted 13.3 percent of all white civilian non-institutional youth, aged 16 to 24.[23] By October 1988 the number of such youth who were out of school without high school diplomas had fallen to 3.4 million, and the undereducation rate of all civilian non-institutional whites, including Hispanics, was 12.7 percent.[24] (See table 1.1 in chapter 1.)

Since 1980, nearly a million non-Hispanic whites have legally immigrated to the United States. They are coming at the rate of about 116,000 per year. About three-quarters of them—756,000—were born in countries in which the languages of non-Hispanic white minorities in the United States are spoken.[25] If the educational attainment of these people is equal to that of pre-1980 immigrants from the same countries, many of these people are well educated. Their daughters and sons are no more likely to be undereducated than white minority youth in 1980. Given the educational attainment of the most recent pre-1980 immigrants and the proportions of native-born vis-à-vis foreign-born white minority youth, it is

Table 7.11
Estimated Numbers and Yearly Average Numbers of Immigrants Born in Countries in Which Non-Hispanic White Minority Languages Are Spoken Admitted to the United States between April 1, 1980, and September 30, 1988, and Numbers Admitted in Fiscal Year 1988, by Country or Group of Countries of Birth

Country of birth	Total	Average per year, 1980—88	Admitted, FY 1988
Total	756,000	89,000	91,379
Total, countries speaking European languages[1]	436,000	51,000	50,318
Austria	4,000	*	514
Belgium	5,000	1,000	581
Brazil	17,000	2,000	2,699
Canada[2]	20,000	2,000	2,416
Czechoslovakia	10,000	1,000	1,482
Denmark	2,000	*	558
Finland	3,000	*	390
France	19,000	2,000	2,524
Germany	59,000	7,000	6,755
Greece	26,000	3,000	2,458
Hungary	7,000	1,000	1,227
Italy	29,000	3,000	2,949
Netherlands	10,000	1,000	1,187
Norway	3,000	*	397
Poland	64,000	8,000	9,507
Portugal	36,000	4,000	3,199
Romania	31,000	4,000	3,875
Soviet Union	53,000	6,000	2,949
Sweden	8,000	1,000	1,156
Switzerland	6,000	1,000	751
Yugoslavia	15,000	2,000	1,941
Other countries	320,000	38,000	41,061
Afghanistan	21,000	2,000	2,899
Arabic-speaking countries[3]	139,000	16,000	17,660
Iran	114,000	13,000	15,246
Israel	29,000	3,000	3,640
Turkey	17,000	2,000	1,642

Source: Derived from Immigration and Naturalization Service, unpublished tabulations.

Note: The numbers of immigrants admitted between April 1 and September 30, 1980, are estimated to be half the totals for fiscal year 1980.

[1]Except English- and Spanish-speaking countries, French- and Dutch-speaking Caribbean islands, and Cape Verde.

[2]Of the total number of immigrants born in Canada, 20.5 percent are estimated to speak a non-English language at home. Bureau of the Census, "Socioeconomic Characteristics of U.S. Foreign-born Population Detailed in Census Bureau Tabulations," p. 7.

[3]Algeria, Bahrain, Egypt, Iraq, Jordan, Kuwait, Lebanon, Libya, Malta, Morocco, Oman, People's Democratic Republic of Yemen, Qatar, Saudi Arabia, Sudan, Syria, Tunisia, United Arab Emirates, and Yemen Arab Republic.

reasonable to assume that the undereducation rate of non-Hispanic white minority youth has fallen nationally at least as much as the undereducation rate of whites in general and that they are maintaining their advantage over white majority youth. This is certainly the case in states such as California to which many highly educated people are immigrating. It may not be the case in Louisiana and other southeastern states in which both white majority and white minority youth have a higher than average risk of undereducation and in which, in any case, the large majority of white minority youth are native born. It may not be the case in states in which less well-educated immigrants are larger proportions of total immigration from countries in which white minority languages are spoken.

The non-Hispanic white population in the United States is projected to grow by 0.6 percent between 1985 and 1990, by 0.4 percent between 1990 and 1995, and by 0.3 percent between 1995 and the year 2000, assuming moderate fertility and mortality and a yearly net immigration of 139,000 non-Hispanic whites.[26] At these rates, the number of non-Hispanic white school-age children and youth will increase from 32.3 million in 1985 to 33.8 million in the year 2000.[27] (See table 1.3 in chapter 1.) Because other groups are growing faster, non-Hispanic white youth will constitute a smaller proportion of the total school-age population in the year 2000. Whether non-Hispanic white minority youth will constitute a smaller proportion of non-Hispanic white youth at risk and whether the risk of undereducation lessens for youth in all states will depend on the characteristics of future immigrants from countries in which white minority languages are spoken and the efforts that are made by school systems to meet the needs of both native-born and foreign-born language minority students. Educational programs that recognize and build upon the strengths that non-Hispanic white minority and other linguistically different youth bring to the classroom will speed the process and encourage more and more of these youth to achieve their educational potential.

NOTES

1. Bureau of the Census, U.S. Department of Commerce, *1980 Census of Population, Detailed Population Characteristics, Part 1, United States Summary* (Washington, D.C.: U.S. Government Printing Office, 1984), pp. 16 and 17.

2. In 1980, 69.1 percent of all language minority people, aged five and older, were native born. Ibid., pp. 12–13.

3. The differences between 19.2 percent for white minority youth and 17.0 percent for white majority youth in Louisiana and between 10.2 percent and 7.7 percent for these groups in North Dakota are significant at the 68 percent confidence level.

4. The rate of foreign-born non-Hispanic white minority youth in Rhode Island—44.0 percent—was higher than their rate in Massachusetts at the 68 per-

cent confidence level; there were about 6,000 foreign-born non-Hispanic white minority youth in all in Rhode Island in 1980.

5. The difference between 15.3 percent for native-born white minority youth in Texas and 12.9 percent for foreign-born youth in that state is not statistically significant.

6. The difference between 14.2 percent for native-born white minority youth and 12.2 percent for white majority youth in Rhode Island is not statistically significant.

7. See pp. 81–88.

8. Bureau of the Census, *Detailed Population Characteristics,* pp. 16 and 17.

9. Ibid., pp. 16, 17, and 18.

10. Bureau of the Census, *Detailed Population Characteristics, Parts 2–52, the States and the District of Columbia* (Washington, D.C.: U.S. Government Printing Office, 1983), tables 197 and 198, various pages.

11. Bureau of the Census, U.S. Department of Commerce, "Socioeconomic Characteristics of U.S. Foreign-born Population Detailed in Census Bureau Tabulations," press release, October 17, 1984, pp. 1–4.

12. Ibid.

13. Ibid., pp. 9–14, and Bureau of the Census, *Detailed Population Characteristics, Part 8, Connecticut*; and *Part 41, Rhode Island,* p. 8.

14. Bureau of the Census, "Socioeconomic Characteristics," pp. 6–7.

15. Bureau of the Census, *Detailed Population Characteristics, Part 41, Rhode Island,* p. 8; and idem, "Socioeconomic Characteristics," pp. 9–14.

16. Bureau of the Census, "Socioeconomic Characteristics," pp. 9–14.

17. Bureau of the Census, *Detailed Population Characteristics, Part 1, United States Summary,* p. 43.

18. Ibid.

19. Bureau of the Census, *Detailed Population Characteristics, Part 20, Louisiana,* p. 23; and *Part 36, North Dakota,* p. 17.

20. Immigration and Naturalization Service, U.S. Department of Justice, unpublished tabulations.

21. Ibid.

22. Immigration and Naturalization Service, U.S. Department of Justice, *Statistical Yearbook of the Immigration and Naturalization Service, 1987* (Washington, D.C.: U.S. Government Printing Office, 1988), pp. 32–34.

23. Bureau of the Census, U.S. Department of Commerce, *School Enrollment—Social and Economic Characteristics of Students: October 1981 and 1980* (Washington, D.C.: U.S. Government Printing Office, 1985), p. 60.

24. Bureau of the Census, U.S. Department of Commerce, *School Enrollment—Social and Economic Characteristics of Students: October 1988 and 1987* (Washington, D.C.: U.S. Government Printing Office, 1990), p. 5.

25. Immigration and Naturalization Service, unpublished tabulations.

26. Bureau of the Census, U.S. Department of Commerce, *Projections of the Hispanic Population: 1983 to 2080* (Washington, D.C.: U.S. Government Printing Office, 1986), pp. 10 and 18.

27. Ibid., p. 14.

8

American Indian, Eskimo, and Aleut Youth Who Are Undereducated

American Indians, Eskimos, and Aleuts are the most likely to be undereducated of all native-born youth in the United States. In 1980 nearly three in ten of American Indian/Alaska Native youth, aged 16 to 24, were not enrolled in school and had not completed the twelfth grade. They were more than twice as likely as white majority youth to be undereducated. The undereducation rate of these youth was 29.2 percent in comparison with 13.0 percent of native-born non-Hispanic whites with monolingual English-speaking backgrounds, 20.4 percent of African Americans, and 26.6 percent of native-born Hispanics.

The strongest factor related to undereducation for American Indians, Eskimos, and Aleuts as a group appears to be poverty, and they are among the poorest of minorities. Those from families with incomes below the poverty level were 1.6 times more likely to be undereducated than those from more economically advantaged families in 1980.

The majority of American Indian, Eskimo, and Aleut youth live in households in which only English is spoken. In 1980 nearly two-thirds of all American Indian/Alaska Native youth, aged 16 to 24, and 60.7 percent of those who were undereducated, lived in such households. The other third were part of a population of more than half a million speakers of American Indian and Alaska Native languages and people living in families with speakers of those languages in the United States in 1980.[1] The largest group of speakers of Native American languages, and a third of all speakers of these languages counted in 1980, consisted of 123,000 speakers of Navajo.[2] Among people who identified themselves as Navajo in

1980, four out of five reported that they speak Navajo at home. They are the exception among members of the largest American Indian tribes. In 1980 there were only three other major tribal groups—the Papago, Pueblo, and Apache people—even half of whose members reported that they still speak their mother tongues in their families.[3]

As among Hispanics, American Indian, Eskimo, and Aleut youth with English language backgrounds are less likely to be undereducated than those from backgrounds in which their tribal languages are spoken. However, the difference may be more a reflection of poverty and other conditions affecting Native American populations who live on reservations or in isolated rural areas where many people speak Native American languages than the effect of the language background of the youth. This seems to be the case in Arizona and New Mexico, two of the three states in which the overall extent of undereducation is greatest; the third state, North Carolina, has the smallest proportion of non-English language-background Native American youth.

American Indians, Eskimos, and Aleuts, even more than Asians and Pacific Islanders, and Hispanics, are not a homogeneous group. They belong to many nations, tribes, and bands with very different traditions. They speak more than 200 distinct languages.[4] A considerable majority of American Indians no longer live on reservations. The quarter who did so in 1980 were divided among 278 different reservations in all areas of the country, the majority with fewer than 500 Indian residents.[5] Most Eskimos and Aleuts in Alaska live in the 209 Alaska Native villages, only three of which had more than 1,000 inhabitants in 1980.[6] American Indians and Alaska Natives are the most rural group in the United States: nearly half in 1980 lived in places with fewer than 2,500 inhabitants.[7]

The risk of undereducation for American Indian, Eskimo, and Aleut youth varies considerably by state, and the variation is related to the differences among the state populations, principally in the extent of poverty. Poverty, in turn, is associated with living patterns. Native American youth in California were up to 1.4 times less likely to be out of school without high school diplomas than those in North Carolina, New Mexico, and Arizona in 1980. American Indian populations in North Carolina, New Mexico, and Arizona are all predominantly rural;[8] large majorities of those in New Mexico and Arizona live on reservations,[9] and Native American youth in those states are the most likely of youth in any of the states with substantial Native American populations to come from families with incomes below the poverty level. In contrast, American Indians in California live predominantly in cities and towns.[10] Very few live on reservations or in rancherías.[11] Native American youth in California are the least likely to come from the poorest families.

Their relative position in comparison with American Indians, Eskimos, and Aleuts elsewhere does not mean that Native American youth in California are less educationally disadvantaged than other groups in California. Native-born Hispanics and Native Americans in California had similar undereducation rates in 1980; they were second only to foreign-born Hispanics in that state and well ahead of African Americans and white majority youth in the likelihood of undereducation. The situation of Native Americans is similar in Oklahoma. Regardless of the differences in their living patterns and poverty, however, American Indian, Eskimo, and Aleut youth in the other five states with the largest Native American populations are the most likely to be out of school without high school diplomas of all native-born youth in those states.

The following sections of this chapter contain discussions of the characteristics and geographical distribution of undereducated American Indian, Eskimo, and Aleut youth in the United States and comparisons of the undereducation rates of this group nationally and in the seven states in which there were at least an estimated 10,000 American Indians, Eskimos, and Aleuts, aged 16 to 24, in 1980. The differences in the likelihood of poverty and the extent of American Indian/Alaska Native language exposure among the youth are examined in relation to the differences in the characteristics and living patterns of American Indian and Alaska Native populations in these states. American Indian/Alaska Native undereducation rates are compared with those of other groups in the seven states. The chapter ends with a consideration of the prospects for these youth in the remainder of this century. Information on American Indians, Eskimos, and Aleuts from the published volumes of the 1980 census supplements the information from the study.

THE NUMBERS AND CHARACTERISTICS OF UNDEREDUCATED AMERICAN INDIANS, ESKIMOS, AND ALEUTS

In 1980 there were 82,000 American Indians, Eskimos, and Aleuts, aged 16 to 24, in the United States who were not enrolled in school and had not completed the twelfth grade, as shown in table 8.1. All but about a thousand of them were born in the United States and 50,000 of them— three out of five—lived in households in which only English is spoken.

Young American Indian, Eskimo, and Aleut women are almost as likely as their brothers to be undereducated. In 1980 men slightly outnumbered women, and 30.4 percent of the former, in comparison with 28.0 percent of the latter, were undereducated, as shown in table 8.2.[12] Among undereducated American Indian and Alaska Native youth, there are about as many teenagers per year of age as 20-to-24-year-olds, but, as with other youth, the 20-to-24-year-olds are more likely to be undereducated. In 1980, 31.0 percent of young adults were undereducated in comparison with 27.2 percent of teenagers.

Table 8.1
**Estimated Numbers and Distribution of Undereducated American Indian,
Eskimo, and Aleut Youth, by Language Background and Selected
Characteristic: United States, 1980**

	Total		English only		Non-English	
Characteristic	Number	Percent	Number	Percent	Number	Percent
Total	82,000	100.0	50,000	100.0	32,000	100.0
Gender						
Males	43,000	52.2	26,000	52.7	17,000	51.4
Females	39,000	47.8	24,000	47.3	16,000	48.6
Age						
16 to 19	36,000	44.1	21,000	43.0	15,000	45.8
20 to 24	46,000	55.9	28,000	57.0	17,000	54.2
Nativity						
Native born	81,000	98.2	49,000	98.0	32,000	98.5
Foreign born	1,000	1.8	1,000	2.0	*	1.5
Poverty status in 1979[1]						
Above poverty level	46,000	56.2	30,000	60.5	16,000	49.5
Below poverty level	32,000	38.4	16,000	32.5	15,000	47.6
Years of schooling completed						
Fewer than 5	2,000	2.6	1,000	1.8	1,000	3.8
5 to 8	16,000	19.1	8,000	16.2	8,000	23.4
9 to 11	64,000	78.4	41,000	82.0	23,000	72.8

Note: Percentages calculated on unrounded numbers. Detail may not add to total number
   or to 100.0 percent because of rounding.

*Fewer than an estimated 1,000 young people.

[1]Not determined for people living in group quarters.

   American Indian, Eskimo, and Aleut youth who live in households in
which one or more people speak a language other than English are more
likely to be undereducated than those who live in monolingual English-speaking households. In 1980, 27.8 percent of the latter and 31.5 percent of the former had discontinued their education before high school
graduation.
   American Indians, Eskimos, and Aleuts are among the poorest peoples

Table 8.2
Estimated Numbers of Undereducated American Indian, Eskimo, and Aleut Youth and American Indian/Alaska Native Undereducation Rates, by Language Background and Selected Characteristic: United States, 1980

Characteristic	Total		English only		Non-English	
	Number	Percent	Number	Percent	Number	Percent
Total	82,000	29.2	50,000	27.8	32,000	31.5
Gender						
Males	43,000	30.4	26,000	29.3	17,000	32.4
Females	39,000	28.0	24,000	26.4	16,000	30.6
Age						
16 to 19	36,000	27.2	21,000	26.3	15,000	28.6
20 to 24	46,000	31.0	28,000	29.2	17,000	34.6
Nativity						
Native born	81,000	29.2	49,000	27.7	32,000	31.6
Foreign born	1,000	31.2	1,000	33.6	*	27.3
Poverty status in 1979[1]						
Above poverty level	46,000	25.2	30,000	24.2	16,000	27.3
Below poverty level	32,000	40.0	16,000	39.9	15,000	40.1

Note: Detail may not add to total because of rounding.

*Fewer than an estimated 1,000 young people.

[1]Not determined for people living in group quarters.

in the United States. Among those for whom poverty was determined in 1980, 27.5 percent had incomes below the poverty level;[13] among youth, aged 16 to 24, 30.1 percent were poor. American Indian, Eskimo, and Aleut youth were as likely as black youth to be poor. They were 1.7 times more likely to be poor than white majority youth, 1.5 times more likely to be poor than Asian/Pacific youth, and 1.3 times more likely to be poor than native-born Hispanic youth in 1980. (See table 3.7 in chapter 3.) Poverty increases the undereducation risk of American Indian, Eskimo, and Aleut youth by a factor of 1.6; two out of five, in comparison with a quarter of their counterparts from more advantaged families, were out of school without high school diplomas in 1980. The poverty status of 6.9 percent of all American Indian and Alaska Native youth and of 5.4 percent of those who were undereducated was not determined in 1980. These were youth living in group quarters.

Undereducated non-English language-background American Indian/ Alaska Native youth are less likely to stay in school, at least through the ninth grade, and more likely to have very low levels of education than their counterparts with monolingual English-speaking backgrounds. In 1980, 72.8 percent of the former and 82.0 percent of the latter had completed from 9 to 11 years of schooling; twice as many of the former as the latter—3.8 percent in comparison with 1.8 percent—had less than a fifth grade education. In years of schooling completed, undereducated Native Americans from monolingual English-speaking homes compare favorably with white majority youth. Those from language minority homes complete about as many years of schooling as other minority youth. (See table 2.6 in chapter 2.)

UNDEREDUCATED AMERICAN INDIAN, ESKIMO, AND ALEUT YOUTH IN THE STATES

Undereducated American Indian, Eskimo, and Aleut youth are found in all regions of the country. In 1980 there were 34 states with at least 1,000 undereducated American Indians and Alaska Natives. The state with the largest number was Arizona where 10,000 lived. Nine thousand lived in California and 8,000 in Oklahoma. (See table 2.8 in chapter 2.)

Undereducated American Indians, Eskimos, and Aleuts are the dominant minorities in four states—Alaska, South Dakota, Montana, and Oklahoma—and the second largest groups after Hispanics in two—New Mexico and Arizona. In Alaska, they constituted a third of the undereducated youth in 1980; they constituted a quarter in South Dakota, 17 percent in New Mexico, 14 percent in Montana, and 12 percent in Arizona. (See table 2.9 in chapter 2.)

There were seven states in which at least an estimated 10,000 American Indians, Eskimos, and Aleuts, aged 16 to 24, lived in 1980. These seven states—Alaska, Arizona, California, New Mexico, North Carolina, Oklahoma, and Washington—were home to 56 percent of the total American Indian population counted in 1980; 81 percent of all Eskimos lived in Alaska, and more than three-quarters of Aleuts lived in Alaska, California, and Washington in 1980.[14] Fifty-five percent of undereducated American Indian and Alaska Native youth lived in these seven states in 1980. The undereducation rates and characteristics of the populations in these seven states are discussed in the following sections.

THE STATE UNDEREDUCATION RATES OF AMERICAN INDIAN, ESKIMO, AND ALEUT YOUTH

The likelihood of American Indians, Eskimos, and Aleuts to be out of school and not high school graduates varies considerably by state, as illustrated in figure 8.1. In 1980, in the states with at least 10,000 Native American youth, the undereducation rates ranged from 23.8 percent in California to 34.3 percent in North Carolina. (See table 3.10 in chapter 3 for rates in all the states with at least 1,000 Native American youth.)

Figure 8.1
Undereducation Rates of American Indian, Eskimo, and Aleut Youth, 1980

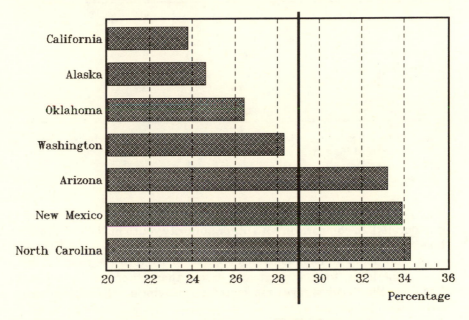

National average

THE CHARACTERISTICS OF AMERICAN INDIAN, ESKIMO, AND ALEUT YOUTH IN THE STATES

There is a wide variation in the poverty rates of American Indian and Alaska Native youth in different states and, with the exception of youth in North Carolina, their likelihood of poverty corresponds to their likelihood of undereducation. In 1980 youth in Arizona whose poverty status was determined were 2.2 times more likely to be poor than those in the neighboring state of California. Nearly half of all Native American youth in Arizona, and 42.3 percent of those in New Mexico, were poor, in comparison with 21.3 percent of those in California, about a quarter of those in North Carolina, Alaska, and Oklahoma, and 28.4 percent of those in Washington, as shown in table 8.3. American Indian youth in North Carolina, while not as likely to be poor as those in Arizona and New Mexico

Table 8.3
Estimated Numbers of American Indian, Eskimo, and Aleut Youth and
Percentages with Selected Characteristics, by Selected State: United States,
1980

State	Number	Percentage	
		In poverty[1]	With NELB[2]
Total, all states	281,000	30.1	36.4
Alaska	13,000	24.8	59.0
Arizona	29,000	47.3	87.6
California	38,000	21.3	22.3
New Mexico	21,000	42.3	90.2
North Carolina	12,000	25.7	8.0
Oklahoma	30,000	24.9	22.6
Washington	12,000	28.4	18.0

Note: Selected states are those with at least an estimated 10,000 American Indians, Eskimos, and Aleuts, aged 16 to 24.

[1]Poverty status not determined for people living in group quarters.

[2]Non-English language background.

and differing in other respects, as will be noted, are just as likely to be un-dereducated. In comparison with other minority youth in North Carolina, however, American Indian youth are just as likely to be poor.[15] They are even more likely to be undereducated, as discussed in the next section. They experience, to an even greater extent than other groups in North Carolina, the disadvantages associated with living in the high poverty rural areas in that state.[16]

American Indians, Eskimos, and Aleuts in some states are more likely to live in households in which their tribal languages are spoken than are youth in other states, and, not surprisingly, exposure to their tribal languages is related to the extent to which groups in the various states live on reservations or in rural communities with less frequent contact with outsiders. Again, North Carolina Indian youth are the exception. Although predominantly rural, few American Indians in North Carolina, according to their responses to the 1980 census, speak or hear Cherokee or other languages of their tribal heritages spoken.[17] Among the Lumbee people, the largest tribal group in North Carolina, fewer than 1 percent reported in 1980 that they speak a language other than English at home.[18]

Very large majorities of Native American youth in Arizona and New Mexico have language minority backgrounds. They are the most likely to live on reservations or tribal trust lands. In 1980 nine out of ten American Indian/Alaska Native youth in New Mexico, and 87.6 percent of those in Arizona, lived in households in which one or more people speak a language other than English at home; tribes in these states, especially the Navajo, maintain their languages and speak them at home to a greater extent than members of other large tribes.[19] Non-English language-background youth also constituted the majority in Alaska where most American Indians and Alaska Natives live in the Alaska Native villages or other Native American areas. In contrast, fewer than a quarter of American Indian, Eskimo, and Aleut youth in Washington, California, and Oklahoma lived in language minority households in 1980; American Indian populations in these states are at least as likely to live in urban areas as in rural areas—those in California are overwhelmingly urban—and fewer live in areas especially established for American Indians. The living patterns of American Indian, Eskimo, and Aleut populations in general in the various states and the characteristics of American Indian tribes that relate to the risk of undereducation are examined below.

THE EDUCATIONAL DISADVANTAGE OF AMERICAN INDIAN, ESKIMO, AND ALEUT YOUTH

Nationally and in five of the states with the largest Native American populations, American Indian and Alaska Native youth are the most likely of all native-born youth to be out of school without high school diplomas; in California and Oklahoma their undereducation rates are similar to those of native-born Hispanics who are second only to foreign-born Hispanics in the extent of undereducation. As shown in table 8.4, the educational disadvantage of American Indian/Alaska Native youth in comparison with whites ranged from 1.7 times for those living in Oklahoma

Table 8.4
Undereducation Rates of American Indian, Eskimo, and Aleut; Native-Born Hispanic; African American; and White Majority Youth, by Selected State: United States, 1980

State	American Indians, Eskimos, & Aleuts	Native-born Hispanics	African Americans	White majority youth
Total, all states	29.2	26.6	20.4	13.0
Alaska	24.6	*	*	10.5
Arizona	33.2	28.7	18.2	12.9
California	23.8	22.8	14.2	11.7
New Mexico	33.9	21.2	*	11.0
North Carolina	34.3	23.8	20.5	18.3
Oklahoma	26.4	27.6	15.7	15.3
Washington	28.3	22.6	15.5	13.0

Note: Selected states are those with at least an estimated 10,000 American Indians, Eskimos, and Aleuts, aged 16 to 24.

*Base number less than an estimated 10,000.

to more than three times for those living in New Mexico in 1980; their disadvantage in comparison with blacks in the five states with at least 10,000 black youth was 1.7 to 1.8 times. In comparison with native-born Hispanics in Arizona, New Mexico, North Carolina, and Washington, the American Indians, Eskimos, and Aleuts were 1.2 to 1.6 times more likely to be undereducated.[20] The educational disadvantage revealed in these differences is only one indicator of problems in the education of American Indian, Eskimo, and Aleut youth that have long festered. The disadvantage, while more severe in states in which many Native American students attend schools on or near reservations, is also present in a state such as California where most of them attend urban schools; it is severe in North Carolina where most American Indian students attend rural schools.

AMERICAN INDIAN AND ALASKA NATIVE STATE POPULATIONS

The differences in the living patterns of American Indian populations in the various states are shown in table 8.5. American Indians in California are the most urbanized and among the least likely to live on reservations. In 1980, 82.5 percent of California Indians lived in urban areas, most of them in central cities or their suburbs;[21] only 4.7 percent lived on reservations or in rancherías.[22] A large majority of American Indians in

Table 8.5
Estimated Numbers of American Indians, Percentages Living in American Indian Areas, and Percentages Living in Urban Areas, by Selected State: United States, 1980

State	Number	Living in American Indian areas	Living in urban areas
Total, all states	1,367,000	27.1	54.6
Alaska	22,000	4.3	47.4
Arizona	152,000	74.9	32.2
California	198,000	4.7	82.5
New Mexico	107,000	77.7	29.7
North Carolina	65,000	7.5	22.2
Oklahoma	169,000	71.5	49.9
Washington	58,000	28.8	57.8

Source: Derived from Bureau of the Census, *American Indian Areas and Alaska Native Villages: 1980*, pp. 4 and 15; and idem, *1980 Census of Population, General Social and Economic Characteristics, Part 1, United States Summary*, p. 12, and selected state parts, table 58, various pages.

Note: Selected states are those with at least an estimated 10,000 American Indians, Eskimos, and Aleuts, aged 16 to 24.

North Carolina also live outside American Indian areas, but the majority live in the country—in places with fewer than 2,500 inhabitants. In 1980 only 7.5 percent of North Carolina Indians lived on the Eastern Cherokee Reservation, the state's only reservation.[23] More than three-quarters of the total population lived in rural areas.[24] In the other states in which the majority of American Indian and Alaska Native youth have monolingual English language backgrounds—Oklahoma and Washington—American Indians are as likely or more likely to live in urban areas as to live in rural areas. In 1980 about half of Oklahoma Indians and 57.8 percent of Washington Indians lived in urban areas.[25] At the same time, 68.7 percent of Oklahoma Indians lived in the historic Indian areas identified for the 1980 census—former reservations that were dissolved before statehood in 1907—and 2.8 percent lived on the Osage Reservation.[26] Of those in Washington, 28.3 percent lived on its 25 reservations or on tribal trust lands.[27]

Large majorities of American Indians in Arizona and New Mexico live on reservations or tribal trust lands, and the populations are also predominantly rural. In 1980 reservations or trust lands were home to 74.9 percent of American Indians in Arizona and 77.7 percent of those in New Mexico;[28] 67.8 percent of Indians in Arizona and 70.3 percent of those in New Mexico lived in rural areas.[29] American Indian and Alaska Native youth in these states, as already indicated, are much more likely to be poor and to have non-English language backgrounds.

In Alaska the majority of Eskimos and Aleuts live in Alaska Native villages, and they are mostly rural populations, as shown in table 8.6. American Indians in Alaska are more likely to live outside the special areas and more, proportionally, live in urban areas. In 1980, 77.8 percent of Eski-

Table 8.6
Estimated Numbers of American Indians, Eskimos, and Aleuts; Percentages Living in Alaska Native Villages or on the Annette Islands Reserve; and Percentages Living in Urban Areas: Alaska, 1980

Group	Number	Living in Alaska Native villages	Living on Annette Isl. Reserve	Living in urban areas
Total	64,000	61.3	1.5	30.2
American Indians	22,000	36.7	4.3	47.4
Eskimos	34,000	77.8	-	19.3
Aleuts	8,000	58.1	0.1	31.3

Source: Derived from Bureau of the Census, *American Indian Areas and Alaska Native Villages: 1980*, p. 4, and idem, *1980 Census of Population, General Social and Economic Characteristics, Part 3, Alaska*,p. 13.

mos, 58.1 percent of Aleuts, and 36.7 percent of American Indians lived in the villages, and another 4.3 percent of Indians lived on the Annette Islands Reserve, Alaska's one reservation;[30] 80.7 percent of Eskimos, 68.7 percent of Aleuts, and 52.6 percent of American Indians lived in rural areas in Alaska.[31]

AMERICAN INDIAN TRIBES

In 1980 there were 21 American Indian tribes with at least an estimated 10,000 members, as shown in table 8.7.[32] Most members of a given tribe are concentrated in one or a few states where their reservations or traditional lands are located. The examples of the Athabaskan in Alaska, the Lumbee in North Carolina, the Pima and Papago in Arizona, and the

Table 8.7
Estimated Numbers of Members of American Indian Tribes, by Selected State and Tribe: United States, 1980 (Numbers in thousands)

Tribe	Total, all states	Alaska	Arizona	Cali-fornia	New Mexico	North Carolina	Oklahoma	Wash-ington
Total, all tribes	1,479	23	154	228	107	66	171	61
Apache	36	*	14	7	4	*	1	1
Athabaskan	10	9	*	*	*	*	*	*
Blackfoot	22	*	*	5	*	*	*	*
Cherokee	232	1	3	51	1	8	59	5
Cheyenne	10	*	*	1	*	*	3	*
Chickasaw	10	*	*	2	*	*	6	*
Chippewa	74	*	*	4	*	*	*	2
Choctaw	50	*	1	8	*	*	24	1
Creek	28	*	*	3	*	*	15	*
Iroquois	38	*	*	3	*	1	1	*
Lumbee	28	*	*	*	*	26	*	*
Navajo	159	*	77	6	58	*	1	*
Paiute	10	*	*	4	*	*	*	*
Papago	13	*	12	1	*	*	*	*
Pima	12	*	10	1	*	*	*	*
Potawatomi	10	*	*	1	*	*	2	*
Pueblo	43	*	9	3	27	*	*	*
Seminole	10	*	*	1	*	*	5	*
Shoshone	10	*	*	1	*	*	*	*
Sioux	79	*	1	7	*	*	1	2
Tlingit	10	7	*	*	*	*	*	1

Source: Derived from Bureau of the Census, *1980 Census of Population, Characteristics of American Indians by Tribes and Selected Areas: 1980*, pp. 1–53.

Note: Selected states are those with at least an estimated 10,000 American Indians, Eskimos, and Aleuts, aged 16 to 24. Tribes are those with at least an estimated 10,000 members.

*Fewer than an estimated 1,000 people.

Navajo in Arizona and New Mexico are readily apparent from the table. However, the largest concentrations of other tribes are found in states that do not have the largest numbers of American Indians overall, such as the Sioux in South Dakota;[33] the Chippewa people in Minnesota, Michigan, Wisconsin, and North Dakota;[34] and the Iroquois in New York.[35] The Cherokee people are widely dispersed throughout the United States. In addition to Oklahoma and California, as shown in the table, there are sizable numbers of Cherokees in Texas, Michigan, and seven other states in all parts of the United States that are not shown in the table.[36]

The wide variety of tribal affiliations of Indians in California, as shown in table 8.7, reflects the movement away from concentration. It reflects the dispersion of Indian peoples from their home reservations to the cities. In 1980, 53,000 American Indians, claiming at least 72 tribal affiliations, lived in Los Angeles County alone.[37]

American Indian tribes differ considerably in educational attainment and, not surprisingly, the two groups whose adult members are least likely to be high school graduates are prominent among American Indians in the states in which Native American youth have the highest undereducation rates. In 1980 fewer than two in five Navajo adults—members of the largest groups in Arizona and New Mexico—and almost as many Lumbee adults—members of the largest group in North Carolina—were high school graduates, as shown in table 8.8. In contrast, Creek, Potawatomi, and Tlingit adults were almost as likely to be graduates as whites; nearly two-thirds of the former and 69.6 percent of non-Hispanic whites had completed high school in 1980.[38]

The extent to which the various tribes still speak their languages differs strikingly. Among the 21 largest tribes, the range was from fewer than 1 percent of Lumbees to 84.8 percent of Navajos who reported in 1980 that they spoke non-English languages at home.[39] As noted above, very large proportions of American Indian young people in Arizona and New Mexico live in households in which non-English languages are spoken, whereas few in North Carolina live in such households.

Indian groups concentrated in the Southwest tend to be poorer than others who are more widely dispersed, such as Potawatomi, Creek, Cherokee, Chickasaw, Iroquois, and Choctaw, although all groups are considerably more likely to be poor than whites, Hispanics, or Asian Americans. In 1980 the poverty rates ranged from 45.5 percent of Navajos and 42.1 to 43.3 percent of Pimas and Papagos to 15.0 percent of Tlingits, as shown in table 8.8.[40] At the same time, the rate of non-Hispanic whites was 8.9 percent; that of Hispanics, 12.4 percent; and that of Asians and Pacific Islanders, 13.1 percent. American Indians, Eskimos, and Aleuts, with a rate of 27.6 percent in the aggregate, were not quite as poor in 1980 as blacks whose poverty rate was 29.8 percent.[41]

Table 8.8
High School Graduation Rates of American Indians, Eskimos, and Aleuts, Aged 25 and Older; Percentages, Aged 5 and Older, Speaking Non-English Languages at Home; and Poverty Rates, by Tribe or Group: United States, 1980

Tribe or group	Graduation rates, adults, aged 25+	% speakers of NELs, aged 5+	Poverty rates[1]
Total	55.8	NA	27.6
Total, all American Indian tribes	55.8	26.1	27.5
Apache	53.9	50.7	34.1
Athabaskan	49.1	22.9	30.7
Blackfoot	62.8	9.8	24.6
Cherokee	58.4	8.2	20.5
Cheyenne	60.3	24.5	34.7
Chickasaw	63.0	7.9	21.1
Chippewa	54.8	10.4	28.2
Choctaw	59.1	16.1	21.3
Creek	65.1	12.4	19.7
Iroquois	59.9	12.5	21.1
Lumbee	37.8	0.7	27.8
Navajo	39.9	84.8	45.5
Paiute	58.5	17.4	25.4
Papago	42.9	72.1	42.1
Pima	45.7	43.4	43.3
Potawatomi	65.0	6.6	18.2
Pueblo	58.3	69.9	31.0
Seminole	64.4	20.6	23.1
Shoshone	51.2	31.4	32.3
Sioux	56.8	25.0	38.8
Tlingit	64.7	13.9	15.0
Eskimo	44.3	NA	28.8
Aleut	58.4	NA	19.5

Source: Derived from Bureau of the Census, *1980 Census of Population, Characteristics of American Indians by Tribes and Selected Areas: 1980*, pp. 203–255 and 309–361; and idem, *1980 Census of Population, General Social and Economic Characteristics, Part 1, United States Summary*, pp. 157, 162, 163, and 168.

Note: Poverty status not determined for people living in group quarters and unrelated individuals under age 15. NEL = non-English language. NA = not available.

UNDEREDUCATED AMERICAN INDIAN, ESKIMO, AND ALEUT YOUTH IN THE REMAINDER OF THIS CENTURY

Almost all of the American Indians, Eskimos, and Aleuts in the United States were born in this country. Their numbers are increasing from natural growth, not immigration, and they are increasing faster than those of whites or blacks. Between 1970 and 1980 the numbers of American Indians increased by 71.8 percent. In comparison, the numbers of whites grew by 6.0 percent and those of blacks grew by 17.3 percent.[42]

American Indians, Eskimos, and Aleuts are a young population. They have larger families than African Americans or non-Hispanic whites. In 1980 half of all American Indians and Alaska Natives were under 24 years old; some groups were even younger, as shown in table 8.9.[43] In comparison, half of blacks were at least 24.9 years old, and half of whites, at least 31.7.[44] The average American Indian family consisted of 3.84 members, but tribal families ranged in size from 4.95 members among the Papago

Table 8.9
Median Ages, Average Numbers of Family Members, and Fertility Rates of American Indians, Eskimos, and Aleuts, by Tribe or Group: United States, 1980

Tribe or group	Median age	Persons per family	Children per 1,000 women, aged 15-44
Total	23.6	3.84	1,700
Total, all American Indian tribes	23.5	3.84	1,688
Apache	21.4	4.12	1,757
Athabaskan	21.4	4.46	1,639
Blackfoot	24.6	3.38	1,711
Cherokee	27.3	3.35	1,664
Cheyenne	19.7	4.81	1,809
Chickasaw	27.6	3.41	1,511
Chippewa	20.7	4.15	1,829
Choctaw	26.1	3.60	1,654
Creek	24.4	3.81	1,479
Iroquois	24.9	3.72	1,586
Lumbee	22.4	4.13	1,881
Navajo	19.3	4.92	1,795
Paiute	21.5	4.10	1,706
Papago	21.1	4.95	1,736
Pima	19.5	4.80	1,902
Potawatomi	24.5	3.81	1,491
Pueblo	21.3	4.62	1,639
Seminole	23.5	3.94	1,549
Shoshone	22.4	4.08	1,519
Sioux	20.3	4.49	1,947
Tlingit	21.4	4.56	1,799
Eskimo	21.3	4.57	1,699
Aleut	24.5	3.62	1,531

Source: Derived from Bureau of the Census, *1980 Census of Population, General Social and Economic Characteristics, Part 1, United States Summary,*pp. 157 and 163; and idem, *1980 Census of Population, Characteristics of American Indians by Tribes and Selected Areas: 1980*, pp. 150–202.

to 3.35 members among the Cherokee.[45] Eskimo families averaged 4.57 family members, and Aleut families, 3.62 members.[46] At the same time, the average African American family consisted of 3.69 family members, and that of non-Hispanic whites, 3.16 family members.[47] The fertility rate of American Indian women averaged 1,688 children per 1,000 women, aged 15 to 44, in 1980. It ranged from 1,947 for Sioux women to 1,479 for Creek women.[48] The fertility rate among Eskimos was 1,699 children per 1,000 women, aged 15 to 44, and among Aleuts, 1,531.[49] The fertility rate of blacks in 1980 was 1,575, and that of whites, 1,232.[50] In 1980 there were 430,000 school-age American Indians, Eskimos, and Aleuts; they constituted 28 percent of the total Native American population of 1.5 million— the highest proportion among all the racial/ethnic groups.[51]

The numbers of American Indians are increasing even faster in certain states and areas than they are nationally as a result of interstate migration and of the movement of many Indians from reservations and rural areas to the cities. Between 1970 and 1980 the numbers of Indians in California increased by 117.6 percent. In some of the states with fewer Indians, there was even greater growth: 184.3 percent in Florida, 135.6 percent in Michigan, and 119.3 percent in Texas.[52] The majorities of American Indians and Alaska Natives in all these states live in urban areas.[53]

American Indian, Eskimo, and Aleut youth are the most likely of all native-born youth to be out of school without high school diplomas. There were 82,000 undereducated American Indians and Alaska Natives, and they constituted three out of ten of their age group in 1980. American Indian and Alaska Native youth living in states in which American Indian populations are largely rural and live on reservations or are otherwise isolated are at even greater risk: in 1980 those in Arizona, New Mexico, and North Carolina were 1.4 times more likely to be undereducated than American Indians and Alaska Natives living in California where most Indians live in inner cities and other urban areas. Those in California, however, were still among the most disadvantaged youth in that state.

Information from the 1990 census will determine how much the numbers of school-age American Indians and Alaska Natives have increased and whether the level of poverty is the same or whether it is decreasing as Native American populations move to the cities. It will reveal whether the numbers of undereducated American Indians, Eskimos, and Aleuts, aged 16 to 24, are growing and whether American Indians and Alaska Natives are less likely, or just as likely, to be undereducated in 1990 as in 1980. As with other minorities, improvement will depend upon whether school reforms embrace the special needs of American Indians, Eskimos, and Aleuts or whether this group will continue to be victims of "crossed purposes and unfulfilled hopes," as a recent *Education Week* report expressed it.[54] The findings of this study confirm once again that there must be substantial changes in the way Native American children are educated.

Change must take place both in schools on reservations where they are served almost exclusively and in schools in urban centers where they are often overlooked among the large numbers of other minorities with competing needs. Without increased attention and resources dedicated specifically to the education of American Indian and Alaska Native children, the population of American Indian, Eskimo, and Aleut youth who are at risk of undereducation can only grow through the remainder of this century.

NOTES

1. Bureau of the Census, U.S. Department of Commerce, *1980 Census of Population, Detailed Population Characteristics, Part 1, United States Summary* (Washington, D.C.: U.S. Government Printing Office, 1984), pp. 16 and 17.

2. Unpublished data from the 1980 census.

3. Bureau of the Census, U.S. Department of Commerce, *1980 Census of Population, Characteristics of American Indians by Tribes and Selected Areas: 1980* (Washington, D.C.: U.S. Government Printing Office, 1989), pp. 203–255.

4. William L. Leap, "American Indian Languages," in *Language in the USA,* ed. Charles A. Ferguson and Shirley Brice Heath (Cambridge, Eng.: Cambridge University Press, 1981), p. 116.

5. Bureau of the Census, U.S. Department of Commerce, *American Indian Areas and Alaska Native Villages: 1980* (Washington, D.C.: U.S. Government Printing Office, 1984), p. 3.

6. Ibid., pp. 4 and 5.

7. Bureau of the Census, U.S. Department of Commerce, *1980 Census of Population, General Social and Economic Characteristics, Part 1, United States Summary* (Washington, D.C.: U.S. Government Printing Office, 1983), p. 13.

8. Bureau of the Census, *General Social and Economic Characteristics, Part 4, Arizona; Part 33, New Mexico;* and *Part 35, North Carolina,* table 58, various pages.

9. Bureau of the Census, *American Indian Areas,* p. 4.

10. Bureau of the Census, *General Social and Economic Characteristics, Part 6, California,* p. 31.

11. Bureau of the Census, *American Indian Areas,* p. 15.

12. The difference is significant at the 68 percent confidence level.

13. Bureau of the Census, *General Social and Economic Characteristics, United States Summary,* pp. 113–114.

14. Bureau of the Census, U.S. Department of Commerce, *Race of the Population by States: 1980* (Washington, D.C.: U.S. Government Printing Office, 1981), pp. 6 and 12.

15. See table 3.12 in chapter 3 for poverty rates by racial/ethnic group and state. The differences between the rates of American Indian, Eskimo, and Aleut youth; Hispanic youth as a group; and non-Hispanic black youth in North Carolina are not statistically significant.

16. Bureau of the Census, *General Social and Economic Characteristics, Part 35, North Carolina,* pp. 61, 67, 75, and 87.

17. There were 65,000 American Indians in North Carolina in 1980, but only 2,000 individuals reported speaking an American Indian or Alaska Native language at home, and another 2,000 lived in homes in which at least one person spoke such a language in 1980. Bureau of the Census, *Race of the Population,* p. 6, and idem, *Detailed Population Characteristics, Part 35, North Carolina,* pp. 19 and 20.

18. Bureau of the Census, *Characteristics of American Indians,* p. 228.

19. Ibid., pp. 203–255.

20. The differences between the undereducation rates of American Indians, Eskimos, and Aleuts and those of native-born Hispanics in Arizona, North Carolina, and Washington are significant at the 68 percent level of confidence.

21. Bureau of the Census, *General Social and Economic Characteristics, Part 6, California,* p. 31.

22. Bureau of the Census, *American Indian Areas,* p. 15.

23. Ibid., p. 24.

24. Bureau of the Census, *General Social and Economic Characteristics, Part 35, North Carolina,* p. 21.

25. Bureau of the Census, *General Social and Economic Characteristics, Part 38, Oklahoma,* p. 17; and *Part 49, Washington,* p. 19.

26. Bureau of the Census, *American Indian Areas,* p. 4.

27. Ibid., p. 15.

28. Ibid.

29. Bureau of the Census, *General Social and Economic Characteristics, Part 4, Arizona,* p. 15; and *Part 33, New Mexico,* p. 15.

30. Bureau of the Census, *American Indian Areas,* p. 4.

31. Bureau of the Census, *General Social and Economic Characteristics, Part 3, Alaska,* p. 15.

32. Bureau of the Census, *Characteristics of American Indians,* pp. 1–53.

33. Ibid., p. 44.

34. Ibid., p. 11.

35. Ibid., p. 22.

36. Ibid., p. 8.

37. Ibid., pp. 57–58.

38. Ibid., pp. 203–255; Bureau of the Census, *General Social and Economic Characteristics, United States Summary,* p. 163.

39. Bureau of the Census, *Characteristics of American Indians,* pp. 203–255.

40. Ibid., pp. 309–361.

41. Bureau of the Census, *General Social and Economic Characteristics, United States Summary,* p. 168.

42. Bureau of the Census, *Race of the Population,* pp. 1 and 12.

43. Bureau of the Census, *Characteristics of American Indians,* pp. 150–202.

44. Bureau of the Census, *General Social and Economic Characteristics, United States Summary,* p. 163.

45. Bureau of the Census, *Characteristics of American Indians,* pp. 150–202.

46. Bureau of the Census, *General Social and Economic Characteristics, United States Summary,* p. 157.

47. Ibid., p. 163.

48. Bureau of the Census, *Characteristics of American Indians,* pp. 150–202.

49. Bureau of the Census, *General Social and Economic Characteristics, United States Summary,* p. 157.

50. Ibid., p. 163.

51. Bureau of the Census, *Detailed Population Characteristics, United States Summary,* pp. 7–8 and 40–51.

52. Bureau of the Census, *Race of the Population,* p. 12.

53. Bureau of the Census, *General Social and Economic Characteristics, Part 11, Florida; Part 24, Michigan;* and *Part 45, Texas,* table 58, various pages.

54. 'Stuck in the Horizon,' A Special Report on the Education of Native Americans, *Education Week* (Washington, D.C.), August 2, 1989, p. 1.

9

Asian and Pacific Islander
Youth Who Are Undereducated

The majority of Asian and Pacific Islander youth in the United States were born in foreign countries. Most come from homes in which non-English languages are spoken, and half of them live in the central cities of metropolitan areas. They are disproportionately poor. Nevertheless, as a group, Asian/Pacific youth are less likely to be out of school without high school diplomas than whites from monolingual English-speaking families who were born in the United States and are considerably more advantaged economically and socially. In 1980 there were 55,000 undereducated Asians and Pacific Islanders, aged 16 to 24. They comprised fewer than one in ten of their age group, and they were 1.3 times less likely than white majority youth and much less likely than other minority youth to be undereducated.

Asian and Pacific Islander youth belong to a group that numbered 3.7 million people in 1980[1] and has been increased by 2 million legal immigrants since then.[2] Asian/Pacific youth are the most likely of all youth to be foreign-born, and the characteristics of those who are foreign-born are very different from those of native-born Asian and Pacific Islander Americans. Asian/Pacific youth are the second most likely, after Hispanics, to have language minority backgrounds. In 1980, 57.3 percent of all Asians and Pacific Islanders, aged 16 to 24, were born outside the United States, and nearly three-quarters lived in households in which one or more people speak a language other than English.

Asians and Pacific Islanders as a group are more likely to be poor than whites, but they are less likely than other minority groups: 13.1 percent of Asians and Pacific Islanders had 1979 incomes below the poverty level, in comparison with 9.4 percent of whites and rates of nearly a quarter and more for other minorities.[3] Young Asians and Pacific Islanders are more likely to be poor than the total population of Asians and Pacific Islanders. One in five of those aged 16 to 24 in 1980 lived in a family whose income was below the poverty level. They were 1.8 times more likely to be poor than white majority youth. Poor Asian/Pacific youth are more than twice as likely to be undereducated as Asians and Pacific Islanders who are not from the poorest families.

Asians and Pacific Islanders are the most urbanized of all the racial/ ethnic groups, and more of them live in the central cities of metropolitan areas than in the suburbs although the proportion in the suburbs is the largest of any of the groups. In 1980 more than nine out of ten Asians and Pacific Islanders in all lived in urban areas—46.3 percent in central cities, 39.6 percent in suburbs of central cities, and 7.3 percent in smaller cities and towns.[4] Asian/Pacific youth in the suburbs are less likely than youth in the central cities to be undereducated— their 1980 rate was 6.5 percent as compared with 8.4 percent for the central city youth—but both groups are less likely to be undereducated than other youth living in the suburbs.[5]

The aggregate national undereducation rate of Asians and Pacific Islanders suggests that all Asian/Pacific youth are doing well educationally in the United States. However, other evidence from the study reveals that this is not the case. Asian and Pacific Islander youth who are undereducated are likely to be very undereducated. In 1980 undereducated Asians and Pacific Islanders were four times more likely than other undereducated youth to have less than a fifth grade education, and they were second only to Hispanics in the proportions failing to complete at least nine years of schooling before discontinuing their education. Moreover, Asians and Pacific Islanders do not have low undereducation rates in all states. In 1980 there were two undereducated Asians and Pacific Islanders in Texas for every one, proportionally, in the other seven states with substantial populations of Asian/Pacific youth. Asian/Pacific youth in Texas are somewhat more likely than white majority youth in that state, and almost as likely as black youth, to be undereducated.

These statistics highlight one of the problems of treating Asians and Pacific Islanders as though they were one homogeneous group. The aggregate national undereducation rate and other statistics that group Asians, with or without Pacific Islanders, conceal a multitude of differences among peoples with contrasting characteristics, backgrounds, and needs, some of whom are doing very well in this country and others of whom are struggling. They reflect the well-being of the majority of the largest Asian groups at the expense of recently arrived Asian immigrants, especially those from Southeast Asia, and at the expense of native Hawaiians in Hawaii, whose condition resembles, in some respects, that of American Indians in continental United States.

Some of the Asian immigrants who have arrived since 1980 are highly educated. They contribute to the economic well-being of their groups and to the general superiority of Asian Americans as a whole on many social and economic indicators, including undereducation rates. Other new immigrants, notably some of those from Southeast Asia, lack even the basic skills. The young people in these groups—and the young women more than the young men—are highly likely to be undereducated. Their presence will be reflected in the 1990 census findings, when it will again be possible to look at the status of Asians and Pacific Islanders as a group and at that of the individual ethnic communities that make up the Asian/Pacific population in the United States.

Depending on the size of other Asian groups, the arrival of new Southeast Asian immigrants affects the state undereducation rates and numbers of undereducated Asian/Pacific youth more in some states than in others. In Texas, for example, immigrants from Vietnam, Cambodia, and Laos constituted a quarter of the Asian/Pacific population in 1980.[6] Since 1980, many new Southeast Asian immigrants have settled in Texas, increasing the size of the population at risk in that state. Other states, especially Massachusetts and Washington, have also received disproportionate numbers of Southeast Asian immigrants since 1980. Nationally, and in these states, the 1990 census and other data sources that are sufficiently large to provide statistics for Asians and Pacific Islanders may well reflect a decline in the educational status of Asians and Pacific Islanders.

The following sections of this chapter contain descriptions of the characteristics of undereducated Asian and Pacific Islander youth as found in the study, the undereducation rates of this group, and some of the differences between them as a group and undereducated white majority and other youth in the United States. Undereducation rates and characteristics of the undereducated Asians and Pacific Islanders in the eight states with at least an estimated 10,000 Asian/Pacific youth in 1980 are examined in relation to the risk of undereducation. The final sections contain an examination of the characteristics and geographical distribution of the major groups of Asian and Pacific Islander peoples and of immigrants from Asian countries who were in the United States in 1980. They also contain information on immigration from Asian countries since 1980, along with a discussion of its potential effect on the numbers and undereducation rates of Asian and Pacific Islander youth in the United States and in the eight states with the largest numbers of these youth. The information on Asian and Pacific Islander peoples in the United States in 1980 is from the 1980 census volumes and other published Bureau of the Census sources. The Immigration and Naturalization Service provided the information on Asian immigration since 1980.

THE NUMBERS AND CHARACTERISTICS OF UNDEREDUCATED ASIAN AND PACIFIC ISLANDER YOUTH

As shown in table 9.1, there were 55,000 Asian and Pacific Islander youth in the United States in 1980 who were out of school and had not completed 12 years of schooling. Forty thousand of them—nearly three-quarters—were born in foreign countries. They were twice as likely to be undereducated as Asian and Pacific Islanders born in the United States, as shown in table 9.2, and there were other differences that are discussed below.

Table 9.1

Estimated Numbers and Distribution of Undereducated Asian and Pacific Islander Youth, by Nativity and Selected Characteristic: United States, 1980

Characteristic	Total		Native born		Foreign born	
	Number	Percent	Number	Percent	Number	Percent
Total	55,000	100.0	15,000	100.0	40,000	100.0
Gender						
Males	25,000	46.4	8,000	53.4	17,000	43.7
Females	29,000	53.6	7,000	46.6	22,000	56.3
Age						
16 to 19	18,000	32.2	6,000	43.1	11,000	28.1
20 to 24	37,000	67.8	9,000	56.9	29,000	71.9
Language background						
English only	11,000	20.8	9,000	59.2	2,000	6.2
Non-English	44,000	79.2	6,000	40.8	37,000	93.8
Poverty status in 1979[1]						
Above poverty level	35,000	64.0	10,000	68.8	25,000	62.1
Below poverty level	18,000	32.0	3,000	22.5	14,000	35.6
Years of schooling completed						
Fewer than 5	9,000	15.7	1,000	7.7	7,000	18.7
5 to 8	13,000	24.1	2,000	12.9	11,000	28.4
9 to 11	33,000	60.2	12,000	79.4	21,000	52.9

Note: Percentages calculated on unrounded numbers. Detail may not add to total because of rounding.

[1]Not determined for people living in group quarters.

Table 9.2
Estimated Numbers of Undereducated Asian and Pacific Islander Youth and Asian/Pacific Undereducation Rates, by Nativity and Selected Characteristic: United States, 1980

Characteristic	Total		Native born		Foreign born	
	Number	Rate	Number	Rate	Number	Rate
Total	55,000	9.8	15,000	6.3	40,000	12.4
Gender						
Males	25,000	9.1	8,000	6.7	17,000	11.0
Females	29,000	10.5	7,000	5.9	22,000	13.9
Age						
16 to 19	18,000	7.5	6,000	6.1	11,000	8.8
20 to 24	37,000	11.5	9,000	6.5	29,000	14.9
Language background						
English only	11,000	7.8	9,000	7.4	2,000	10.0
Non-English	44,000	10.5	6,000	5.2	37,000	12.6
Poverty status in 1979[1]						
Above poverty level	35,000	8.6	10,000	5.4	25,000	11.4
Below poverty level	18,000	17.2	3,000	12.7	14,000	18.8

Note: Detail may not add to total because of rounding.

[1]Not determined for people living in group quarters.

Among native-born undereducated Asian/Pacific youth, men outnumber women in proportions similar to those of white majority men to women—53.6 percent to 46.4 percent in 1980; among foreign-born undereducated Asian/Pacific youth, women are the majority—56.3 percent to 43.7 percent in 1980. The difference between the 1980 undereducation rates of native-born Asian/Pacific women and men—5.9 percent and 6.7 percent, respectively—is not statistically significant; nevertheless, native-born Asian/Pacific women, like their white majority sisters, appear to have an advantage. In contrast, foreign-born women are more likely to be undereducated than men; their 1980 rate was 13.9 percent in comparison to 11.0 for men.

Foreign-born undereducated Asian/Pacific youth are especially likely to be older, perhaps because more older than younger youth immigrate, and few who come in their late teens or older enter school in this country. In 1980 young adults, aged 20 to 24, outnumbered teenagers by a factor of more than two to one per year of age. Among the native-born, the factor was only 1.1, the same as that among white majority youth. Foreign-born Asian/Pacific young adults, in contrast, were 1.7 times more likely to be undereducated than their teenage counterparts. There was little, if any, difference in the rates of older and younger native-born Asian/Pacific youth.

The majority of Asian and Pacific Islander youth live in language minority households—73.9 percent did so in 1980. However, like African Americans and whites, and unlike Hispanics and American Indians, Eskimos, and Aleuts, native-born Asians and Pacific Islanders who live in homes in which one or more people speak a language other than English are less likely than native-born Asians and Pacific Islanders who live in monolingual English-speaking homes to be out of school without high school diplomas. In 1980 the comparative undereducation rates were 5.2 percent for those with language minority backgrounds and 7.4 percent for those with English monolingual backgrounds. (See table 3.2 in chapter 3.)

There is a strong relationship between nativity and language background among Asians and Pacific Islanders. In 1980, 92.3 percent of all foreign-born Asian/Pacific youth lived in households in which one or more people speak a language other than English at home, but only 49.2 percent of native-born youth lived in such households. Among undereducated foreign-born youth, 93.8 percent, and among undereducated native-born youth, 40.8 percent, lived in language minority households. There were 44,000 undereducated Asians and Pacific Islanders in language minority households; 84.1 percent of them were foreign born.

Although Asians and Pacific Islanders as a group are more likely to be poor than white majority youth, the most serious economic disadvantage plagues foreign-born Asian/Pacific youth. Native-born Asian and Pacific Islander youth are not much more likely to be poor than non-Hispanic whites. Their rate was 12.3 percent in comparison with 11.1 percent of white majority and 11.3 percent of non-Hispanic white minority youth who were from families with 1979 incomes below the poverty level.[7] Asian/Pacific youth born outside the United States are twice as likely to come from families with incomes below the poverty level; in 1980 their rate was 25.8 percent, about the same as those of foreign-born Hispanic and black youth. (See table 3.7 in chapter 3.)

Poverty is an even greater risk factor for native-born Asians and Pacific Islanders than it is for majority whites. In 1980 native-born youth from poor families were 2.4 times more likely to be undereducated than those from more economically advantaged families. Among white majority youth the ratio was 2.1. Foreign-born Asians and Pacific Islanders from poor families were 1.6 times more likely to be undereducated than those from more advantaged families. (See table 3.6 in chapter 3.)

The poverty status of 49,000 Asian/Pacific youth—8.8 percent of the total 16-to-24-year-old group—was not determined because they lived in group quarters in 1980. This group included about 2,000 undereducated Asians and Pacific Islanders.

Surprisingly, in view of their overall favorable undereducation rates, Asian and Pacific Islanders who are undereducated are more likely than other youth to be very undereducated; they are the likeliest of all youth to have completed fewer than five years of schooling and the second likeliest, after Hispanics, to have completed fewer than nine years. (See table 2.6 in chapter 2.) Again, the differences between native-born and foreign-born youth are considerable. Native-born Asians and Pacific Islanders who were not high school graduates were about as likely as white majority and other native-born white youth in 1980 to have completed at least nine years of schooling before discontinuing their education. They were 1.5 times more likely to have done so than foreign-born Asians and Pacific Islanders who were somewhat less likely to have completed at least nine years than foreign-born whites.[8] In 1980 nearly four out of five native-born but only a little more than half of foreign-born Asian/Pacific youth had completed at least nine years of schooling. By the measure of completion of at least five years, native-born as well as foreign-born Asians and Pacific Islanders—but especially those who are foreign born—are seriously disadvantaged. Native-born Asians and Pacific Islanders are the most likely of all native-born youth, and foreign-born Asians and Pacific Islanders are among the most likely of foreign-born youth, to have completed no more than four years of schooling. The 1980 proportion of native-born undereducated Asian/Pacific youth with less than a fifth grade education was 7.7 percent; that of foreign-born youth was 18.7 percent. In comparison, 2.7 percent of undereducated white majority youth and 10.8 percent of undereducated foreign-born non-Hispanic white youth, including those with monolingual English-speaking backgrounds, had completed fewer than five years of schooling. Fifty-six percent of all Asians and Pacific Islanders with fewer than five years of schooling were foreign-born women.

UNDEREDUCATED ASIAN AND PACIFIC ISLANDER YOUTH IN THE STATES

Like Asians and Pacific Islanders in general, the largest group of undereducated Asian/Pacific youth in the United States live in California. In 1980 there were 17,000 undereducated Asian/Pacific youth in California. They constituted three out of ten of undereducated Asians and Pacific Islanders in the United States. The second largest group—8,000—lived in Hawaii. Asians and Pacific Islanders are the majority population in Hawaii;[9] undereducated Asian/Pacific youth are the largest proportion of undereducated youth there. In all, there were 23 states with at least 1,000 undereducated Asians and Pacific Islanders in 1980. Undereducated

Asian/Pacific youth constituted 47.1 percent of undereducated youth in Hawaii in 1980; their proportion was less than 3 percent in other states. (See tables 2.8 and 2.9 in chapter 2.)

In addition to California and Hawaii, the other states with at least 10,000 Asian/Pacific youth, aged 16 to 24, in 1980 were Illinois, Massachusetts, New Jersey, New York, Texas, and Washington. Sixty-eight percent of undereducated Asian/Pacific youth and three-quarters of all the Asians and Pacific Islanders in the United States in 1980 lived in those eight states.[10] The undereducation rates and characteristics of Asian/Pacific youth and the characteristics of the various Asian and Pacific Islander populations and Asian immigrant populations in those states are discussed in the following sections of this chapter.

THE STATE UNDEREDUCATION RATES OF ASIAN AND PACIFIC ISLANDER YOUTH

As illustrated in figure 9.1, Asians and Pacific Islanders in Texas are much more likely than Asian/Pacific youth in the other seven states with

Figure 9.1
Undereducation Rates of Asian and Pacific Islander Youth, 1980

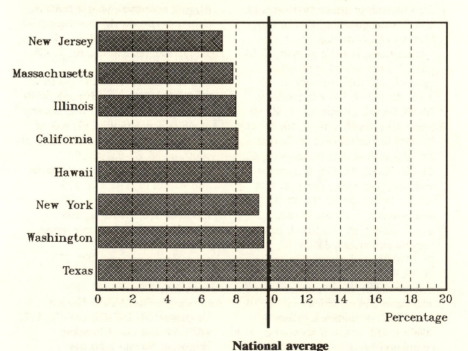

at least 10,000 Asian/Pacific youth in 1980 not to be enrolled in school and not to have completed 12 years of schooling. In 1980 one in six Asian/Pacific youth in Texas was undereducated, almost twice as many, proportionately, as in the other states. The undereducation rates of Asians and Pacific Islanders in California, Hawaii, Illinois, Massachusetts, New Jersey, New York, and Washington ranged from 7.2 percent to 9.6 percent in 1980, but these differences are not statistically significant. In all of these states, Asian/Pacific youth are less likely than, or only as likely as, white majority youth in the same states to be undereducated. In Texas, their 1980 rate—17.0 percent—was somewhat higher than that of whites and approached that of African Americans; the rate of white majority youth was 14.7 percent, and that of African Americans, 19.2 percent.[11] (See table 3.9 in chapter 3.)

THE CHARACTERISTICS OF ASIAN AND PACIFIC ISLANDER YOUTH IN THE STATES

Asian/Pacific youth in Texas differ from those in the other states, as shown in table 9.3. They are more likely to be poor and foreign born and are among the most likely to live in language minority households. In all of these characteristics they differed significantly in 1980 from Asian/Pacific youth in California and Hawaii. They differed significantly from those in New York and New Jersey, and probably from those in Washington and Illinois, on the poverty measure.[12] They differed from those in

Table 9.3
Estimated Numbers of Asian and Pacific Islander Youth and Percentages with Selected Characteristics, by Selected State: United States, 1980

State	Number	Percentage		
		In poverty[1]	Foreign born	With NELB[2]
Total, all states	559,000	20.1	57.3	73.9
California	207,000	19.1	56.3	78.1
Hawaii	89,000	10.9	18.5	50.2
Illinois	21,000	20.7	77.8	86.5
Massachusetts	10,000	26.4	67.3	81.9
New Jersey	11,000	10.8	73.3	82.9
New York	45,000	18.4	77.3	86.0
Texas	20,000	29.6	78.4	84.0
Washington	20,000	23.3	54.7	63.3

Note: Selected states are those with at least an estimated 10,000 Asians and Pacific Islanders, aged 16 to 24.

[1]Poverty status not determined for people living in group quarters.

[2]Non-English language background.

Washington in nativity and language background. Underlying these differences are differences among the Asian and Pacific Islander populations in the various states.

ASIAN PEOPLES IN THE UNITED STATES

In 1980 there were 3.7 million Asians and Pacific Islanders in the United States.[13] As shown in table 9.4, 3.5 million of them were Asians. The largest groups consisted of Chinese, 812,000; Filipinos, 782,000; and Japanese, 716,000. In addition, there were 387,000 Asian Indians, 357,000 Koreans, and 245,000 Vietnamese. Asian American groups are heavily concentrated in certain states. In 1980, 40 percent of Chinese lived in California; another 18 percent lived in New York. Forty-six percent of Filipinos lived in California and 17 percent in Hawaii. Thirty-eight percent of Japanese lived in California and a third in Hawaii. Seventeen percent of Asian Indians lived in New York, 15 percent in California, 10 percent in Illinois, and 8 percent in New Jersey. Nearly three in ten Koreans lived in California where more than a third of Vietnamese and Cambodians and a quarter of Laotians also lived in 1980.[14]

Table 9.4
Estimated Numbers of Asians, by Selected State and Group: United States, 1980 (Numbers in thousands)

Group	Total, all states	California	Hawaii	Illinois	Massachusetts	New Jersey	New York	Texas	Washington
Total, all Asians	3,467	1,247	453	171	52	108	327	130	105
Asian Indian	387	60	1	37	9	31	68	23	4
Cambodian (Kampuchean)	16	6	*	1	*	*	*	1	2
Chinese	812	326	56	29	25	23	147	27	18
Filipino	782	358	132	44	3	24	36	16	26
Hmong	5	1	*	*	*	*	*	*	*
Indonesian	10	5	*	*	*	*	1	*	*
Japanese	716	269	240	18	4	10	25	12	27
Korean	357	103	17	24	5	13	33	14	13
Laotian	48	12	1	3	1	*	1	3	2
Pakistani	16	3	*	2	*	1	3	1	*
Thai	45	13	1	3	1	1	4	3	1
Vietnamese	245	85	3	6	3	3	6	28	9

Source: Derived from Bureau of the Census, Asian and Pacific Islander Population by State: 1980, pp. 12–13.

Note: Selected states are those with at least an estimated 10,000 Asians and Pacific Islanders, aged 16 to 24.

*Fewer than an estimated 1,000 people.

Texas is the only one of the eight states with large Asian populations in which the Vietnamese outnumbered other groups in 1980. Vietnamese constituted 21 percent of the Asian population; including Cambodians, Hmongs, and Laotians, Indochinese made up a quarter of all the Asians in Texas in 1980. The proportions of Indochinese in the other states ranged from 12.7 percent in Washington to 1.1 percent in Hawaii. The 1980 populations of Asian Americans in six of the other seven states were dominated by Chinese, Filipinos, and Japanese, the largest groups nationally. Asian Indians were the largest group in New Jersey.[15]

The Vietnamese—the largest Asian group in Texas—and other Indochinese populations differ considerably from the Asian populations that predominate in the other states. They are the most recent Asian arrivals and the least prepared to adjust rapidly to their new homes and to begin to make their way economically. Moreover, unlike immigrant members of the other, longer-established Asian groups who are able to join U.S. ethnic enclaves directly from their home countries, many Indochinese immigrants have experienced refugee camps abroad and dispersion in this country. As shown in table 9.5, more than nine out of ten Indochinese in the United States in 1980 were immigrants, and nine out of ten of them had arrived between 1975 and 1980.[16] Vietnamese men, aged 25 and older,

Table 9.5
Percentages of Asians Who Are Foreign Born; High School Graduation Rates of Men and Women, Aged 25 and Older; and Poverty Rates of Individuals, Aged 15 and Older, by Asian Group: United States, 1980

| Group | Foreign born | Graduation rates, adults, 25+ | | Poverty rates[1] |
		Men	Women	
Total, all Asians	62.1	79.3	71.8	12.1
Asian Indian	70.4	88.8	71.5	10.6
Cambodian (Kampuchean)	93.9	49.9	32.0	48.7
Chinese	63.3	75.2	67.4	13.3
Filipino	64.7	73.1	75.1	6.9
Hmong	90.5	27.8	17.1	62.8
Indonesian	83.4	93.7	84.8	20.1
Japanese	28.4	84.2	79.5	6.6
Korean	81.9	90.0	70.6	12.5
Laotian	93.7	38.0	23.9	65.9
Pakistani	85.1	92.7	75.3	13.4
Thai	82.1	93.7	61.3	14.2
Vietnamese	90.5	71.3	53.6	33.5

Source: Derived from Bureau of the Census, "More of Asian and Pacific Islander Families Have at Least Two Workers Than Do Other U.S. Families, Census Bureau Says," table 1.

[1]Rates for non-institutional population, aged 15 and older.

were as likely to be high school graduates as white men—71.3 percent as compared with 69.6 percent—but only half of Cambodian men, 38.0 percent of Laotian men, and 27.8 percent of Hmong men had completed 12 or more years of schooling. Among the women, the rates ranged from 53.6 percent of Vietnamese women to 17.1 percent of Hmong women, in comparison with 68.1 percent of white women.[17] More recent immigrants from Vietnam are less well educated than earlier immigrants. Among adults who had immigrated between 1975 and 1980, 60.8 percent were high school graduates, and 10.6 percent had completed fewer than five years of schooling. In comparison 66.6 percent of the 1970–74 Vietnamese immigrants were high school graduates, and 8.8 percent had less than fifth grade educations. The earlier immigrants were 1.7 times more likely to be college graduates than the 1975–80 immigrants.[18]

Indochinese poverty rates parallel their levels of education and recency of arrival. The Vietnamese were 3.6 times more likely to be poor than whites in 1980. A third of those who were at least 15 years of age had incomes below the poverty level in comparison with 9.4 percent of whites. The other groups were much worse off: half of the Cambodians and as a many as two-thirds of the Hmongs and Laotians were poor.[19]

Among other Asian groups, fewer are recent immigrants, educational attainment is considerably higher, and poverty, considerably lower. In 1980 the poverty rates of people, aged 15 and older, in the longer-established groups ranged from 6.6 percent for the Japanese and 6.9 percent for the Filipinos—well below that of whites—to 13.3 percent for the Chinese and 13.4 percent for the Pakistanis.[20] The Japanese are largely native born: in 1980 fewer than three in ten were born in Japan or elsewhere abroad. The high school graduation rates of Japanese American women and men are well above those of white women and men. The majority of members of the other major Asian American groups are foreign born, but the overall proportions of foreign-born people and the proportions of recent immigrants among them are considerably less than among the Indochinese groups. About two-thirds of the Chinese and Filipinos, seven in ten Asian Indians, and eight in ten Koreans in 1980 were born abroad. Among the immigrants, 54.6 percent of those born in Taiwan, 52.3 percent of those born in Korea, and 43.7 percent of those born in India had arrived in the United States as recently as 1975; only a third of immigrants from Hong Kong and the Philippines, and 27.2 percent of those from mainland China, were recent arrivals.[21] The educational attainment of Chinese, Filipinos, Asian Indians, and Koreans in the United States, like that of the Japanese, is also well above that of whites in the United States, as shown in table 9.5. Their high school graduation rates in 1980 ranged from 90.0 percent for Korean men to 73.1 for Filipino men and from 75.1 for Filipino women to 70.6 for Korean women. Moreover, many members of these groups are college graduates. In 1980 the college graduation rates ranged from 41.2 percent of Filipino women to 22.0 percent of Korean women and from two-thirds of Asian Indian men to a third of Filipino men.[22] In contrast, 13.3 percent of white women and 21.3 percent of white men, aged 25 and older, were college graduates.[23]

There has been a veritable "brain drain" of highly educated immigrants from some of the Asian countries. Among people born in India, aged 25 and older, in the United States in 1980, two-thirds were college graduates; three in ten of those born in Taiwan, nearly as many of those born in Pakistan, and two in five of those born in Hong Kong and the Philippines were college graduates.[24] These people adjust quickly to life in their new home. They find professional employment and contribute to the generally favorable economic levels of their groups.

PACIFIC ISLANDER PEOPLES IN THE UNITED STATES

There were 260,000 Pacific Islanders living in the United States in 1980, as shown in table 9.6. The largest group—172,000—consisted of native Hawaiians, seven out of ten of whom lived in Hawaii. The other major groups were Samoans, 40,000, and Guamanians, 31,000. More than half of the Guamanians and nearly half of the Samoans lived in California.[25]

In contrast with all the Asian American groups except the Japanese, Pacific Islanders living in the United States are largely native-born citizens. In 1980, as shown in table 9.7, among people in the three major groups, all but 1.6 percent of Hawaiians, 9.5 percent of Guamanians, and 35.6 percent of Samoans were born in their native islands, another state if not Hawaii, or another outlying U.S. area if not Guam or American Samoa.[26]

Hawaiian and Guamanian men are about as likely as white men, and Hawaiian women are about as likely as white women, to be high school graduates. Samoan men lag behind white men. Guamanian women and, especially, Samoan women lag behind white women. In 1980, 67.0 percent of Hawaiian women, 64.7 percent of Guamanian women, and 56.6 percent

Table 9.6
Estimated Numbers of Pacific Islanders in the United States and in California and Hawaii, by Group, 1980

Group	Total, all states	California	Hawaii
Total, all Pacific Islanders	260,000	66,000	138,000
Guamanian	31,000	17,000	2,000
Hawaiian	172,000	24,000	118,000
Samoan	40,000	18,000	14,000

Source: Derived from Bureau of the Census, *Asian and Pacific Islander Population by State: 1980*, pp. 14–15.

Table 9.7
Percentages of Pacific Islanders Who Are Foreign Born; High School
Graduation Rates of Men and Women, Aged 25 and Older; and Poverty
Rates of Individuals, Aged 15 and Older, by Pacific Islander Group: United
States, 1980

| | | Graduation rates, adults, 25+ | | |
Group	Foreign born	Men	Women	Poverty rates[1]
Total, all Pacific Islanders	11.8	69.4	65.2	16.4
Guamanian	9.5	71.2	64.7	13.9
Hawaiian	1.6	70.0	67.0	14.4
Samoan	35.6	65.7	56.6	25.5

Source: Derived from Bureau of the Census, "More of Asian and Pacific Islander Families
Have at Least Two Workers Than Do Other U.S. Families, Census Bureau Says," table 2.

[1]Rates for non-institutional population, aged 15 and older.

of Samoan women, aged 25 and older, were high school graduates in comparison with 68.1 percent of white women in the age group. Among men,
aged 25 and older, 71.2 percent of Guamanians, 70.0 percent of Hawaiians, and 65.7 percent of Samoans were high school graduates; the comparable rate of white men in 1980 was 69.6 percent.[27]

Pacific Islanders are more likely than whites and all but the most recent
Asian immigrants to be poor. Among people in the three major groups,
Samoans are the poorest. About 14 percent of Hawaiians and Guamanians and a quarter of Samoans, aged 15 and older, had 1979 incomes below
the poverty level in comparison with 9.4 percent of whites and an average
of 12.1 percent for the Asian groups.[28]

IMMIGRATION FROM ASIA SINCE 1980

Since April 1980, 2 million people have immigrated to the United States
from Asian countries, and they are continuing to arrive at the rate of
about 235,000 per year, as shown in table 9.8. The largest groups consist
of people born in the Philippines, 396,000; Vietnam, 337,000; China, Taiwan, and Hong Kong, 355,000; Korea, 289,000; India, 211,000; Laos,
130,000; and Cambodia (Kampuchea), 107,000.[29]

The arrival of Asian immigrants has dramatically increased the sizes
of certain Asian American groups, especially the groups from Southeast
Asia. Since 1980, immigration of people born in Cambodia and Laos has
increased the numbers of Cambodians nearly eightfold and the numbers
of Laotians, nearly fourfold. Post-1980 immigrants born in Vietnam have
increased the numbers of Vietnamese 2.4 times. Moreover, these numbers

Table 9.8
Estimated Numbers and Yearly Average Numbers of Immigrants Born in Asian and Pacific Island Countries Admitted to the United States between April 1, 1980, and September 30, 1988, and Numbers Admitted in Fiscal Year 1988, by Selected Country of Birth

Country of birth	Total	Average per year, 1980—88	Admitted, FY 1988
Total	2,014,000	237,000	229,488
Total, all Asian countries	1,998,000	235,000	227,673
Bangladesh	9,000	1,000	1,325
Burma	8,000	1,000	803
Cambodia (Kampuchea)	107,000	13,000	9,629
China and Taiwan	309,000	36,000	38,387
Hong Kong	46,000	5,000	8,546
India	211,000	25,000	26,268
Indonesia	10,000	1,000	1,342
Japan	35,000	4,000	4,512
Korea	289,000	34,000	34,703
Laos	130,000	15,000	10,667
Malaysia	8,000	1,000	1,250
Pakistan	46,000	5,000	5,438
Philippines	396,000	47,000	50,697
Thailand	48,000	6,000	6,888
Vietnam	337,000	40,000	25,789
Total, all Pacific Island countries	16,000	2,000	1,815
Fiji	8,000	1,000	1,028

Source: Derived from Immigration and Naturalization Service, unpublished tabulations.

Note: The numbers of immigrants admitted between April 1 and September 30, 1980, are estimated to be half the totals for fiscal year 1980.

do not include the children of Cambodians, Laotians, and Vietnamese born in the refugee camps in Thailand who further swell the numbers of ethnic Cambodians, Laotians, and Vietnamese in the United States.[30]

Although substantial, the numbers of immigrants born in the Philippines, China, Taiwan, and Hong Kong, India, and Korea who have come to the United States since 1980 are proportionally much smaller in comparison with the 1980 U.S. populations of these groups. The increases in the Filipino, Chinese, Asian Indian, and Korean populations because of immigration ranged from 44 percent for Chinese to 80 percent for Koreans between 1980 and 1988.

Immigration of people born in Cambodia, Laos, and Vietnam peaked in 1982 and 1983 while immigration from Hong Kong, Korea, the Philippines, and India appears to be rising and that from China and Taiwan to

be fluctuating. However, one in five of all Asians admitted to the United
States in 1988 was born in Cambodia, Laos, or Vietnam.[31] Indochinese
constitute even more substantial proportions of Asian immigrants moving into certain states, as indicated in the following sections.

Immigrants tend to settle where other members of their groups are located. Thus Asian immigration is felt especially in the states that already
have substantial Asian American populations. The Asians admitted in
1987 who were born in one of the eleven countries that contributed the
largest numbers of 1987 immigrants were no exception: seven in ten
planned to reside in the eight states with at least 10,000 Asian and Pacific
Islander youth in 1980, as shown in table 9.9. More than a third of the
1987 Asian immigrants—76,600—were headed for California. Another
11.6 percent planned to reside in New York, 5.1 percent in Illinois, and
5.1 percent in Texas. Except for Pakistanis, the largest numbers of each
of the groups planned to reside in California. The largest numbers of immigrants born in Pakistan planned to live in New York.[32]

The proportions of the 1987 immigrants from various Asian countries
intending to reside in certain states roughly parallel the proportions of the
various Asian populations in those states in 1980, with two exceptions.
Since only about 4,000 Japanese immigrated to the United States in 1987,

Table 9.9
**Immigrants Admitted to the United States in Fiscal Year 1987, by Selected
State of Intended Residence and Country of Birth**

Country of birth	Total, all states	Cali-fornia	Hawaii	Illinois	Massa-chusetts	New Jersey	New York	Texas	Wash-ington
Total, all Asian countries	212,761	76,600	5,735	10,876	5,769	8,705	24,601	10,858	6,370
Cambodia (Kampuchea)	12,460	3,953	18	354	1,320	18	589	652	1,075
China	25,841	10,088	583	786	908	603	7,542	648	471
Hong Kong	4,706	1,963	105	169	196	143	1,034	178	73
India	27,803	4,770	15	2,883	673	3,144	4,241	1,852	271
Korea	35,849	9,999	912	1,910	509	1,582	4,012	1,493	1,348
Laos	6,828	2,245	29	175	170	10	130	486	257
Pakistan	6,319	1,022	13	626	76	448	1,376	618	34
Philippines	50,060	24,833	3,784	2,820	268	1,889	2,602	1,471	1,397
Taiwan	11,931	5,148	95	367	233	610	1,480	935	220
Thailand	6,733	2,460	37	255	347	59	418	371	395
Vietnam	24,231	10,119	144	531	1,069	199	1,177	2,154	829

Source: Derived from Immigration and Naturalization Service, *Statistical Yearbook of the
Immigration and Naturalization Service, 1987*, pp. 32–34.

Note: Selected states are those with at least an estimated 10,000 Asians and Pacific Islanders, aged 16 to 24, in 1980.

their proportions are disregarded. The large influx of Cambodians, Laotians, and Vietnamese meant that Indochinese constituted the largest group, with Massachusetts or Washington as their planned state of residence, and the second largest group, after Filipinos, headed for California. These groups constituted 44.4 percent of intended Massachusetts immigrants, 33.9 percent of intended Washington immigrants, and 21.3 percent of intended California immigrants.[33] The Indochinese immigrants headed for Massachusetts in 1987 represented a group nearly seven-tenths the size of the total Indochinese population resident in Massachusetts in 1980, which, at that time, constituted 7.1 percent of all Asians there. The Indochinese, the largest group of Asians and a quarter of Texas Asians in 1980, constituted three in ten of 1987 Asian immigrants who intended to reside in Texas.[34]

UNDEREDUCATED ASIAN AND PACIFIC ISLANDER YOUTH IN THE REMAINDER OF THIS CENTURY

In 1980 Asian and Pacific Islander youth were 1.3 times less likely than white majority youth to be undereducated, and there were only 55,000 undereducated Asians and Pacific Islanders in the United States. The favorable undereducation rate of Asian/Pacific youth and the small number of undereducated Asians and Pacific Islanders reflect the educational and economic well-being of the Asian groups that were dominant among Asian and Pacific Islander Americans through the seventies. However, recent immigration and population growth are changing the composition of the Asian and Pacific Islander population. Immigrants from Cambodia, Laos, and Vietnam—the least well-educated among Asians coming to the United States—are an increasing proportion of the total population. Because of population growth and the age distribution of immigrants, Cambodians, Hmongs, Laotians, and Vietnamese are an even larger proportion of the school-age Asian/Pacific population. Population growth is also increasing the proportion of school-age Hawaiians, Guamanians, Samoans, and other Pacific Islanders. All of these groups are poorer than the older-established Asian American groups. The young people among them are more at risk of undereducation.

Indochinese constituted 8.4 percent of the 3.7 million Asians and Pacific Islanders of all ages and 12.6 percent of the school-age population in 1980; Pacific Islanders constituted 7.0 percent of the total and 8.8 percent of the school-age population.[35] Since 1980, 2 million immigrants born in Asian countries and 16,000 Fijians, Tongans, and other Pacific Islanders have been legally admitted to the United States. Nearly three out of ten of these post-1980 Asian and Pacific Islander immigrants were born in Cambodia, Laos, or Vietnam.[36] An estimated 293,000 of those admitted between 1980 and 1985 were aged 5 to 17 in 1985, and of them, 43.7 percent were born in Indochina.[37]

The natural growth of the Indochinese and Pacific Islander populations is greater than that of the older-established Asian American populations, such as Japanese, Chinese, and Filipino Americans, and it is greater than the natural population growth of non-Hispanic whites. These groups are younger, and a larger proportion of them are women in the child-bearing years; they have larger families and higher fertility rates. In 1980 half of the Cambodians, Guamanians, Hawaiians, and Vietnamese were aged 24 or younger, as shown in table 9.10; half of the Hmongs, Laotians, and Samoans were no more than teenagers. In contrast, half of all Chinese, Filipinos, and Asian Indians were at least 28 years old, and half of the Japanese were in their thirties or older. The average family of Hmongs, Laotians, Samoans, and Vietnamese consisted of at least five people and that of Cambodians, of 4.62 people, in comparison with fewer than four people in the average Chinese, Japanese, or Asian Indian family. Samoan women, aged 15 to 44, had a fertility rate of 1,918 children per thousand, and the rates of Guamanian, Hawaiian, and Vietnamese women were higher than 1,500 per thousand. Among the other groups, the fertility rates ranged from 917 for the Japanese to 1,324 for the Asian Indians.[38] In 1980 half of non-Hispanic whites were at least 31.7 years old, the average family consisted of 3.16 people, and the fertility rate was 1,232 children per 1,000 women, aged 15 to 44.[39]

Even without further immigration, Indochinese and Pacific Islanders will constitute a greater proportion of the population of Asians and Pacific Islander Americans in the future. They will contribute disproportionately to the growth in the size of the Asian/Pacific school-age population and to its increasing share of the total school-age population in the United States. The sons and daughters of well educated Filipinos, Chinese, Japanese, Koreans, and Asian Indians in economically advantaged families are likely to complete their schooling and follow their parents into higher education. The expectations may not be so bright for the daughters and sons of less well-educated Indochinese whose lot in the United States is likely to be insecurity and economic struggle. They are less bright for poor Hawaiians, Guamanians, and Samoans. These groups swell the size of the numbers of Asian and Pacific Islander youth who are at risk.

The changes in the Asian and Pacific Islander population affect some states more than others. More than a third of the Asian immigrants admitted to the United States in 1987 intended to reside in California and another third in the other seven states with the largest Asian populations in 1980. California population experts estimate that Asians and Pacific Islanders, who constituted 5.5 percent of that state's total population in 1980,[40] will probably constitute 10 percent of California's population by the end of the century; they will exceed African Americans in numbers as the state's second largest minority group, after Hispanics.[41] However, because of the size of its native-born and longer-established Asian Ameri-

Table 9.10
Median Ages, Average Numbers of Family Members, and Fertility Rates of Asians and Pacific Islanders, by Group: United States, 1980

Group	Median age	Persons per family	Children per 1,000 women, aged 15-44
Total	28.4	3.98	1,185
Total, all Asians	28.8	3.96	NA
Asian Indian	29.6	3.45	1,324
Cambodian (Kampuchean)	22.4	4.62	NA
Chinese	29.8	3.65	968
Filipino	28.4	4.20	1,275
Hmong	16.3	5.82	NA
Indonesian	27.2	3.29	NA
Japanese	33.5	3.59	917
Korean	25.9	4.88	1,216
Laotian	16.9	5.36	NA
Pakistani	26.8	3.33	NA
Thai	27.1	5.09	NA
Vietnamese	21.5	5.16	1,549
Total, all Pacific Islanders	23.1	4.25	NA
Guamanian	23.0	3.94	1,575
Hawaiian	24.3	4.10	1,590
Samoan	19.2	5.16	1,918

Source: Derived from Bureau of the Census, "More of Asian and Pacific Islander Families Have at Least Two Workers Than Do Other U.S. Families, Census Bureau Says," tables 1 and 2; idem, *1980 Census of Population, General Social and Economic Characteristics, Part 1, United States Summary*, pp. 157 and 163.

NA = not available.

can populations, and because well educated as well as less well educated immigrant groups continue to flow into the state, the risk of undereducation for California's Asian/Pacific youth as a whole may actually decrease. The same cannot be said for other states, such as Massachusetts, Washington, and Texas, where immigrant Indochinese and their native-born children constitute, and will continue to constitute, increasing proportions of the Asian and Pacific Islander populations, replacing more advantaged groups. It cannot be said for Hawaii, where native Hawaiians are increasing in numbers and native Hawaiian youth already exceed the numbers of Filipinos, the second largest overall Asian/Pacific group after the Japanese in Hawaii,[42] and where poverty puts native Hawaiians at a special risk in comparison to white, Japanese, and Filipino Americans in Hawaii.[43]

When the 1990 census data from the sample become available in 1993, it will be possible to assess the overall changes in the undereducation rates and numbers of undereducated youth among Asians and Pacific Islanders as a whole and to examine the educational and economic status of individual Asian and Pacific Islander groups after a decade of new immigration and population growth. As shown by the analysis in this chapter, the former must be interpreted in the light of the latter. Otherwise, the special needs of the newest Asian immigrants and of Pacific Islander groups such as native Hawaiians in Hawaii may be overlooked. Without special help for the neediest among them, the undereducation rates of Asian and Pacific Islander youth and the numbers who are undereducated, up to now so low, may grow.

NOTES

1. Bureau of the Census, U.S. Department of Commerce, *Asian and Pacific Islander Population by State: 1980* (Washington, D.C.: U.S. Government Printing Office, 1983), p. 8.

2. Immigration and Naturalization Service, U.S. Department of Justice, unpublished tabulations. The number of Asian/Pacific immigrants admitted between April 1 and September 30, 1980, is estimated to be half the total for FY 1980. The total does not include immigrants born in Near Eastern countries whom the service classifies as Asians.

3. Bureau of the Census, U.S. Department of Commerce, *1980 Census of Population, General Social and Economic Characteristics, Part 1, United States Summary* (Washington, D.C.: U.S. Government Printing Office, 1983), pp. 113–114 and 126.

4. Ibid., p. 13.

5. Ibid., pp. 97–98.

6. Bureau of the Census, *Asian and Pacific Islander Population*, pp. 12–13.

7. The difference between 12.3 percent of Asians and Pacific Islanders and 11.1 and 11.3 percent of whites is significant at the 68 percent confidence level.

8. The difference between 52.9 percent for foreign-born Asian/Pacific youth and 57.2 percent for foreign-born whites is significant at the 68 percent confidence level.

9. Bureau of the Census, *Asian and Pacific Islander Population*, p. 8.

10. Ibid.

11. The difference between 17.0 percent for Asian/Pacific youth and either 14.7 percent for white majority youth or 19.2 percent for African American youth in Texas is significant at the 68 percent confidence level.

12. The difference between 29.6 percent for Asian/Pacific youth in Texas and either 23.3 percent for this group in Washington or 20.7 percent in Illinois is significant at the 68 percent confidence level.

13. Bureau of the Census, *Asian and Pacific Islander Population*, p. 8.

14. Ibid., pp. 12–13.

15. Ibid.

16. Bureau of the Census, U.S. Department of Commerce, "More of Asian and Pacific Islander Families Have at Least Two Workers Than Do Other U.S. Fami-

lies, Census Bureau Says," press release, April 8, 1988, table 1; and idem, "Socio-economic Characteristics of U.S. Foreign-Born Population Detailed in Census Bureau Tabulations," press release, October 17, 1984, p. 6.

17. Bureau of the Census, "Asian and Pacific Islander Families," table 1; and idem, *1980 Census of Population, Detailed Population Characteristics, Part 1, United States Summary* (Washington, D.C.: U.S. Government Printing Office, 1984), p. 43.

18. Bureau of the Census, *Detailed Population Characteristics*, p. 13.

19. Bureau of the Census, "Asian and Pacific Islander Families," table 1; and idem, *Detailed Population Characteristics*, p. 551.

20. Bureau of the Census, "Asian and Pacific Islander Families," table 1.

21. Ibid.; and Bureau of the Census, "Socioeconomic Characteristics," pp. 1–2.

22. Bureau of the Census, "Asian and Pacific Islander Families," table 1.

23. Bureau of the Census, *Detailed Population Characteristics*, p. 43.

24. Bureau of the Census, "Socioeconomic Characteristics," pp. 5–6.

25. Bureau of the Census, *Asian and Pacific Islander Population*, pp. 14–15.

26. Bureau of the Census, "Asian and Pacific Islander Families," table 2.

27. Ibid., table 2; and Bureau of the Census, *Detailed Population Characteristics*, p. 43.

28. Bureau of the Census, "Asian and Pacific Islander Families," tables 1 and 2; and idem, *Detailed Population Characteristics*, p. 505.

29. Immigration and Naturalization Service, unpublished tabulations.

30. Of the 6,733 immigrants born in Thailand who were admitted to the United States in FY 1987, 3,745 were refugees, 3,660 of them under ten years of age. Immigration and Naturalization Service, U.S. Department of Justice, *Statistical Yearbook of the Immigration and Naturalization Service, 1987* (Washington, D.C.: U.S. Government Printing Office, 1988), pp. 6 and 53.

31. Immigration and Naturalization Service, unpublished tabulations.

32. Immigration and Naturalization Service, *1987 Yearbook*, pp. 32–34.

33. Ibid.

34. Bureau of the Census, *Asian and Pacific Islander Population*, pp. 12–13; and Immigration and Naturalization Service, *1987 Yearbook*, pp. 32–34.

35. Bureau of the Census, "Asian and Pacific Islander Families," tables 1 and 2.

36. Immigration and Naturalization Service, unpublished tabulations.

37. Dorothy Waggoner, "Foreign Born Children in the United States in the Eighties," *NABE Journal* 12 (Fall 1987): 32–33.

38. Bureau of the Census, "Asian and Pacific Islander Families," table 1; and idem, *General Social and Economic Characteristics*, p. 157.

39. Bureau of the Census, *General Social and Economic Characteristics*, p. 163.

40. Bureau of the Census, *Asian and Pacific Islander Population*, p. 8.

41. Laird Harrison, "State Reports More Asians Than Blacks," *Asian Week* (San Francisco), April 8, 1988.

42. Native Hawaiians constituted 12.3 percent of the total Asian/Pacific population and 36.6 percent of youth, aged 15 to 24, in Hawaii in 1980; there were an estimated 26,000 native Hawaiian youth and an estimated 24,000 Filipino youth. Bureau of the Census, *Asian and Pacific Islander Population*, pp. 8–9; and *General Social and Economic Characteristics, Part 13, Hawaii*, p. 64.

43. Bureau of the Census, *General Social and Economic Characteristics, Part*

13, Hawaii, p. 69. Poor Asian/Pacific youth in Hawaii were two to three times more likely to be undereducated than their counterparts from more economically advantaged backgrounds in 1980.

Appendix A: The Source and Accuracy of the Data

The original data for this study are the result of a special analysis of the Five Percent Public-Use Microdata Sample (PUMS) of the 1980 decennial census. Unless another source is cited, the information discussed is from the special analysis.

The information from the special analysis has been supplemented by information from the published volumes and other published sources for the 1980 census, information from the Census Bureau's current population surveys on school enrollment and educational attainment of the U.S. population since 1980, and information from other Census Bureau sources. It has also been supplemented by information on immigrants since 1980 from the 1987 report of the Immigration and Naturalization Service (INS) and unpublished INS tabulations of the numbers of immigrants legally admitted to the United States since 1980 by country of birth, including admissions in fiscal year 1988.

The microdata samples of the 1980 census are samples of the census sample of about 19 percent of the households in the 50 states and the District of Columbia, which received the long form of the 1980 census. Appendix C contains the questions from the long form used to construct the classification variables for the special analysis.

The Five Percent PUMS contains the responses of over a quarter of the households that received the census long form or about 1 percent of all U.S. households. It contains the records of over 11 million individuals and more than 4 million housing units.[1] It yields information on every state separately and provides sufficient precision for separate analysis of the characteristics of undereducated 16-to-24-year-old African Americans; American Indians, Eskimos, and Aleuts; Asians and Pacific Islanders; Hispanics; and two groups of non-Hispanic whites—white majority youth and youth with non-English language backgrounds (non-Hispanic white minority youth)—in the nation and in each state in which there were at least an estimated 10,000 young people in a given group in 1980.

Because the data for the study are based on a sample, the results are estimates. They may differ from the results that would have been produced if the questions on the long form had been asked in all households and the data from all households included in the study. The degree of potential difference between estimates and the "true" numbers or percentages attributable to the fact that the data are from a sample and not from a 100 percent survey—the sampling error—is measured by the standard error of a given estimate or percentage.

Standard errors are used to produce confidence intervals or ranges within which the "true" numbers or percentages are posited. A confidence interval that is plus or minus two standard errors provides 95 percent certainty that the "true" number or percentage is within that range. For example, the estimate of 5,883,000 undereducated youth, aged 16 to 24, in the United States in 1980 that resulted from the special analysis has a standard error of 14,584; at the 95 percent confidence level, the "true" number is somewhere between 5,854,000 and 5,913,000. The estimate of 9,000 for Vermont has a standard error of 589, and the "true" number for that state is, with 95 percent confidence, between 8,000 and 10,000. Similarly, the undereducation rate for the nation in 1980, estimated to be 15.4 percent, has a standard error of four hundredths of a percent and is, therefore, almost certainly between 15.3 and 15.5 percent. The rate for Vermont, estimated to be 10.1 percent, has an error of seven-tenths of a percent; at the 95 percent confidence level, the "true" undereducation rate of 16-to-24-year-olds in Vermont is between 8.8 and 11.4 percent.

The instances in which differences between the undereducation rates of groups that are statistically significant only at the 68 percent confidence level (plus or minus one standard error) are discussed in the text are footnoted. Otherwise, all differences meet the higher standard. Moreover, with few exceptions, the rates for different groups are not compared unless their base numbers—the sizes of the groups within which individuals with the described characteristics are found—are estimated to be at least 10,000. Rates calculated on smaller bases have such large standard errors that the comparisons would have little value.

Data gathered from 100 percent surveys, as well as data from samples, are subject to non-sampling errors. They are subject to variances that cannot be accounted for through the use of standard errors. If certain populations are undercounted or certain groups systematically understate or overstate certain characteristics, the results will not present an accurate picture of the size or the proportion of groups with those characteristics. These conditions frequently affect the counts of minorities. They suggest that absolute numbers should be treated with caution.

One condition that affects the 1980 census and other U.S. population counts is the presence of undocumented foreign-born workers and others. The Census Bureau estimates that about 2 million undocumented people of all ages were counted in the 1980 census.[2] There is no way to determine how many were not counted or how many were young people, aged 16 to 24, who should be added to the undereducated group.

The 1980 census was conducted on April 1. The census counts used in this study do not include, therefore, youth who arrived from Cuba in the Mariel boat lift later that spring or the large numbers of Southeast Asians who immigrated after the passage of the Refugee Act of 1980 and whose characteristics may be very different from those of the 16-to-24-year-old members of their groups identified in the 1980 census.

The published volumes of the 1980 census and other Census Bureau sources contain discussions of the accuracy of the information used to supplement the data from the special analysis. They contain formulas and error tables for calculating standard errors. The estimated number of 4.2 million undereducated youth derived from the October 1988 current population survey, for example, has a standard error of 101,000, and thus the "true" number of undereducated youth in 1988 may be anywhere from 4.0 to 4.5 million at the 95 percent level of confidence. The estimated number for undereducated Hispanic youth, 1.2 million, has an error of 48,000, and the "true" number of undereducated Hispanics is probably between 1.1 and 1.3 million. The undereducation rates for all youth and for Hispanics from the same source are estimated to be 12.9 percent and 35.8 percent, respectively; with errors of three-tenths of a percent and 1.5 percent, the "true" rates are almost certainly between 12.2 percent and 13.5 percent for all youth and 32.8 percent and 38.7 percent for Hispanics.

The INS numbers are actual counts of individuals admitted to the United States each fiscal year. In adding the numbers of legal immigrants since the census was taken on April 1, 1980, the number for fiscal year 1980—October 1, 1979, to September 30, 1980—was divided in half.

NOTES

1. Bureau of the Census, U.S. Department of Commerce, *Census of Population and Housing, 1980: Public-Use Microdata Samples Technical Documentation* (Washington, D.C.: U.S. Government Printing Office, 1983), p. 3.

2. Robert Warren and Jeffrey S. Passel, "Estimates of Illegal Aliens from Mexico Counted in the 1980 United States Census" (Paper presented at the annual meeting of the Population Association of America, Pittsburgh, Pennsylvania, April 14–16, 1983).

Appendix B: Definitions

The following definitions are used in this study. Appendix C contains the questions from the long form of the 1980 decennial census that are referred to in the definitions. These questions were the basis for the variables that were especially constructed for this study.

EDUCATIONAL DELAY

Educational delay affects students who are older than their classmates. It is measured by the proportion of students enrolled in a given grade who are two or more years older than the modal age—the age of the largest number of students in that grade.

HIGH SCHOOL GRADUATION RATE

The high school graduation rate is the proportion of adults in a given group who have completed 12 years of schooling. Whether or not completion of 12 years of schooling should be understood to include completion by an alternate method such as passing the GED (General Educational Development) test or only completion of a "regular" school program and receipt of a high school diploma depends on the source of the data. (See "Undereducated Youth.")

LANGUAGE BACKGROUND

English language-background individuals are those from households in which only English is spoken, that is, those from monolingual English-speaking households. Non-English language-background or language minority people are those who speak languages other than English at home themselves and those who speak only English at home but live in language minority households, that is, in households in which one or more other individuals speaks a non-English language. The information on language used for the special analysis comes from the responses to question 13a (appendix C), which were disaggregated by household to identify monolingual English-speaking households and language minority households. Information on the specific non-English language backgrounds of language minority people, based on responses about the non-English languages spoken at home and contained in the published census volumes, supplements the information from the special analysis in the chapter on non-Hispanic white minority youth.

NATIVITY

Native-born individuals are those born in one of the fifty states, the District of Columbia, Puerto Rico, or an outlying U.S. area and people born abroad of American parents, as identified in questions 11 and 12 (appendix C). Foreign-born individuals are all others. Published information on foreign-born populations in 1980 by countries of birth is used to supplement the information from the special analysis in the chapters on African American, Hispanic, and non-Hispanic white minority youth.

POVERTY RATE

The poverty rate is the proportion of a given group with a family or individual income below the poverty threshold. (See "Poverty Status.")

POVERTY STATUS

Poverty status is determined by whether the family income of an individual living in a family or the individual income of someone not living in a family was above or below the poverty threshold for families of their size and age distribution, as established by the federal government. In 1980 the average poverty threshold for a family of four was a 1979 income of $7,412.[1]

Poverty status is not determined for people living in group quarters, that is, military barracks or other military group quarters, institutions of various kinds, and college dormitories—the institutional population—or for unrelated individuals under age 15. In 1980 it was not determined for 2.8 million, or 7.4 percent, of 16-to-24-year-old youth. They included 8.8 percent of the Asians and Pacific Islanders; 8.4 percent of the African Americans; 7.8 percent of the white majority youth; 6.9 percent of the American Indians, Eskimos, and Aleuts; 4.3 percent of the Hispanics; and 3.9 percent of the non-Hispanic white minority youth in the age group. Poverty status was not determined for 288,000 undereducated young people, 4.9 percent of that group.

PROJECTIONS OF POPULATION GROWTH

Projections are forecasts of the size of given population in the future using various assumptions about fertility, mortality, and net immigration. The projections may be high or low depending on which assumptions are believed to be the most probable. Projected populations always differ from actual future populations. In particular, they cannot take into account future political or economic developments abroad or changes in immigration legislation or other unforeseeable developments in the United States that may affect migration to and from this country.

The Census Bureau provides projections for Hispanics, non-Hispanic whites, blacks, and other races in the aggregate.[2] To consider the possible future growth of the American Indian, Eskimo, and Aleut and the Asian and Pacific Islander school-age populations separately and to compare their potential growth with that of white and black school-age populations, three measures of population growth found in the published data from the 1980 census are used, namely, (1) the median age, the age of members of a group that divides it into two equal parts;[3] (2) family size, the average number of members of a single family, consisting of a householder and one or more other people living in the same household who are related by blood, marriage, or adoption;[4] and (3) the fertility rate, the number of children ever born per 1,000 women in a given age group—in this case women aged 15 to 44.[5] Population growth is also affected by mortality, and some of the same groups that are younger than the majority and have large families and high birth rates also have higher mortality rates than the majority. Mortality rates primarily affect projections of the total population.

RACIAL/ETHNIC GROUPS

Hispanics are identified by a "yes" response to question 7 (appendix C). All others are non-Hispanics. They are classified according to their responses to question 4 (appendix C) as white; black, that is, African American; American Indian, Eskimo, and Aleut; and Asian and Pacific Islander. The non-Hispanic white category consists of two groups, as follows: (1) white majority individuals who are native-born non-Hispanic whites from monolingual English-speaking households and (2) non-Hispanic white minority people who are non-Hispanic whites from households in which one or more people speak a language other than English, that is, language minority households. Asians and Pacific Islanders are Japanese, Chinese, Filipino, Korean, Vietnamese, Asian Indian, Hawaiian, Guamanian, Samoan, and others who identified themselves as Asians or Pacific Islanders by writing in an Asian or Pacific Island ethnicity or national origin in responses to question 4. Other non-Hispanics are non-Hispanics not identified with any of the four categories of responses to question 4 and foreign-born whites from monolingual English-speaking households. In 1980 there were 51,000 non-Hispanics, aged 16 to 24, not identified by race and 227,000 foreign-born English language-background non-Hispanic whites, aged 16 to 24.

The detailed responses to question 4, for American Indians and Asians and Pacific Islanders, and to question 7, for Hispanics, are the basis for the information on the American Indian, Asian/Pacific, and Hispanic subgroups from the published 1980 census volumes used to supplement the information from the special analysis in the chapters on those groups.

In the special analysis, the racial/ethnic groups are mutually exclusive. However, in much of the published information from the 1980 census and other census sources, the racial groups are mutually exclusive on the basis of the responses to question 4 and similar questions, but Hispanics are separately identified. All tables using published data in which the racial/ethnic groups are not mutually exclusive list Hispanic ethnicity as a separate variable and indicate that Hispanics may be of any race. "African American," alternating with "black," is used throughout to refer to non-Hispanic blacks; in the text, it may also refer to all blacks, including black Hispanics, in instances in which published sources are used in which the racial/ethnic groups are not mutually exclusive.

REGIONS AND SUBREGIONS OF THE UNITED STATES

The geographical subdivisions used tables 3.9 and 3.11 are those of the Bureau of the Census. The Northeast consists of two subregions: New England, composed of the states of Maine, New Hampshire, Vermont, Massachusetts, Rhode Island, and Connecticut; and Mid Atlantic, composed of New York, New Jersey, and Pennsylvania. The Midwest also has two subregions: East North Central, with Ohio, Indiana, Illinois, Michigan, and Wisconsin; and West North Central, with Minnesota, Iowa, Missouri, North and South Dakota, Nebraska, and Kansas. The South consists of three subregions: South Atlantic, with the District of Columbia and Delaware, Maryland, Virginia, West Virginia, North and South Carolina, Georgia, and Florida; East South Central, with Kentucky, Tennessee, Alabama, and Mississippi; and West South Central, with Arkansas, Louisiana, Oklahoma, and Texas. The two subregions of the West are the Mountain, which is composed of Montana, Idaho, Wyoming, Colorado, New Mexico, Arizona, Utah, and Nevada; and the Pacific, which consists of Washington, Oregon, California, Alaska, and Hawaii.

UNDEREDUCATED YOUTH

Undereducated youth are youth who are not enrolled in school and have not completed twelve years of schooling. In the special analysis, the universe consists of youth, aged 16 to 24, in the fifty states and the District of Columbia in 1980. The undereducated are those who were not enrolled between February 1 and April 1, 1980, and had not completed twelve years by the time the census was taken on April 1. The census form specified that individuals who had passed a high school equivalency test, such as the GED test, should indicate that they had completed twelve years of schooling. Thus in this study, undereducated youth are not only out-of-school youth who have not completed twelve years in a regular high school, as evidenced by a diploma, but they also are youth who have not received an alternate credential such as that obtained by passing the GED test. Questions 8, 9, and 10 on the census long form identify undereducated individuals.

Undereducated youth in the information from the published volumes of the 1980 census used to determined the extent of undereducation by urbanicity are civilian youth, aged 16 to 19. Undereducated youth in the information from the yearly current population surveys of school enrollment (the October CPSs) are civilian youth not living in group quarters, that is, civilian non-institutional youth, aged 16 to 24, or, for the data on years of schooling completed, those aged 14 to 24. In the CPS, the questions on educational attainment apply only to progress in "regular" schools, and completion means obtaining a high school diploma or other credential recognized within the regular school system.[6]

UNDEREDUCATION RATE

The undereducation rate is the proportion of a given group of youth who are not enrolled in school and have not completed the twelfth grade at a given time. It corresponds to the "status" dropout rate, as defined and differentiated from the "event" and "cohort" dropout rates by the National Center for Education Statistics.[7] The rate is expressed as a percentage.

UNDEREDUCATION RISK FACTOR

An undereducation risk factor is the extent to which higher undereducation rates may be associated with a given characteristic such as poverty. It is calculated by dividing the higher rate by the lower one. Thus poor youth were 2.1 times more likely to be undereducated than youth in more economically advantaged circumstances in 1980 (28.1 percent divided by 13.7 percent).

URBANICITY

Urbanicity is the extent to which a given group lives in urban areas rather than in rural areas, as defined by the census. Urban areas are metropolitan areas, consisting of a central city or cities and the surrounding suburbs or urban fringe areas, and all other places with populations of at least 2,500. Rural areas are all other areas. Rural farms are places of an acre or more that produced at least $1,000 in agricultural income in 1979.[8]

YEARS OF SCHOOLING COMPLETED

Years of schooling completed are the number of years completed by undereducated young people before discontinuing their education. The information comes from question 9 (appendix C), the highest grade of regular school ever attended, and question 10 (appendix C), whether the highest grade was completed. In the special analysis, undereducated youth are grouped into those who have completed zero to 4 years, 5 to 8 years, and 9 to 11 years of schooling. In the published information from the current population surveys of school enrollment, undereducated youth are grouped into those who have completed zero to 8 years and 9, 10, and 11 years of schooling.

NOTES

1. Bureau of the Census, U.S. Department of Commerce, *1980 Census of Population, General Social and Economic Characteristics, Part 1, United States Summary* (Washington, D.C.: U.S. Government Printing Office, 1983), pp. B-22–B-23.
2. See Bureau of the Census, U.S. Department of Commerce, *Projections of the Hispanic Population: 1983 to 2080* (Washington, D.C.: U.S. Government Printing Office, 1986).
3. Bureau of the Census, *General Social and Economic Characteristics*, p. B-4.
4. Ibid., p. B-2.
5. Ibid., p. B-10.

6. Bureau of the Census, U.S. Department of Commerce, *School Enrollment—Social and Economic Characteristics of Students: October 1988 and 1987* (Washington, D.C.: U.S. Government Printing Office, 1990), p. 191. The same limitation applies to data from the March CPSs on educational attainment. Idem, *Educational Attainment in the United States: 1987 and 1986* (Washington, D.C.: U.S. Government Printing Office, 1988), pp. 77–78.

7. National Center for Education Statistics, U.S. Department of Education, *Dropout Rates in the United States: 1988* (Washington, D.C.: U.S. Government Printing Office, 1989), pp. ix–x and 2.

8. Bureau of the Census, *General Social and Economic Characteristics,* pp. A-1–A-2.

Appendix C: Questions from the Long Form of the 1980 Census of Population Used for the Special Analysis of Undereducated Youth

4. Is this person — *Fill one circle.*	○ White ○ Asian Indian ○ Black or Negro ○ Hawaiian ○ Japanese ○ Guamanian ○ Chinese ○ Samoan ○ Filipino ○ Eskimo ○ Korean ○ Aleut ○ Vietnamese ○ Other — *Specify* ○ Indian (Amer.) *Print* *tribe* → _ _ _ _ _ _ _ _ _ _ _ _ _ _ _ _ _ _
7. Is this person of Spanish/Hispanic origin or descent? *Fill one circle.*	○ No (not Spanish/Hispanic) ○ Yes, Mexican, Mexican-Amer., Chicano ○ Yes, Puerto Rican ■ ○ Yes, Cuban ○ Yes, other Spanish/Hispanic
8. Since February 1. 1980, has this person attended regular school or college at any time? *Fill one circle. Count nursery school, kindergarten, elementary school, and schooling which leads to a high school diploma or college degree.*	○ No, has not attended since February 1 ○ Yes, public school, public college ○ Yes, private, church-related ○ Yes, private, not church-related
9. What is the highest grade (or year) of regular school this person has ever attended? *Fill one circle.* *If now attending school, mark grade person is in. If high school was finished by equivalency test (GED), mark "12."*	**Highest grade attended:** ○ Nursery school ○ Kindergarten Elementary through high school *(grade or year)* 1 2 3 4 5 6 7 8 9 10 11 12 ○ ○ ○ ○ ○ ○ ○ ○ ○ ○ ○ College *(academic year)* ■ 1 2 3 4 5 6 7 8 or more ○ ○ . . . Never attended school — *Skip question 10*
10. Did this person finish the highest grade (or year) attended? *Fill one circle.*	○ Now attending this grade *(or year)* ○ Finished this grade *(or year)* ○ Did not finish this grade *(or year)*

11. **In what State or foreign country was this person born?**
    Print the State where this person's mother was living
    when this person was born. Do not give the location of
    the hospital unless the mother's home and the hospital
    were in the same State.

    -

    Name of State or foreign country; or Puerto Rico, Guam, etc.

12. *If this person was born in a foreign country –*
    a. **Is this person a naturalized citizen of the**
       United States?

         Yes, a naturalized citizen
         No, not a citizen
    ■   Born abroad of American parents   ■

13a. **Does this person speak a language other than**
     English at home?

          Yes   No, only speaks English – *Skip to 14*

Bibliography

Boyer, Ernest L. *High School: A Report on Secondary Education in America.* New York: Harper and Row, 1983.

Bureau of the Census. U.S. Department of Commerce. *American Indian Areas and Alaska Native Villages: 1980.* 1980 Census of Population. Supplementary reports. PC80-S1-13. Washington, D.C.: U.S. Government Printing Office, 1984.

———. *Asian and Pacific Islander Population by State: 1980.* 1980 Census of Population. Supplementary reports. PC80-S1-12. Washington, D.C.: U.S. Government Printing Office, 1983.

———. *Census of Population and Housing, 1980: Public-Use Microdata Samples Technical Documentation.* Washington, D.C.: U.S. Government Printing Office, 1983.

———. *Educational Attainment in the United States: March 1982 to 1985.* Current population reports. Series P-20, no. 415, by Rosalind R. Bruno. Washington, D.C.: U.S. Government Printing Office, 1987.

———. *Educational Attainment in the United States: March 1987 and 1986.* Current population reports. Series P-20, no. 428, by Robert Kominski. Washington, D.C.: U.S. Government Printing Office, 1988.

———. "More of Asian and Pacific Islander Families Have at Least Two Workers Than Do Other U.S. Families, Census Bureau Says." Press release, April 8, 1988.

———. *1980 Census of Population, Characteristics of American Indians by Tribes and Selected Areas: 1980.* PC80-2-1C. Washington, D.C.: U.S. Government Printing Office, 1989.

———. *1980 Census of Population, Detailed Population Characteristics, Parts 1–52, United States Summary, the States, and the District of Columbia.*

PC80-1-D1-D52. Washington, D.C.: U.S. Government Printing Office, 1983-84.

———. *1980 Census of Population, General Social and Economic Characteristics, Parts 1–52, United States Summary, the States, and the District of Columbia.* PC80-1-C1-C52. Washington, D.C.: U.S. Government Printing Office, 1983.

———. *Persons of Spanish Origin by State: 1980.* 1980 Census of Population. Supplementary reports. PC80-S1-7. Washington, D.C.: U.S. Government Printing Office, 1982.

———. *Poverty in the United States, 1986.* Current population reports. Series P-60, no. 160. Washington, D.C.: U.S. Government Printing Office, 1988.

———. *Projections of the Hispanic Population: 1983 to 2080.* Current population reports. Series P-25, no. 995, by Gregory Spencer. Washington, D.C.: U.S. Government Printing Office, 1986.

———. *Race of the Population by States: 1980.* 1980 Census of Population. Supplementary reports. PC80-S1-3. Washington, D.C.: U.S. Government Printing Office, 1981.

———. *School Enrollment—Social and Economic Characteristics of Students: October 1981 and 1980.* Current population reports. Series P-20, no. 400, by Rosalind R. Bruno. Washington, D.C.: U.S. Government Printing Office, 1985.

———. *School Enrollment—Social and Economic Characteristics of Students: October 1982.* Current population reports. Series P-20, no. 408, by Paul M. Siegel and Rosalind R. Bruno. Washington, D.C.: U.S. Government Printing Office, 1986.

———. *School Enrollment—Social and Economic Characteristics of Students: October 1983.* Current population reports. Series P-20, no. 413, by Robert Kominski. Washington, D.C.: U.S. Government Printing Office, 1987.

———. *School Enrollment—Social and Economic Characteristics of Students: October 1985 and 1984.* Current population reports. Series P-20, no. 426, by Rosalind R. Bruno. Washington, D.C.: U.S. Government Printing Office, 1988.

———. *School Enrollment—Social and Economic Characteristics of Students: October 1986.* Current population reports. Series P-20, no. 429, by Rosalind R. Bruno. Washington, D.C.: U.S. Government Printing Office, 1988.

———. *School Enrollment—Social and Economic Characteristics of Students: October 1988 and 1987.* Current population reports. Series P-20, no. 443, by Rosalind R. Bruno. Washington, D.C.: U.S. Government Printing Office, 1990.

———. "Socioeconomic Characteristics of U.S. Foreign-Born Population Detailed in Census Bureau Tabulations." Press release, October 17, 1984.

Center for Education Statistics. U.S. Department of Education. *Who Drops Out of High School? Findings from High School and Beyond.* Contractor report, by Stephen M. Barro and Andrew Kolstad. Washington, D.C.: U.S. Government Printing Office, 1987.

Fernández, Ricardo R., and Shu, Gangjian. "School Dropouts: New Approaches to an Enduring Problem." *Education and Urban Society* 20 (August 1988): 363–386.

Harrison, Laird. "State Reports More Asians Than Blacks." *Asian Week* (San Francisco), April 8, 1988.

Immigration and Naturalization Service. U.S. Department of Justice. *Statistical Yearbook of the Immigration and Naturalization Service, 1987.* Washington, D.C.: U.S. Government Printing Office, 1988.

————. Unpublished tabulations.

Intercultural Development Research Association. *Texas School Dropout Survey Project: A Summary of Findings.* San Antonio, 1986.

Johnston, William B. *Workforce 2000: Work and Workers for the 21st Century.* Indianapolis: Hudson Institute, 1987.

Kolstad, Andrew J., and Owings, Jeffrey A. "High School Dropouts Who Change Their Minds about School." Paper presented at the annual meeting of the American Educational Research Association, San Francisco, April 16, 1986.

Kominski, Robert. "Estimating the National High School Dropout Rate." *Demography* 27 (May 1990): 303–311.

Leap, William L. "American Indian Languages." In *Language in the USA,* edited by Charles A. Ferguson and Shirley Brice Heath. Cambridge, Eng.: Cambridge University Press, 1981.

Levin, Henry M. *The Costs to the Nation of Inadequate Education: A Report Prepared for the Select Committee on Equal Educational Opportunity of the United States Senate,* January 1972. Washington, D.C.: U.S. Government Printing Office, 1972.

Mann, Dale. "Can We Help Dropouts? Thinking about the Undoable." In *School Dropouts: Patterns and Policies,* edited by Gary Natriello. New York: Teachers College Press, 1987.

National Center for Education Statistics. U.S. Department of Education. *Digest of Education Statistics 1982,* by W. Vance Grant and Leo J. Eiden. Washington, D.C.: U.S. Government Printing Office, 1982.

————. *Digest of Education Statistics, 1989.* Washington, D.C.: U.S. Government Printing Office, 1989.

————. *Dropout Rates in the United States: 1988.* NCES 89-609, by Mary J. Frase. Washington, D.C.: U.S. Government Printing Office, 1989.

National Center for Education Statistics. U.S. Department of Health, Education, and Welfare. *The Educational Disadvantage of Language-Minority Persons in the United States, Spring 1976.* NCES bulletin 78-121, by Leslie J. Silverman. July 26, 1978.

————. *Place of Birth and Language Characteristics of Persons of Hispanic Origin in the United States, Spring 1976.* NCES bulletin 78-135, by Dorothy Waggoner. October 20, 1978.

Office of Educational Research and Improvement. U.S. Department of Education. *Dealing with Dropouts: The Urban Superintendents' Call to Action,* by the Office of Educational Research and Improvement's Urban Superintendents Network. Washington, D.C.: U.S. Government Printing Office, 1988.

Sherraden, Michael W. "School Dropouts in Perspective." *The Educational Forum* 51 (Fall 1986): 15–31.

"Stuck in the Horizon." A Special Report on the Education of Native Americans. *Education Week* (Washington, D.C.), August 2, 1989.

U.S. Department of Education. "State Education Performance Chart, 1982 and 1989." Reprinted in *Education Week* (Washington, D.C.), May 9, 1990.

Valdivieso, Rafael, and Galindo, Martha, eds. *"Make Something Happen": Hispanics and Urban High School Reform.* Volume 2. Washington, D.C.: Hispanic Policy Development Project, 1984.

Waggoner, Dorothy. "Foreign Born Children in the United States in the Eighties." *NABE Journal* 12 (Fall 1987): 23–49.

——. "Language Minorities in the United States in the 1980s: The Evidence from the 1980 Census." In *Language Diversity, Problem or Resource?*, edited by Sandra Lee McKay and Sau-ling Cynthia Wong. New York: Newbury House Publishers, 1988.

——. *Volume 1: Magnitude of the Problem—Census Analysis. Texas School Dropout Survey Project.* San Antonio: Intercultural Development Research Association, 1986.

Warren, Robert, and Passel, Jeffrey S. "Estimates of Illegal Aliens from Mexico Counted in the 1980 United States Census." Paper presented at the annual meeting of the Population Association of America, Pittsburgh, April 14–16, 1983.

Wehlage, Gary G., and Rutter, Robert A. "Dropping Out: How Much Do Schools Contribute to the Problem?" In *School Dropouts: Patterns and Policies,* edited by Gary Natriello. New York: Teachers College Press, 1987.

William T. Grant Foundation Commission on Work, Family and Citizenship. *The Forgotten Half: Pathways to Success for America's Youth and Young Families.* Washington, D.C., 1988.

Index

About the Author

DOROTHY WAGGONER is a specialist in language minority statistics and bilingual education. Prior to her retirement from the Federal Government, she held positions in the Office of Bilingual Education and Minority Languages Affairs and the National Center for Education Statistics of the U.S. Department of Education. She chaired an interagency committee charged with planning the language questions for the 1980 census. Dr. Waggoner has written extensively on the numbers and characteristics of language minority populations and their educational needs.